MANCHESTER uNITED
THE OFFICIAL REVIEW 1996

MANCHESTER UNITED
THE OFFICIAL REVIEW 1996

Contributors
Alex Ferguson | **Brian Kidd** | **Jim Ryan** | **Eric Harrison**
The players and staff at Manchester United

Andy Mitten | **Alex Leith** | **Jim Drewett**
Bill Mowbray | **Adam Bostock** | **Justyn Barnes**
Roland Jones | **Alexis Szabo** | **Rachel Jervis**

Photographs
Action Images | **John Peters** | **Ryan Giggs' mother**

Design
Tim Barnes | **Vernon Adams**

First published in 1996 by

Manchester United Books

an imprint of

André Deutsch Ltd
106 Great Russell Street | London | WC1B 3LJ

in association with

Manchester United Football Club Plc
Old Trafford | Manchester | M16 0RA

CIP data for this title is available from the British Library

ISBN 0233 99018 6

Produced by **Zone Ltd**.

Printed and bound in Italy by **Editoriale Bortolazzi-STEI**.

CONTENTS

ALEX FERGUSON
1995/96

THE MANAGER'S VIEW

demonstrates to the millions of youngsters who follow the game what can be achieved if you pass the ball skilfully and effectively.

Much was made in mid-season of Newcastle United's 12-point lead. While we had to admire the Tynesiders for the way they took control of the proceedings, we knew from our own bitter experience how things might change for them and how easy it would be for them to fritter away their points advantage.

In the end, experience proved to be a telling factor. Having gone through the major disappointments of 1992 and 1995, we knew what to expect from the final nailbiting weeks of the season. Most of our players knew only too well the feelings they were hoping to avoid. You can be certain that Newcastle United will learn from this year's events, and we already know who will be the biggest threat to our Championship crown in 1996/97.

In a team game, it's not always wise or fair to single out an individual for his contribution. But when it comes to influence and inspiration, there can be no bigger individual than Eric Cantona.

Many, many words have already been written about Eric this season and it's hard to find new accolades for this extraordinary player. Suffice it to say that as Eric's manager, I'm delighted with the way he has performed for the team in 1995/96. It was fitting that he scored a stunning goal to win the FA Cup. He has directed so much of our play and helped the younger players to find their feet this season.

Some pundits suggested we couldn't win the title with kids, but they reckoned without the force of a rejuvenated Eric Cantona and the respect and admiration our "kids" have for him as a footballer.

It is a pleasure to be writing the introduction to Manchester United's Offical Review in the knowledge that United are the double Double winners.

In terms of excitement and drama, I thought the 1994/95 League title race would take some beating. But this year's was equally thrilling, if not more so. I say that not because ultimately we were successful this time, but because there were three great clubs challenging for the Championship: Manchester United, Newcastle United and Liverpool.

As I said many times during the campaign, it was pleasing to see the teams who play the game in the best manner leading the way in the Premiership table. If nothing else, it

To call them "kids" is condescending, anyway. Brought up in the traditions of Manchester United, the likes of Paul Scholes, David Beckham, Nicky Butt and the Neville brothers are mature young men who are more than capable of winning trophies. They're good enough, so they're old enough.

If age was such an important issue, football would have been kept waiting for some of its greatest talents; the teenage Duncan Edwards, George Best and Pelé spring to mind. In many respects, our Double triumph is as much a victory for youth as it is for Manchester United.

One of the greatest things about winning the Championship is that it gives us the chance to play in the world's greatest club competition, the European Champions' Cup. We're determined to improve on our recent performances in that competition and show the rest of Europe that British football is not as far behind the continent's as people would have us believe.

It wasn't so long ago that Liverpool, Forest and Aston Villa monopolised the European Cup for England, and we would dearly love to spearhead a return to those halcyon days. The Bosman ruling will present some difficulties for managers, but in Europe it gives me the chance to field my strongest team regardless of where my players were born. It's only right that the team which wins the domestic Championship should be allowed to compete at full strength for the prestigious title of European Champions.

Whatever happens next season, it is comforting to think that we will have you, our wonderful supporters, to back us all the way. Your enthusiasm and passion played a key part in winning the historic double Double this year, and will give us a headstart in our bid to retain it.

Alex Ferguson CBE

AUGUST

1 | 2 | 3 | 4 | 5 | 6 | 7 | 8 | 9 | 10 | 11 | 12 | 13 | 14 | 15 | 16 | 17 | 18 | 19 | 20 | 21 | 22 | 23 | 24 | 25 | 26 | 27 | 28 | 29 | 30 | 31

AUGUST

THE MONTH IN REVIEW

The United boys came back from their holidays to find it was hotter in England than it had been in Florida and Torremolinos – not the sort of weather that makes the heart yearn for Brian Kidd's gruelling cobweb-dusting training routines. England was in the grip of a heatwave, with temperatures sitting stubbornly in the high nineties and a hosepipe ban leaving front gardens looking brown and tatty. But there was work to be done...

May 1995 had seen United's double hopes evaporate into nothing on two consecutive weekends in London. First up had been that excruciating 1–1 draw with West Ham, where only a mixture of bad luck, bad finishing and inspired goalkeeping had stopped a victory and a hat-trick of Championship wins. Then to Wembley for the FA Cup final and a mugging from Everton.

To make matters worse, back at the Cliff three of the old guard were gone. Paul Ince had been lured by the lire and jetted off to Milan to play for Inter. A week into the season, Andrei Kanchelskis zapped down the M62 to Everton after legal wranglings of OJ-like proportions. And Mark Hughes, for so long a symbol of the spirit and determination of the team, had gone to Chelsea of all places.

With no major replacements signed over the summer (Ajax star Marc Overmars was lined up to replace Kan Kan, but the £10 million price tag was deemed too much), United fans shook their heads in disbelief and tried to work out what sort of a team Fergie was going to field. Some even called up a local radio poll to say Fergie should quit – though most of the callers turned out to be City supporters.

What's worse, Eric Cantona – banned until October – got extremely miffed with the FA when they banned him from playing reserve matches. Only Fergie's last-minute intervention kept "le Dieu" at Old Trafford at all. To the press, United's Championship challenge was in disarray. Behind the scenes, however, it was business as usual. It would be time for Fergie's Fledglings to earn their wings.

United started off their pre-season matches with a trip to Kuala Lumpur, where they beat the Malaysian side Selangor 4–1 and 2–0 in a tournament called the Glamoir Invitational Cup. It was so hot in the Shah Alam stadium that many of the players lost two litres of fluid during the game. But what the heck, it was worth it to get the season's first silverware in the cabinet.

Overmars: over-priced, and over there

Malaysian fans go batty over the boys in red

Then a whistle-stop tour of the British Isles saw a jet-lagged side go down 1–0 to Birmingham City before beating Bradford, East Fife and Oldham, and snatching a 2–2 draw with Shelbourne in Dublin. Fergie gave a run-out to many of his teenage stars and experimented with a trendy five-at-the-back defence.

However, when the season proper started Fergie might have reflected that he'd packed too many games into the pre-season tour. A trip to Villa Park saw United's young side ripped apart by three goals before half time. Despite rallying in the second period, they were unable to turn things round and found the net only once through David Beckham. Fergie's three centre backs formation experiment was clearly not working.

What was needed was a couple of easyish home games. West Ham and Wimbledon, within three days of one another, provided the Old Trafford opposition. United played badly but scraped through to beat the Hammers 2–1 with a Keane goal. Then they beat Wimbledon 3–1 with a leisurely continental-style display culminating in a brace of goals for Keane.

The final match of the month saw a perfect chance for revenge over Blackburn, near neighbours and the last season's title snatchers... and United took them on in style. A great, battling performance at Ewood Park saw the Reds

"They're a young side, they'll get better."
ALEX FERGUSON

steamroller Ray Harford's men, despite seeing Roy Keane sent off in the second half for (allegedly) diving. It was 100-mile-an-hour stuff, which saw United rise to third in the table behind a Tony Yeboah-inspired Leeds and Keegan's Newcastle. Things weren't looking brilliant.

But they weren't looking all that bad, either.

The price of fame

SELANGOR 1
MANCHESTER UNITED 4

Monday 31 July 1995 | 8.45 pm | Shah Alam Stadium | Att: 51,286

HOME TEAM

- 23. V Murugan
- 20. Scott Ollenshaw
- 2. Allen Davidson
- 16. Ismail Ibrahim
- 5. K Gunalan
- 12. K Sanbagamaran
- 8. Josip Bolik
- 4. Mahmet Durakuc
- 10. David Mitchell
- 7. Sharil Arshat
- 6. P Maniam

SUBSTITUTES

- 3. A Talib Sucaahman
- 9. Ruddi Suparman
- 18. Yogeswaran

SCORER

Ollenshaw | 79 mins

MATCH REPORT

The opening game of the Reds' busy pre-season schedule took place in the impressive 80,000 capacity Shah Alam stadium, just outside the Malaysian capital of Kuala Lumpur. Wearing the new grey kit for the first time, United took things easy in the first half against Malaysia's most popular side. The majority of the 51,286-strong crowd soon had something to celebrate, when Captain Bruce headed United in front on 48 minutes.

The young United side dominated throughout the second half, and further goals from Butt, Pallister and a cracker from Sharpe sealed an easy 4–1 victory over Selangor.

VISITORS

- 1. Peter Schmeichel
- 2. Paul Parker
- 3. Denis Irwin
- 4. Steve Bruce
- 5. Lee Sharpe
- 6. Gary Pallister
- 7. Brian McClair
- 8. Roy Keane
- 9. Nicky Butt
- 10. Paul Scholes
- 11. Gary Neville

SUBSTITUTES

- 12. David Beckham
- 14. Terry Cooke
- 15. Phil Neville

SCORERS

Bruce | 48 mins
Butt | 55 mins
Pallister | 64 mins
Sharpe | 76 mins

Pictures from top:
United in Malaysia | Meeting Birmingham City at St Andrews | Keane out-flanks East Fife | Nicky Butt at Boundary Park

SELANGOR 0
MANCHESTER UNITED 2
Saturday 2 August 1995 | 8.45 pm | Shah Alam Stadium | Att: 22,612

HOME TEAM

1. Emad Hassan
2. Samsul Amri Borhan
3. Talib Sulaiman
4. Mehmet Durakovic
6. P Manham
10. Kalla Goroes
11. Azrin Shaazainl
12. K Sanbagamaran
15. Dollah Salleh
16. Zainal Abidin
17. Ismak Ibraaim

SUBSTITUTES

5. K Gunalan
7. David Mitchell
8. Sharil Arsat

VISITORS

1. Peter Schmeichel
2. Paul Parker
3. Denis Irwin
4. Steve Bruce
6. Gary Pallister
9. Brian McClair
16. Roy Keane
19. Nicky Butt
21. Phil Neville
22. Paul Scholes
29. Ben Thornley

SUBSTITUTES

22. Terry Cooke
28. David Beckham
25. Kevin Pilkington

SCORERS

Bruce | 18 mins
Scholes | 29 mins

MATCH REPORT

Despite ticket prices being reduced to just £2.50, the Malaysian public didn't warm to the idea of seeing United play Selangor in the same stadium for the second time in 48 hours. The resulting crowd of 22,612 looked lost in the mammoth stadium, and the ones who stayed away probably did the right thing.

Bruce put the Reds a goal up against the lacklustre Malaysians and Scholes made it two with a powerful effort just before the break.

United couldn't add to their tally, and there was more chance of seeing Cantona come on as sub as there was of seeing Selangor score.

The 6–1 aggregate victory rounded off a satisfying week in Malaysia. At least we had already won one trophy this season.

BIRMINGHAM CITY 1
MANCHESTER UNITED 0
Monday 7 August 1995 | 7.45 pm | St Andrews | Att: 13,849

HOME TEAM

1. Ian Bennett
2. Scott Hiley
3. John Frain
4. Mark Ward
5. Andy Edwards
6. Liam Daish
7. Jonathon Hunt
8. Steve Claridge
9. Ian Muir
10. Richard Forsyth
11. Paul Tait

SUBSTITUTES

12. Ricky Otto
13. Richard Price
15. Chris Whyte

SCORER

Daish | 12 mins
Whyte | 44 mins

VISITORS

1. Peter Schmeichel
2. Paul Parker
3. Denis Irwin
4. Steve Bruce
5. Lee Sharpe
6. Gary Pallister
9. Brian McClair
16. Roy Keane
19. Nicky Butt
22. Paul Scholes

SUBSTITUTES

25. Gary Neville
29. Ben Thornley
Parker | 85 mins
28. David Beckham
26. Terry Cooke

MATCH REPORT

Sitting in the smart new surroundings of St Andrews, you could have been forgiven for thinking you were at Old Trafford – such is the resemblance on two sides of the ground.

However, football fans would always prefer quality football on the park to quality facilities off it and tonight the football wasn't up to scratch. The only goal of the night came from the Blues against a United side who may have had vision, but lacked penetration in attack.

BRADFORD CITY 0
MANCHESTER UNITED 1
Wednesday 9 August 1995 | 7.45 pm | Pulse Valley Parade | Att: 13,457

HOME TEAM

1. Gavin Ward
2. Richard Huxford
3. Wayne Jacobs
4. Graham Mitchell
5. Nicky Mohan
6. John Ford
7. Tommy Wright
8. Eddie Youds
9. Ian Ormondroyd
10. Carl Shutt
11. Neil Grayson

SUBSTITUTES

14. Chris Kamara
17. Shaun Murray
18. Neil Tolson

VISITORS

1. Peter Schmeichel
2. Paul Parker
3. Denis Irwin
4. Steve Bruce
5. Lee Sharpe
9. Brian McClair
15. Graeme Tomlinson
16. Roy Keane
19. Nicky Butt
25. Gary Neville
26. David Beckham

SUBSTITUTES

20. Terry Cooke
    Beckham
22. Paul Scholes
    Tomlinson
21. Phil Neville

SCORER

Keane | 38 mins

MATCH REPORT

Ince may have departed, but Roy Keane and his new sidekick Nicky Butt showed the heart of United's midfield will be ticking away as normal this season.

Performances to date suggest that the two are working well together. Indeed, it was the Keane/Butt combination which resulted in Keane grabbing the only goal of the evening match at a near-capacity Valley Parade stadium.

The Cork man let rip with a ferocious drive past the keeper in the 38th minute, but barely a minute later he was involved in a fracas in the centre circle.

Matters soon cooled. United kept their composure to hold out for a win.

SHELBOURNE 2
MANCHESTER UNITED 2
Friday 11 August 1995 | 7.30 pm | Tolka Park | Att: 12,000

HOME TEAM

1. Alan Gough
2. Greg Costello
3. Tommy Dunne
4. Mick Neville
5. Ray Duffy
6. Gary Howlett
7. Brian Flood
8. Alan Byrne
9. Vinny Arkins
10. Stephen Geoghan
11. John O'Rourke

SUBSTITUTES

12. Karl Wilson
13. David Smith
14. Declan Geoghegan

SCORERS

Geoghan | 12 mins
O'Rourke | 52 mins

VISITORS

25. Kevin Pilkington
2. Paul Parker
3. Denis Irwin
4. Steve Bruce
5. Lee Sharpe
9. Brian McClair
16. Roy Keane
19. Nicky Butt
20. Terry Cooke
27. Gary Neville
15. Graeme Tomlinson

SUBSTITUTES

21. Phil Neville
28. David Beckham
    Cooke
18. Simon Davies

SCORERS

Butt | 27 mins
Beckham | 66 mins

MATCH REPORT

News of Eric leaving (and staying) may have been making headlines, but the rest of the first team had other things on the agenda – starting with a friendly against Shelbourne of Dublin.

The Shelbourne side, who had been trounced 3–0 earlier in the week in the UEFA Cup by a team of Icelandic fishermen, started positively and even went a goal up.

Sharpe levelled affairs but the Dublin side went ahead once again after a mix-up in the United defence.

David Beckham saved our blushes when he grabbed a late equaliser, but it was a performance United would have to learn from, even though it was a friendly.

EAST FIFE 0
MANCHESTER UNITED 4

Sunday 13 August 1995 | 3.00 pm | Bayview Park | Att: 7,000

HOME TEAM

1. Lindsay Hamilton
2. John McStay
3. Alex Hamill
4. John Cusack
5. Dave Beeton
6. Mark Donaghy
7. Ronnie Hildersley
8. Kenny Balmaine
9. Benny Andrew
10. Steve Hutchin
11. Gilbert Allen

SUBSTITUTES

13. Dean Robertson
15. Phil Gartshaw
16. Derek Long

VISITORS

25. Kevin Pilkington
2. Paul Parker
3. Denis Irwin
4. Steve Bruce
5. Lee Sharpe
9. Brian McClair
16. Roy Keane
22. Paul Scholes
27. Gary Neville
26. David Beckham
29. Ben Thornley

SUBSTITUTES

20. Terry Cooke
    Pilkington
21. Phil Neville
    Irwin
30. John O'Kane

SCORERS

Beckham | 29/72 mins
McClair | 39 mins
Sharpe | 59 mins

MATCH REPORT

East Fife hadn't seen a sight like it for years. Thousands of visiting supporters descending on the town of Methill in glorious sunshine.

A capacity crowd of 7,000 at Bayview Park certainly got value for money, as another classy young red side put in four goals without reply.

United dominated from the whistle against the Scottish part-timers, and Beckham put us a goal up after 29 minutes when he drove home a brilliant shot from 20 yards.

McClair added a second 10 minutes later with a simple tap-in from a Cooke cross.

Sporting a new haircut, "Razor" Sharpe made it three on the hour when he stabbed the ball home at the second attempt.

Beckham got his name on the scoresheet once again when he hit an almost identical goal to his first (a few of those would be nice in the Premiership), and the crowd went home happy.

OLDHAM ATHLETIC 0
MANCHESTER UNITED 2

Tuesday 15 August 1995 | 7.45 pm | Boundary Park | Att: 12,000

HOME TEAM

1. Paul Gerrard
2. Richard Jobson
3. Neil Pointon
4. Craig Fleming
5. Steve Redmond
6. Paul Rickers
7. Rick Holden
8. Darren Beckford
9. Scott McNiven
10. Paul Bernard
11. Gunner Halle

SUBSTITUTES

12. Chris Makin
    Halle
13. John Hallworth
    Gerrard
14. Mark Brennan
    McNiven

SCORER

Jobson 56 mins, o.g.

VISITORS

25. Kevin Pilkington
3. Denis Irwin
5. Lee Sharpe
6. Gary Pallister
9. Brian McClair
16. Roy Keane
18. Simon Davies
28. David Beckham
19. Nicky Butt
23. Phil Neville
27. Gary Neville

SUBSTITUTES

21. Pat McGibbon
    Davies
29. Ben Thornley
    Sharpe
30. John O'Kane
    Irwin

SCORER

Sharpe | 26 mins

MATCH REPORT

Boundary Park was the venue for our final pre-season outing in a game held to celebrate Oldham's centenary.

At times the game was played at a leisurely pace. The 4,500 Reds in the Rochdale Road End had little to shout about until Sharpe, keeping his record of a goal in every two pre-season games, put us one up after 28 minutes.

Oldham defender Jobson sealed defeat for his side with an unfortunate own goal in the second half.

ASTON VILLA 3
MANCHESTER UNITED 1

HOME TEAM

1. Mark Bosnich
2. Gary Charles
4. Gareth Southgate
5. Paul McGrath
7. Ian Taylor
8. Mark Draper
9. Savo Milosevic
11. Andy Townsend
14. Alan Wright
16. Ugo Ehiogu
18. Dwight Yorke

SUBSTITUTES

10. **Tommy Johnson**
    Milosevic | 51 mins
20. **Riccardo Scimeca**
    Yorke | 87 mins
13. **Nigel Spink**

SCORERS

Taylor | 13 mins
Draper | 26 mins
Yorke | 37 mins

REFEREE

R Hart | Darlington

VISITORS

	RATING
1. Peter Schmeichel	6
2. Paul Parker	6
3. Denis Irwin	6
5. Lee Sharpe	6
6. Gary Pallister	6
9. Brian McClair	6
16. Roy Keane	6
19. Nicky Butt	6
22. Paul Scholes	6
23. Phil Neville	6
27. Gary Neville	6

SUBSTITUTES

24. **David Beckham** Neville, P	45 mins	7
30. **John O'Kane** Pallister	59 mins	6
18. **Simon Davies**	

SCORER

Beckham | 84 mins

MATCH REPORT

United's season got off to a disastrous start away to Villa, where we conceded three first-half goals. The United players looked stunned and so did the travelling fans as Taylor, Draper and Yorke bagged the goals against a desperate-looking United side.

Fergie's half-time pep-talk clearly woke the players up, and the second 45 minutes saw the Reds play some intelligent and attractive football. Butt and Keane ran the midfield, enabling Beckham and Sharpe to attack the wings. However, Villa's defence stood firm and looked strong, with Paul McGrath playing his part as usual. Our consolation came in the final stages of the game when the fresh legs of young David Beckham dispatched a powerful and late-dipping 25-yard strike.

The game was a real shock, but with the quality of the squad at Old Trafford, surely things could only get better.

IN THE PAPERS

"They began by experimenting with the three-at-the-back system which so many managers had predicted would become fashionable in the Premiership this season. Alex Ferguson said afterwards that his players were quite comfortable playing that way, and had proved it in three or four pre-season matches. That is not how it looked in yesterday's first half."
SUNDAY TELEGRAPH

"Admittedly, United – who sent on youngster David Beckham for Phil Neville at half time – lifted their game while Villa appeared to move down a gear. United began to play like a side who could so easily have won their second consecutive double last season."
SUNDAY MIRROR

"No Ince, no Hughes, no Kanchelskis – no chance. United were simply ripped apart as Villa sent the deposed champions crashing to their worst League defeat in three years. Three goals in a blistering first half."
DAILY EXPRESS

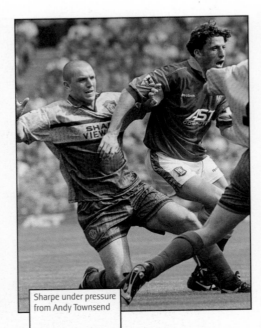

Sharpe under pressure from Andy Townsend

Little Yorkie jumps with big Pally

"These were bad goals to lose. They were all down to individuals' mistakes rather than the fault of the system. But you have to give credit to Aston Villa. They worked ever so hard to close us down."

ALEX FERGUSON

17

MANCHESTER UNITED 2
WEST HAM UNITED 1

HOME TEAM

		RATING
1.	Peter Schmeichel	7
3.	Denis Irwin	8
4.	Steve Bruce	8
5.	Lee Sharpe	7
6.	Gary Pallister	7
9.	Brian McClair	7
16.	Roy Keane	8
19.	Nicky Butt	8
20.	Gary Neville	7
22.	Paul Scholes	8
24.	David Beckham	7

SUBSTITUTES

17.	Andy Cole Scholes	69 mins	7
29.	Ben Thornley McClair	84 mins	7
25.	Kevin Pilkington	

SCORERS

Scholes | 50 mins
Keane | 68 mins

REFEREE

D J Gallagher | Banbury

VISITORS

1.	Ludek Miklosko
2.	Tim Breacker
3.	Julian Dicks
4.	Steve Potts
6.	Martin Allen
7.	Ian Bishop
8.	Marc Rieper
9.	Tony Cottee
10.	John Moncur
16.	Don Hutchison
20.	Danny Williamson

SUBSTITUTES

5.	Alvin Martin
30.	Les Sealey
11.	Marco Boogers Williamson	73 mins

SCORER

Bruce | 56 mins (o.g.)

MATCH REPORT

Roy Keane galvanised United's season with a winning goal against West Ham, much to the relief of everyone.

It wasn't all plain sailing though, as the Hammers levelled the score following a Scholes goal five minutes after the break.

Up until that goal, United had often threatened but failed to break down the visitors' weak defence. With the score at one a-piece, Keane came into his own. His surging runs showed that he is enjoying his new-found responsibility in the absence of Ince. When it came in the 68th minute, Keane's goal was simple and yet significant for the three points that came from it.

For their part, West Ham's battling display was overshadowed by the late sending off of Marco Boogers for a wild lunge on Gary Neville.

IN THE PAPERS

"Roy Keane provided the kick-start to Manchester United's spluttering season as he proved there can be life after Ince. The Irishman was an inspirational figure, claiming the goal which gave nervy United an important victory. It was a sweet moment in an interesting match soured only by the late dismissal of Hammers' summer signing Marco Boogers for an appalling challenge on his English debut." **TODAY**

"That carrot-topped terror Paul Scholes put United ahead early in the second half, only to see Bruce wipe out the lead with an own-goal... The players wore black armbands as a mark of respect to Johnny Carey, who played in every position bar outside left for United. Ferguson could have done with a player like that last night." **GUARDIAN**

"If this performance is to offer a true guideline of Fergie's future in the Championship race, goal king Cole is going to be badly needed. But Ferguson's joy at the win was softened at the last minute, when full back Gary Neville survived a horror tackle that could have put him out of soccer for weeks." **SUN**

Scholesy draws attention to himself

"West Ham
tried to make it
difficult with
five in midfield,
but we were
persistent and
succeeded in
the end."
ALEX FERGUSON

19

MANCHESTER UNITED 3
WIMBLEDON 1

HOME TEAM

		RATING
1.	Peter Schmeichel	7
3.	Denis Irwin	7
4.	Steve Bruce	7
5.	Lee Sharpe	6
6.	Gary Pallister	7
16.	Roy Keane	8
17.	Andy Cole	7
19.	Nicky Butt	7
20.	Gary Neville	7
22.	Paul Scholes	9
24.	David Beckham	7

SUBSTITUTES

		RATING
11.	Ryan Giggs Cole | 71 mins	7
2.	Paul Parker	
18.	Simon Davies Scholes | 82 mins	7

SCORERS

Keane | 27/79 mins
Cole | 59 mins

REFEREE

A J Hill | Blackpool

VISITORS

13.	Paul Heald
3.	Alan Kimble
4.	Vinny Jones
7.	Oyvind Leonhardsen
8.	Robbie Earle
9.	Efan Ekoku
10.	Dean Holdsworth
12.	Gary Elkins
15.	Alan Reeves
16.	Andy Thorn
21.	Chris Perry

SUBSTITUTES

32.	Steve Talboys Leonhardsen | 82 mins
14.	Jon Goodman Elkins | 45 mins
25.	Gary Blissett Ekoku | 82 mins

SCORER

Earle | 64 mins

MATCH REPORT

A splendid strike from Andy Cole, sandwiched between a brace from Keane, underlined United's best performance to date this season.

It was an occasion when the youngsters, Scholes, Butt, Beckham and Gary Neville, really came into their own and showed the benefits of their extended runs in the first team. Keane was thriving once again in a stadium which was subdued, due to the major re-development of the North Stand and the ban on visiting supporters.

United went ahead after 27 minutes when Keane exchanged passes with Scholes on the edge of the box and curled the ball around the Dons' keeper.

Cole added a second early in the second half, when he drilled the ball under keeper Heald from an impossible angle.

Wimbledon did manage to pull a goal back on 65 minutes through Robbie Earle, but any hopes of getting back into the match were killed off with a second from Keane 10 minutes from time.

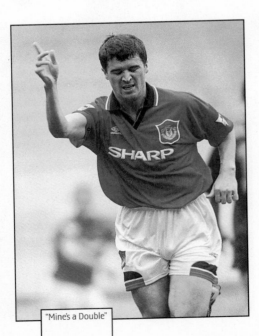

"Mine's a Double"

IN THE PAPERS

"'Cole's goal was typical and an exceptionally good one,' said Ferguson, clearly delighted by all he had seen. 'He had his back to goal when he got the ball, but turned a defender twice before hitting a perfect shot inches inside the post. He will definitely be in the team for Blackburn on Monday.'" **SUNDAY EXPRESS**

"Keane's double strike – he only scored twice in the League last season – took his tally to three in three games. And his youngsters shone through again. Proud Fergie declared: 'Playing against Wimbledon is your initiation as a man. It's always a test. You have to grow up in these games, and they did not let me or themselves down.'" **SUNDAY MIRROR**

"After scoring the winner against West Ham in midweek, Roy Keane was the main inspiration for a Manchester United performance that suggested the 3–1 defeat at Aston Villa on the opening day of the season may prove to be nothing more sinister than an embarrassing hiccup." **SUNDAY TELEGRAPH**

"If anybody launched more leisurely attacks yesterday than Manchester United, they must have been in an armchair. Not that this was necessarily a bad thing. Some of the relaxed networks of passing which they opened up were of the type that United will have to hone if they are to make any progress in Europe this season." **SUNDAY TIMES**

Beckham
speed-walks
out of trouble

On a clear day, you
can see to Fergie

BLACKBURN ROVERS 1
MANCHESTER UNITED 2

HOME TEAM

1. Tim Flowers
4. Tim Sherwood
5. Colin Hendry
6. Graeme Le Saux
7. Stuart Ripley
15. Matty Holmes
25. Ian Pearce
20. Henning Berg
23. David Batty
16. Chris Sutton
10. Alan Shearer

SUBSTITUTES

22. **Mark Atkins**
Holmes | 58 mins
13. **Bobby Mimms**
10. **Mike Newell**
Ripley | 82 mins

SCORER

Shearer | 59 mins

REFEREE

D Elleray | Harrqw-on-the-Hill

VISITORS

		RATING
1.	Peter Schmeichel	7
3.	Denis Irwin	7
4.	Steve Bruce	7
5.	Lee Sharpe	6
6.	Gary Pallister	8
16.	Roy Keane	8
17.	Andy Cole	8
19.	Nicky Butt	8
20.	Gary Neville	7
22.	Paul Scholes	9
24.	David Beckham	7

SUBSTITUTES

2. **Paul Parker**
11. **Ryan Giggs** — 7
Beckham | 76 mins
18. **Simon Davies** — 7
Scholes | 76 mins

SCORERS

Sharpe | 46 mins
Beckham | 72 mins

MATCH REPORT

In front of a watching nation, United showed that they will be challenging for the title once again by beating champions Blackburn in their own back yard.

The score was goalless after an action-packed first half, but United took the lead 30 seconds after the re-start through Sharpe. Blackburn responded like champions and drew level through the clinical Shearer a dozen minutes later. But United were always the better side and, in another goal-mouth scramble, Beckham turned and curled a quite stunning shot past Flowers.

The packed United end was bouncing to strains of "Boom, Boom, Boom, everybody say Keano," but it was Keane, the driving force in the United team since the opening day defeat by Villa, who made the only bad news of the night when he was sent off.

Keane was harshly booked for fouling Holmes, but received his marching orders when the referee judged him to have dived for a penalty. It was an unusual decision, and only slightly soured a wonderful evening for Manchester.

Beckham puckers up and shoots

IN THE PAPERS

"Roy Keane was controversially sent off as United plunged champions Blackburn into early season gloom. Keane, dismissed for the first time in his career in the FA Cup semi final last April, was at the centre of a diving storm. 'It was all played at 100mph and it was a wonderful advert for English football', claimed David Elleray." **DAILY STAR**

"The kids were all fight, all bite and all right on the night. Not even Alan Shearer's third goal in four games could prevent Fergie's babes at Ewood securing the greatest victory of their short careers. It was more than that, in fact. It was one of the greatest performances turned in by any Manchester United side since Alex Ferguson took charge." **SUN**

"United's general passing and movement were superior throughout and Andy Cole, now fully recovered from shin-splints, produced his best centre-forward play since Alex Ferguson signed him from Newcastle. An instinctive chip by David Beckham won the match for United after Alan Shearer had shown a glimpse of his better England form, with a firmly driven response to the goal Lee Sharpe scored at the very start of the second half." **GUARDIAN**

"Tempers flared 16 minutes from the end after Roy Keane crashed dramatically to the ground as Colin Hendry challenged for the ball." **DAILY MAIL**

Cole gets stuck in

Corner flags quiver as Sharpey scores

AUGUST STATS

PLAYER RECORDS

home | away

■ PREMIERSHIP ■ UEFA CUP ■ COCA COLA CUP ■ FA CUP

■ FULL APPEARANCE
▲ CAME ON AS SUB

■ SCORER
▲ SCORED AS SUB

	Matches	Full Appearances	Sub Appearances	Goals
1. Peter Schmeichel	▮▮▮▮	4	0	0
2. Paul Parker	▮	1	0	0
3. Denis Irwin	▮▮▮▮	4	0	0
4. Steve Bruce	▮▮▮	3	0	0
5. Lee Sharpe	▮▮▮▮	4	0	1
6. Gary Pallister	▮▮▮▮	4	0	0
7. Eric Cantona		0	0	0
9. Brian McClair	▮▮	2	0	0
11. Ryan Giggs	▲▲	0	2	0
12. David May		0	0	0
15. Graham Tomlinson		0	0	0
16. Roy Keane	▮▮▮▮	4	0	3
17. Andy Cole	▮▮▲	2	1	1
18. Simon Davies	▲▲	0	2	0
19. Nicky Butt	▮▮▮▮	4	0	0
20. Gary Neville	▮▮▮▮	4	0	0
21. Patrick McGibbon		0	0	0
22. Paul Scholes	▮▮▮▮	4	0	1
23. Philip Neville	▮	1	0	0
24. David Beckham	▲▮▮▮	3	1	2
25. Kevin Pilkington		0	0	0
27. Terry Cooke		0	0	0
29. Ben Thornley	▲	0	1	0
30. John O'Kane	▲	0	1	0

Match columns: Aston Villa, West Ham United, Wimbledon, Blackburn Rovers

PLAYER OF THE MONTH

ANDY COLE

AVERAGE PERFORMANCE RATING: 7.7

FA CARLING PREMIERSHIP

as at 28 August 1995

		Home					Away						
	Pld	W	D	L	F	A	W	D	L	F	A	Pts	GD
■ Leeds United	3	2	0	0	3	0	1	0	0	2	1	9	+4
■ Newcastle United	3	1	0	0	3	0	2	0	0	5	1	9	+7
■ Manchester United	4	2	0	0	5	2	1	0	1	3	4	9	+2
■ Wimbledon	3	1	0	0	3	2	1	0	1	4	3	6	+2
■ Liverpool	3	1	0	0	1	0	1	0	1	3	2	6	+2
■ Aston Villa	3	1	0	0	3	1	1	0	1	2	6	6	+1
■ Arsenal	3	0	1	0	1	1	1	1	0	2	0	5	+2
■ Nottingham Forest	3	0	2	0	1	1	1	0	0	4	3	5	+1
■ Middlesbrough	2	1	0	0	2	0	0	1	0	1	1	4	+2
■ Everton	3	0	1	0	2	2	0	1	0	0	0	4	-2
■ Coventry City	3	1	1	0	2	1	0	0	1	0	3	4	-2
■ Sheffield Wednesday	3	1	0	1	2	3	0	0	1	0	1	3	-2
■ Blackburn Rovers	4	1	0	1	2	2	0	2	2	4	4	3	-2
■ Bolton Wanderers	3	1	0	1	3	4	0	0	1	2	3	3	-2
■ Queens Park Rangers	3	1	0	1	3	0	0	0	1	0	1	3	-3
■ Chelsea	3	0	1	0	0	0	0	1	1	0	2	2	-2
■ West Ham United	3	0	0	1	1	2	0	1	1	2	3	1	-2
■ Manchester City	3	0	1	0	1	1	0	0	2	1	3	1	-2
■ Tottenham Hotspur	3	0	0	2	1	4	0	1	0	1	1	1	-3
■ Southampton	2	0	0	1	3	4	0	0	1	0	1	0	-2

1 | 2 | 3 | 4 | 5 | 6 | 7 | 8 | 9 | 10 | 11 | 12 | 13 | 14 | 15 | 16 | 17 | 18 | 19 | 20 | 21 | 22 | 23 | 24 | 25 | 26 | 27 | 28 | 29 | 30

SEPTEMBER

THE MONTH IN REVIEW

September saw the evenings begin to draw in, the steamy summer temperatures finally drop and United crash disastrously in not one but two cup competitions. Winter had come early to Old Trafford.

United had finished August well with the away victory at Blackburn – sweet revenge after the previous season's title heartbreak. September began with an away fixture against the side that had not only stolen the FA Cup at Wembley in May, but had also lured away one of the Reds' star players. A match against Everton, and new boy Kanchelskis, was bound to be a highly charged affair... and so it proved.

With Kanchelskis no longer blocking his path into the first team, it was Lee Sharpe who was United's hero... and the home fans' villain. Sharpe scored an early goal for United and then, to the Everton fans' horror, with Kanchelskis flying down the wing he sent the Russian tumbling with a strong tackle.

Kanchelskis fell awkwardly and dislocated his shoulder. That was that for the former United winger. To add insult to injury for the furious Goodison crowd, Sharpe scored again. United went on to win 3–2 and move into second place behind Newcastle on goal difference. "It was supposed to be the Andrei Kanchelskis show," said the *Observer*, "but Lee Sharpe stole it."

This was the month that Hindu statues mysteriously drank milk in temples around the world. United set off for Russia and what was supposed to be the start of a long campaign in Europe. The first round of the UEFA Cup had pitted the Reds against Rotor Volgograd. A clean sheet was vital and a clean sheet was kept, with United showing maturity beyond their years. The second leg, two weeks later, didn't go so well. United suddenly found themselves two goals down after 24 minutes and, despite a huge cavalry charge in the second half, couldn't climb the mountain. Scholes pulled one back on the hour and, incredibly, Schmeichel headed home a Giggs cross with one minute to go. It was enough to preserve United's 39-year run of being unbeaten at Old Trafford in Europe; enough to salvage a little pride; but it wasn't enough to stay in Europe.

The two weeks between the UEFA Cup

SEPTEMBER
NUMBER ONES

SINGLE
You Are Not Alone
Michael Jackson

ALBUM
The Great Escape
Blur

FILM
Apollo 13

A nightmare for Kan-Kan against his old club

matches had seen the good, the bad and the ugly from United. The good came from an unbelievably young side (including Scholes, Cooke, Beckham, Butt and Philip Neville) that had Bobby Charlton drooling after their 3–0 League win against Bolton at Old Trafford. "I can't remember anything as good as these kids" he said, and he was including the Busby Babes he'd been a part of nearly 40 years earlier. But just four days later at the same venue, United lost by the same score to practically-bottom-of-the-second-division York in one of the biggest Cup shocks in the history of the game.

A victory was necessary at the weekend to dispel the blues. But the "ugly" and uncharacteristically unambitous Reds looked like they were happy to go for a draw against Sheffield Wednesday at Hillsborough. When a Pembridge free kick ricocheted off a defender and over Schmeichel, all looked lost, but the ball hit the bar and the game finished 0–0. Nevertheless, with Newcastle playing the following day, the single point was enough to put United in familiar territory: the top-of-the-table spot. They were pushed back down again 24 hours later, when Newcastle made no mistake of their win at home to Chelsea. But it

Get yourself some York life, mate: Beckham can run but he can't hide

didn't seem to matter, because the next match was at home to Liverpool on 1 October. The first of October: the date that every United fan had had imprinted on his or her mind for months. That was the day when the Magnificent Seven would return... the day Cantona was coming back!

> ## "I asked to see one of Fergie's celebrating Babes after the match. Sorry, I was told, they've already gone to bed."
>
> PETER FITTON OF THE SUN, AFTER THE BOLTON MATCH.

So near and yet UEFA: Butt deals with defeat

EVERTON 2
MANCHESTER UNITED 3

HOME TEAM

1. Neville Southall
4. David Unsworth
5. Dave Watson
6. Gary Ablett
10. Barry Horne
11. Anders Limpar
18. Joe Parkinson
34. Paul Holmes
17. Andrei Kanchelskis
12. Daniel Amokachi
8. Paul Rideout

SUBSTITUTES

3. Andy Hinchcliffe
   Kanchelskis | 14 mins
13. Jason Kearton
19. Stuart Barlow

SCORERS

Limpar | 27 mins
Rideout | 55 mins

REFEREE

G Poll | Tring

VISITORS

	RATING
1. Peter Schmeichel	7
20. Gary Neville	8
3. Denis Irwin	7
4. Steve Bruce	8
6. Gary Pallister	7
5. Lee Sharpe	8
16. Roy Keane	7
19. Nicky Butt	7
17. Andy Cole	8
22. Paul Scholes	7
24. David Beckham	7

SUBSTITUTES

2. Paul Parker	
11. Ryan Giggs	8
Scholes | 66 mins	
18. Simon Davies	7
Cole | 73 mins	

SCORERS

Sharpe | 3/49 mins
Giggs | 74 mins

MATCH REPORT

United fans let their feelings be known about Kanchelskis when he took to the field in an Everton shirt to howls of derision from the travelling Red army. The Ukrainian didn't last long though, as he was withdrawn, injured, after just 14 minutes of this blood-and-thunder Manc/Scouse derby.

By that time United were ahead, thanks to a Sharpe goal after just three minutes. Everton levelled after 27 minutes when a Pallister back-pass was intercepted by Limpar who beat Schmeichel with a crisp, perfectly placed shot.

The game was played in a style more akin to a crucial Cup-tie. But for all the action, there was a price to pay: eight bookings and one Everton sending-off. That man Sharpe put United ahead just after the break when he disposessed Cole and planted the ball firmly past Southall.

United's game? Not yet. The Toffeemen hit back immediately through Rideout, who knocked in the rebound off Limpar's long-range shot. Neither team was settling for a draw, and a goal from the United substitute Giggs with 16 minutes of the game left sealed a smashing match.

Amokachi in a Gary sandwich

IN THE PAPERS

"Two-goal hero Lee Sharpe, a part-time male model, turned Goodison Park into his own catwalk, despite jeers from irate Evertonians every time he touched the ball following Kanchelskis' painful departure."
MAIL ON SUNDAY

"Match winner Ryan Giggs ended his Premiership hell to shoot Manchester United to the top of the table... Giggs, without a League goal for a year, replaced Paul Scholes and broke his duck with a classy left-footer." **PEOPLE**

"These kids proved they can do a man's job. They stood up to the pressure of an Everton side who have a special talent for closing down and preventing the opposition from expressing themselves... The midfield was a hotly contested war zone. Barry Horne and Joe Parkinson for Everton and Roy Keane and Nicky Butt for United made it a no-go area." **DAILY STAR**

"It was supposed to be the Andrei Kanchelskis show, but Lee Sharpe stole it..."
OBSERVER

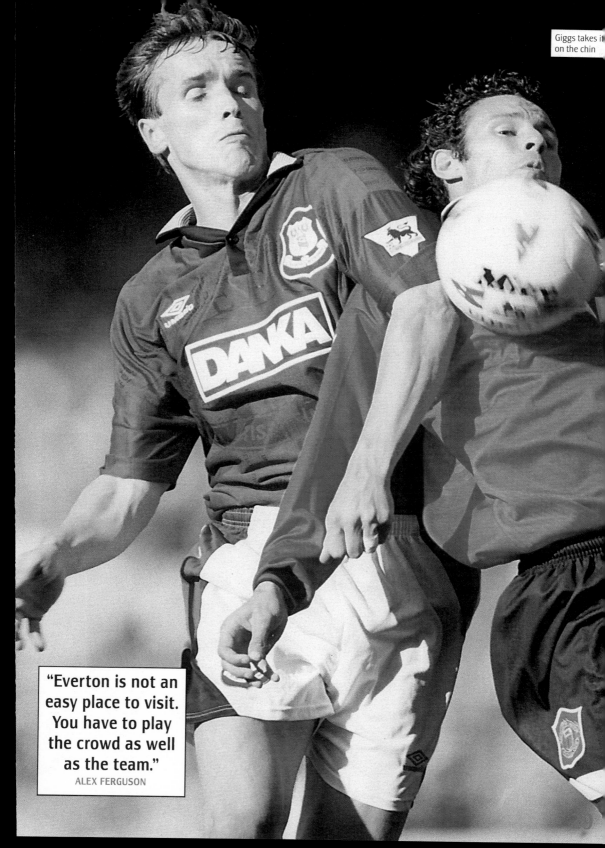

"Everton is not an easy place to visit. You have to play the crowd as well as the team."

ALEX FERGUSON

ROTOR VOLGOGRAD 0
MANCHESTER UNITED 0

HOME TEAM

1. Andrei Samorukov
2. Alexander Shmarko
3. Valery Burlatchenko
4. Vladimir Gerastchenko
5. Alexander Estchenko
6. Sergey Junenko
7. Igor Korniets
8. Vladimir Nidergaus
9. Oleg Veretennikov
10. Valery Esipov
11. Alexander Zernov

SUBSTITUTES

12. Alexander Berketov
13. Igor Menstchikov
14. Alexander Tsarenko
15. Andrey Krivov
    Zernov | 79 mins
16. Eugeny Tchinenov

REFEREE

P Mikkelsen | Denmark

VISITORS   RATING

1. Peter Schmeichel   8
2. Gary Neville   8
3. Denis Irwin   8
4. Steve Bruce   8
5. Lee Sharpe   7
6. Gary Pallister   8
7. David Beckham   8
8. Nicky Butt   8
9. Paul Scholes   8
10. Roy Keane   7
11. Ryan Giggs   9

SUBSTITUTES

12. Paul Parker   7
    Scholes | 70 mins
13. Kevin Pilkington
14. Phil Neville
15. Simon Davies   7
    Keane | 23 mins
16. Terry Cooke

MATCH REPORT

Fergie's young troops survived their own siege of Stalingrad despite losing midfield general Keane after just 23 minutes. With six players aged 21 or below, the young United team suppressed Volgograd for the majority of the match and created enough chances of their own to have won the game.

Volgograd grew in confidence as the game wore on, and Schmeichel was called into action often enough to scare the 140 travelling fans as it drew to a close. A result which should have left United content, and suggested there would be no real problems on the return leg at Old Trafford.

IN THE PAPERS

"This team, for all its youth, has the drive and conviction not to fail. In the second half, they had their moments of good fortune and had to defend with purpose as Volgograd at last began to ask serious questions of them." **TIMES**

"Giggs, playing in his first full game of the season, was majestic. His pace, vision and close control mesmerised the Russians…" **DAILY STAR**

"It was fascinating if not thrilling stuff. United sensibly got bodies behind the ball, aware that to leave themselves outnumbered could be dangerous." **DAILY TELEGRAPH**

Doing it the Lee way

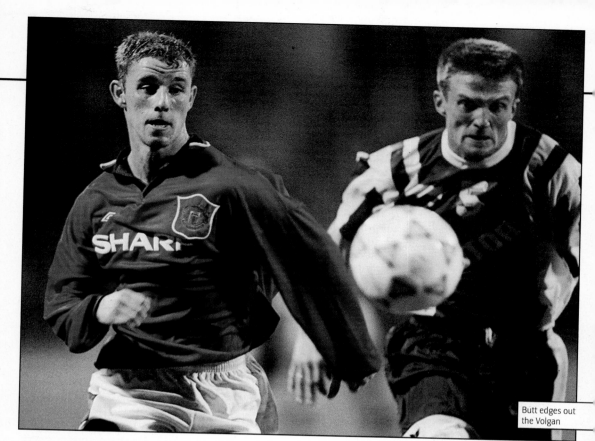

Butt edges out
the Volgan

Head still, eye
on the ball and
follow through

MANCHESTER UNITED 3
BOLTON WANDERERS 0

HOME TEAM

		RATING
1.	Peter Schmeichel	8
2.	Paul Parker	7
23.	Phil Neville	7
4.	Steve Bruce	8
6.	Gary Pallister	8
5.	Lee Sharpe	7
19.	Nicky Butt	8
24.	David Beckham	8
11.	Ryan Giggs	8
22.	Paul Scholes	8
27.	Terry Cooke	8

SUBSTITUTES

18.	Simon Davies	7
	Cooke | 74 mins	
25.	Kevin Pilkington	
21.	Patrick McGibbon	

SCORERS

Scholes | 17/85 mins
Giggs | 33 mins

REFEREE

S W Dunn | Bristol

VISITORS

1.	Keith Branagan
2.	Scott Green
3.	Jimmy Phillips
5.	Gudni Bergsson
8.	Richard Sneekes
10.	John McGinlay
11.	Alan Thompson
14.	Fabian De Freitas
7.	David Lee
21.	Chris Fairclough
22.	Gerry Taggart

SUBSTITUTES

6.	Alan Stubbs	
	McGinlay | 71 mins	
13.	Aidan Davidson	
15.	Mark Patterson	
	Taggart | 53 mins	

MATCH REPORT

Bolton only travelled 10 miles south to Manchester for this derby against United, but they met such overwhelming skill they may well have felt they'd gone all the way to Milan or Madrid.

With Giggs back to his brilliant best and Beckham in splendid form, Bolton were chasing the youngsters' shadows for the full 90 minutes. Scholes claimed two goals either side of Giggs's brilliant 34th-minute effort in a game which delighted the Old Trafford crowd. The young side, including Terry Cooke on his debut, were such a joy to behold that United legend Bobby Charlton enthused: 'I can't remember seeing anything as good as that. I was moved.' Quite.

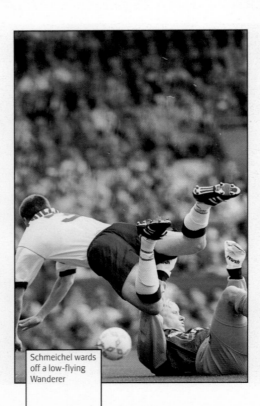

Schmeichel wards off a low-flying Wanderer

IN THE PAPERS

"Bobby Charlton can't remember anything as good, as breathtaking as the way United's babes created a second goal of sheer beauty in the 34th minute. David Beckham arrowed a pass to debut boy Terry Cooke, who manufactured a Maradona-style back-heel pass to Paul Scholes without a care that 32,812 people were watching." **OBSERVER**

"Burnden Park is 10 miles down the road, but this was the first time in 16 seasons that Bolton had come to this famous ground in search of points. You would not have thought so." **SUNDAY TIMES**

"Ferguson included eight players aged 21 or under in United's 14. Their performances, notably that of the rapidly maturing David Beckham, gave a fresh twist to the line about boys against men." **INDEPENDENT**

"I asked to see one of Fergie's celebrating babes after the match, but I was told they had gone to bed!" **SUN**

Terry Cooke makes his debut

"It was a wonderful performance by our players today."
ALEX FERGUSON

33

MANCHESTER UNITED 0

YORK CITY 3

HOME TEAM RATING

1.	Kevin Pilkington	6
2.	Paul Parker	6
3.	Denis Irwin	7
4.	Patrick McGibbon	6
5.	Lee Sharpe	6
6.	Gary Pallister	7
7.	Phil Neville	6
8.	David Beckham	6
9.	Brian McClair	6
10.	Simon Davies	6
11.	Ryan Giggs	7

SUBSTITUTES

12.	Steve Bruce	7
	Davies	56 mins	
14.	Terry Cooke	6
	Neville	46 mins	
15.	Graeme Tomlinson	

REFEREE

J Rushton | Stoke

VISITORS

1.	Dean Kiely
2.	Andy McMillan
3.	Wayne Hall
4.	Nigel Pepper
5.	Steve Tutill
6.	Tony Barras
7.	Graeme Murty
8.	Darren Williams
9.	Paul Barnes
10.	Nick Peverell
11.	Scott Jordan

SUBSTITUTES

12.	Paul Atkin
	Barnes	89 mins
13.	Andy Warrington
14.	Paul Baker
	Peverell	67 mins

SCORERS

Barnes | 24/51 mins
Barras | 53 mins

MATCH REPORT

United were humiliated in front of an Old Trafford crowd by York City, a team from the bottom of the Endsleigh League Division Two.

In the first game of the season's Coca-Cola Cup campaign, Barnes started what was to become a landslide when he put the visitors ahead after 24 minutes. Despite a determined onslaught, United could make no dent in the York defence. As Red frustrations grew, McGibbon was sent off just after the break for a professional foul on his debut appearance. Barnes increased the misery a minute later with a penalty that made it 2–0. As if things couldn't get worse, Barras struck a third goal for York a couple of minutes later. A night best forgotten.

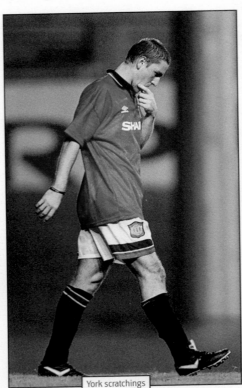

York scratchings

IN THE PAPERS

"The bombs were detonated without compassion as the team at the bottom of the Second Division blitzed the Premiership high-flyers, and you could feel every bit of pain inflicted on Fergie's fresh-faced kids." **DAILY MIRROR**

"Alan Little's side played forceful and skilful football and, from the start, took the game to the home team. United's team changes put them in disarray and Pilkington in their goal spent a great deal of time fielding back-passes." **GUARDIAN**

"United manager Alex Ferguson had warned his youngsters they could not afford to be blasé about facing the Yorkshire side." **DAILY MAIL**

"York sent Manchester United crashing to defeat in one of the most sensational cup upsets of all time. At the end, York received a standing ovation from United's shell-shocked fans as they deservedly milked every second of their unbelievable achievement." **DAILY STAR**

"Oh, the terrible shame and embarrassment of it all." **SUN**

United's defence
stretched again

A nightmare come true

SHEFFIELD WEDNESDAY 0
MANCHESTER UNITED 0

HOME TEAM

- 13. Kevin Preston
- 2. Peter Atherton
- 3. Ian Nolan
- 4. Mark Pembridge
- 5. Dan Petrescu
- 8. Chris Waddle
- 9. David Hirst
- 12. Andy Pearce
- 14. Marc Degryse
- 16. Graham Hyde
- 17. Des Walker

SUBSTITUTES

- 10. Mark Bright
  Hirst | 86 mins
- 11. John Sheridan
- 29. Lee Briscoe
  Pembridge | 81 mins

REFEREE

K W Burge | Tonypandy

VISITORS

		RATING
1.	Peter Schmeichel	9
2.	Paul Parker	6
3.	Denis Irwin	6
4.	Steve Bruce	7
6.	Gary Pallister	6
9.	Brian McClair	6
11.	Ryan Giggs	8
18.	Simon Davies	6
19.	Nicky Butt	7
22.	Paul Scholes	7
24.	David Beckham	7

SUBSTITUTES

23.	Phil Neville	
26.	Chris Casper	
27.	Terry Cooke	7
	Davies	67mins	

MATCH REPORT

A week before Eric Cantona returned to action in a United shirt, the Reds moved up to pole position in the Premier League with a point at Hillsborough.

However, this was a lacklustre performance from United. The young players who had contributed so much in recent weeks looked lightweight and ineffective. Wednesday's Chris Waddle was allowed to patrol the midfield and spray passes around which frequently threatened to unlock the United defence.

Eventually it was the old-timers, Bruce and Pallister, who earned United a point when they fulfilled their task of containing Hirst, Degryse, Waddle and Pembridge.

IN THE PAPERS

"United were composed and intermittently dangerous for the first 30 minutes. But they adopted a much more passive approach in the middle third of the match, when attack was less of a concern than containment."
INDEPENDENT ON SUNDAY

"United rarely threatened, but the Owls were stretched by a couple of menacing United breakaways in the first half."
NEWS OF THE WORLD

"Alex Ferguson is set to welcome back wild child Eric Cantona and reckons his well-behaved kids are all about to blossom! Quite frightening, considering his babes moved to the top of the table without the French genius anywhere in sight."
SUNDAY MIRROR

"The placid tempo was rudely disturbed by Wednesday hitting the bar. Pembridge's free kick ballooned off a red shirt and left Schmeichel no more than a sunbathing spectator." **OBSERVER**

Scrambled legs

Parker keeps tabs on Hirst

"We've done very well so far and we've got ability. It doesn't surprise me at all that we are top... "

ALEX FERGUSON

37

MANCHESTER UNITED 2
ROTOR VOLGOGRAD 2

HOME TEAM | RATING

		RATING
1.	Peter Schmeichel	10
2.	John O'Kane	7
3.	Phil Neville	8
4.	Steve Bruce	8
5.	Lee Sharpe	8
6.	Gary Pallister	8
7.	David Beckham	8
8.	Nicky Butt	9
9.	Andy Cole	8
10.	Roy Keane	7
11.	Ryan Giggs	9

SUBSTITUTES

12.	Paul Scholes	9
	O'Kane I 26 mins	
13.	Kevin Pilkington	
14.	Brian McClair	
15.	Terry Cook	7
	Beckham I 82 mins	
16.	Chris Casper	

SCORERS

Scholes I 59 mins
Schmeichel I 89 mins

REFEREE

B Henemann I Germany

VISITORS

1.	Andrei Samorukov
2.	Alexander Shmarko
3.	Valery Burlatchenko
4.	Alexander Berketov
5.	Alexander Estchenko
6.	Sergey Junenko
7.	Igor Korniets
8.	Vladimir Nidergaus
9.	Oleg Veretennikov
10.	Valery Esipov
11.	Alexander Zernov

SUBSTITUTES

12.	Sergei Ilushin
	Zernov I 73 mins
13.	Alexander Tsarenko
	Estchenko I 69 mins
14.	Andrey Krivov
	Nidergaus I 77 mins
15.	Eugeny Tchinenov

SCORERS

Nidergaus I 16 mins
Veretennikov I 24 mins

MATCH REPORT

Once again, Manchester United failed in Europe. Conceding two goals at home to a Russian side of questionable pedigree showed that United still hadn't learned from their lessons in European competition.

The Russians outclassed United for the first half hour and took the lead after just 16 minutes through Nidergaus. The fear and embarrassment doubled in the 25th minute, when Veretennikov picked up on an error from Bruce and cannoned the ball past Schmeichel.

The next hour saw United sustain a charge on the Rotor goal, but the mistakes had already been made. United poured forward in waves and Scholes pulled a goal back on 59 minutes. Bruce and Pallister both came close to scoring, but it was to no avail.

United came back with an equaliser at the very end, when Schmeichel of all people spared us from losing our first home game in European competition.

Success in Europe slips away

IN THE PAPERS

"They were the brave hearts of Europe. They died with their boots on and up to their necks in rotten luck. But they still rescued a famous record boasted by United for 39 years." **SUN**

"They were warriors to a man. Brave hearts who sweated every last drop to repel the invaders from Russia." **DAILY MIRROR**

"Rotor needed everybody they had, as well as luck, to keep the ball out until two minutes before time, when the Danish keeper headed Giggs' corner past his counterpart." **DAILY TELEGRAPH**

"Sweeper Alexander Shmarko was penalised for hand ball and, though the offence was clearly inside the penalty area, the free kick was awarded outside. That summed up United's misery." **DAILY MAIL**

Schmeichel's first-ever goal for United

"I'm disappointed at the result, obviously. But I can have no complaints about the performance of my players in the second half."

ALEX FERGUSON

SEPTEMBER STATS

PLAYER RECORDS

home | away

■ PREMIERSHIP ■ UEFA CUP ■ COCA COLA CUP ■ FA CUP

FULL APPEARANCE / CAME ON AS SUB
SCORER / SCORED AS SUB

Opponents (left to right): Aston Villa · West Ham United · Wimbledon · Blackburn Rovers · Everton · Rotor Volgograd · Bolton Wanderers · York City · Sheffield Wednesday · Rotor Volgograd

No.	Player	Full Appearances	Sub Appearances	Goals
1.	Peter Schmeichel	9	0	1
2.	Paul Parker	4	1	0
3.	Denis Irwin	8	0	0
4.	Steve Bruce	8	1	0
5.	Lee Sharpe	9	0	3
6.	Gary Pallister	10	0	0
7.	Eric Cantona	0	0	0
9.	Brian McClair	4	0	0
11.	Ryan Giggs	5	3	2
12.	David May	0	0	0
15.	Graeme Tomlinson	0	0	0
16.	Roy Keane	7	0	3
17.	Andy Cole	4	1	1
18.	Simon Davies	2	5	0
19.	Nicky Butt	9	0	0
20.	Gary Neville	6	0	0
21.	Patrick McGibbon	1	0	0
22.	Paul Scholes	8	1	3
23.	Philip Neville	4	0	0
24.	David Beckham	9	1	2
25.	Kevin Pilkington	1	0	0
26.	Chris Casper	0	0	0
27.	Terry Cooke	1	3	0
29.	Ben Thornley	0	1	0
30.	John O'Kane	1	1	0

PLAYER OF THE MONTH

RYAN GIGGS

AVERAGE PERFORMANCE RATING: **8.3**

FA CARLING PREMIERSHIP

as at 23 September 1995

	Pld	Home W	D	L	F	A	Away W	D	L	F	A	Pts	GD
▲ Manchester United	7	3	0	0	8	2	2	1	1	6	6	16	6
■ Newcastle United	6	3	0	0	7	1	2	0	1	5	2	13	9
▲ Liverpool	7	4	0	0	10	2	1	0	2	3	3	15	8
▲ Arsenal	7	2	2	0	7	4	2	1	0	3	0	15	6
▲ Aston Villa	7	3	1	0	7	2	1	1	1	2	3	14	4
▼ Leeds United	7	2	0	1	4	3	2	1	1	8	6	13	3
▲ Middlesbrough	7	2	1	0	4	1	1	2	1	3	3	12	3
■ Nottingham Forest	7	1	2	0	4	3	1	3	0	7	6	11	2
▼ Wimbledon	7	2	1	1	8	8	1	0	2	4	5	10	-1
▲ Chelsea	6	1	2	0	5	2	1	1	1	3	3	9	3
▲ Tottenham Hotspur	6	1	0	2	3	5	1	2	0	5	3	8	0
■ Sheffield Wednesday	7	1	1	2	3	6	1	1	1	5	3	8	-1
■ Blackburn Rovers	7	2	1	1	8	4	0	0	3	2	7	7	-1
■ Everton	7	1	0	2	4	5	1	1	2	5	5	7	-1
■ Queens Park Rangers	6	1	0	2	1	6	1	0	2	3	3	6	-5
▼ Coventry City	7	1	2	0	3	2	0	1	3	4	12	6	-7
■ West Ham United	7	1	1	2	5	7	0	1	2	2	4	5	-4
▼ Southampton	7	1	1	1	5	5	0	1	3	2	9	5	-7
▼ Bolton Wanderers	7	1	1	1	4	5	0	0	4	4	12	4	-9
▼ Manchester City	7	0	1	3	1	5	0	0	3	2	6	1	-8

OCTOBER

1 | 2 | 3 | 4 | 5 | 6 | 7 | 8 | 9 | 10 | 11 | 12 | 13 | 14 | 15 | 16 | 17 | 18 | 19 | 20 | 21 | 22 | 23 | 24 | 25 | 26 | 27 | 28 | 29 | 30 | 31

OCTOBER

THE MONTH IN REVIEW

The French were causing a stir wherever they went in October. But while controversial nuclear tests continued in the Pacific, it was the massive explosion of emotion that greeted Eric's return which caused the commotion in Manchester. The first of October saw the return of the king, when Eric Cantona was allowed to grace the field once more after eight months in the footballing wilderness...

And what a setting for his comeback: Liverpool at Old Trafford. Traditionally the fixture of the year for both sets of fans, this was the fixture of the decade and Cantona needed just 68 seconds to show us all what we'd been missing. With the crowd still waving their *tricolore* flags, Cole found the Frenchman drifting into space on the left. Cantona's perfect "croix" found Butt, and the youngster beat Babb with a deft flick before volleying United fans into seventh heaven.

But just like the three remaining Beatles were doing at the time, Liverpool staged a come-back. Fowler sneaked a couple of goals to threaten a win, but Eric hadn't finished yet. His godlike pass put Giggs free in the box, Redknapp fouled, Eric stepped up to take the spot kick, and up the pole he joyously climbed. A 2–2 draw

wasn't the best of results with Newcastle winning at Everton, but Eric was back.

A few days later OJ Simpson walked free, and if United were going to get out of jail in the Coca-Cola Cup then they'd need just as much luck... only unlike OJ, they only had 90 minutes to overcome the odds. United needed to win 4–0 but could only muster 3–1, despite the best of starts which saw Cantona set up SuperScholes for a goal in the seventh minute. Bye bye Coca-Cola Cup. Next stop the derby.

England's match with Norway meant there was a mid-month break before the City game, but Fergie wanted to give Eric a bit of match practice. So he played him in a Reserve match against Leeds and 21,500 fans turned up at Old Trafford! Unfortunately the pace and excitement was too much for Eric who hobbled off after 15 minutes with a knee injury. For the record, United won 2–0.

No Eric against City in the Old Trafford derby meant that there was precious little penetration in the United attack. Scholes showed what a prospect he is by nodding in a Giggsy-special corner after only four minutes, but United's biggest hero on the day was City striker Niall Quinn, who missed a couple of sitters. Nice one, big lad! Still, the win kept United in second place, four points behind the Geordies, and put smiles on the faces of the red half of Manchester.

With Newcastle in blistering form, United had to be at their best to keep

OCTOBER
NUMBER ONES

SINGLE
Fairground
Simply Red

ALBUM
(What's the Story)
Morning
Glory?
Oasis

FILM
Clueless

A thoughtful Robbo looks at what he left behind

It ain't worth a thing if it ain't got that swing

within coat-tail distance. As news came in that Newcastle were thrashing Wimbledon, things weren't looking too clever at Stamford Bridge. United were 2–1 up and Hoddle's men were pounding on the door for an equaliser. Chelsea's goal came from Mark Hughes, of course. Then Giggs scored a cor-blimey stunner and McClair wrapped things up after coming on with five minutes to go, leaving Chelsea at the end of a drubbing when they'd probably deserved at least a draw. Full marks to Paul Scholes for two early goals, taking his October tally to five.

United's last match in the month of Eric looked like it was going to be all about a new arrival, but in the end the biggest

> ## "Old Trafford's Theatre of Dreams was turned into a temple of worship. For them, this was the second coming and Eric, their Messiah, had not disappointed."
>
> TODAY

Fred le Red hails Eric le Roi

story was the return of a familiar face. Boro manager Bryan Robson's return to the ground he knows so well drew a heart-warming reception from the crowd, though Brazilian star Juninho wasn't ready to make his debut for Middlesbrough at Old Trafford. But Robbo's hard-working team looked like they could do with the Brazilian's skills, and United won 2–0 despite having Roy Keane sent off after 29 minutes for throwing a punch at Jan Fjørtoft. Not a brilliant victory, then: it was sealed with a much-needed last gasper from Andy Cole. But an important win, which took United to within one point of Newcastle.

MANCHESTER UNITED 2
LIVERPOOL 2

HOME TEAM

		RATING
1.	Peter Schmeichel	8
20.	Gary Neville	8
23.	Phil Neville	8
4.	Steve Bruce	8
5.	Lee Sharpe	7
6.	Gary Pallister	8
16.	Roy Keane	7
19.	Nicky Butt	8
11.	Ryan Giggs	9
7.	Eric Cantona	8
17.	Andy Cole	7

SUBSTITUTES

2.	Paul Parker	
22.	Paul Scholes	8
	P Neville | 73 mins	
24.	David Beckham	7
	Butt | 46 mins	

SCORERS

Butt | 1 min
Cantona | 70 mins (pen)

REFEREE

D Elleray | Harrow-on-the-Hill

VISITORS

1.	David James
4.	Jason McAteer
6.	Phil Babb
12.	John Scales
22.	Steve Harkness
25.	Neil Ruddock
15.	Jamie Redknapp
17.	Steve McManaman
9.	Ian Rush
16.	Michael Thomas
23.	Robbie Fowler

SUBSTITUTES

8.	Stan Collymore
19.	Marc Kennedy
26.	Tony Warner

SCORER

Fowler | 32/53 mins

MATCH REPORT

The King is back. Cantona received a legend's reception from those lucky enough to have tickets before he got down to doing what he does best: entertaining.

Cantona took just 67 seconds to burst down the left and spin in a cross for Butt, who lifted the ball over the keeper James. Cue ecstasy all around the stadium.

But Liverpool were always going to provide stern opposition. As the game took shape, they took control in midfield and Fowler comprehensively beat Schmeichel with a terrific shot.

It was Fowler who gave the scousers the lead on 52 minutes. United were down but definitely not out. After 69 minutes, Giggs was bought down by Redknapp and referee Elleray awarded a penalty to United. And who else but the maestro could step forward and coolly sweep the ball into the net?

Pally and Brucey up to mischief

IN THE PAPERS

"In the end it was neither fish nor foul – nor sardine, nor seagull, as the man himself might have put it. Eric Cantona made a goal and scored a goal, but his welcome home party ended in anti-climax." **INDEPENDENT**

"On his first appearance for nearly nine months, Cantona was offered the perfect chance to put his name up in lights and start the party. A penalty for Manchester and United's specialist spot-kicker not only bought a somewhat fortunate equaliser – it caused an eruption." **SUN**

"Few could deny Cantona's triumph, given his colourful contribution to this special occasion – Liverpool being the few. The Manchester United faithful went wild. Old Trafford's Theatre of Dreams was turned into a temple of worship. For them this was the second coming and Eric, their Messiah, had not disappointed." **TODAY**

"In the second half, Alex Ferguson shuffled and reshuffled his formation, bringing on first Beckham and then Scholes as avoidance of defeat promised to become a belated pursuit of victory." **GUARDIAN**

The King
is back...

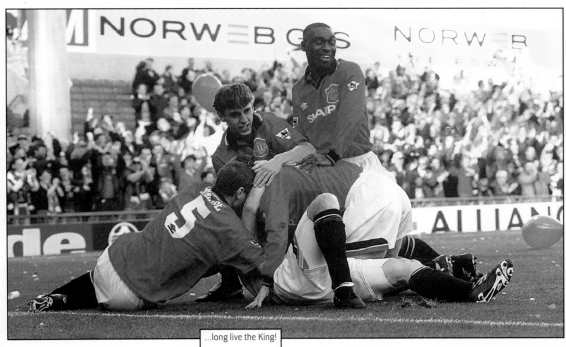

...long live the King!

YORK CITY 1

MANCHESTER UNITED 3

HOME TEAM

1. Andy Warrington
2. Andy McMillan
3. Wayne Hall
4. Nigel Pepper
5. Steve Tutill
6. Tony Barras
7. Paul Atkin
8. Darren Williams
9. Paul Barnes
10. Nick Peverell
11. Scott Jordan

SUBSTITUTES

12. Scott Oxley
13. Glen Naylor
    Peverell | 90 mins
14. Paul Baker
    Barnes | 87 mins

SCORER

Jordan | 39 mins

REFEREE

J T Winter | Middlesborough

VISITORS

		RATING
1.	Peter Schmeichel	7
2.	Gary Neville	8
3.	Lee Sharpe	6
4.	Steve Bruce	6
5.	Terry Cooke	7
6.	Garry Pallister	7
7.	Eric Cantona	7
8.	David Beckham	6
9.	Andy Cole	7
10.	Paul Scholes	8
11.	Ryan Giggs	7

SUBSTITUTES

12.	Phil Neville	7
	Sharpe	67 mins	
14.	Brian McClair	
15.	Roy Keane	7
	Cooke	53 mins	

SCORERS

Scholes | 7/80 mins
Cooke | 14 mins

MATCH REPORT

With a mountain to climb from the shattering 3–0 defeat two weeks before, United set out in this game as they intended to go on, with two goals in the first 15 minutes.

The first came when Cantona picked out Scholes after seven minutes and the young striker buried his effort past rookie-keeper Warrington. Five minutes later, Terry Cooke collected his first senior goal when he stabbed home a cross from Cole.

Despite the initial onslaught, York refused to surrender and staggered the United fans with a goal of their own from Jordan after 38 minutes. Suddenly United needed to score three again. Despite a repeat of the UEFA Cup barrage against Volgograd, United couldn't penetrate the York goal for the third time until the 79th minute, when Scholes grabbed his second. Not even another late dash up-field by Schmeichel could rob York of their historic, two-legged giant-killing act.

Goal hero
Paul Scholes

IN THE PAPERS

"Despite their victory at Bootham Crescent last night, United could not redress their first-leg humiliation and it was the home supporters, who had given Cantona such a convivial welcome for his first away match since his return, who were euphoric at the final whistle." **GUARDIAN**

"Cantona emphasised his prowess as a footballer by delivering a low cross that Paul Scholes controlled and then drove past the helpless Warrington. Minutes later United had taken another step towards their soccer salvation with Scholes, a hard-working focal point for their efforts, accepting the role of provider." **DAILY MAIL**

"Ferguson gambled by playing an attacking formation with only three specialised defenders. York, with Andy Warrington, 19, making his debut in goal, were a bag of nerves in the early stages. When Paul Scholes and Terry Cooke made it 2–0, United looked to be coasting towards an overall victory." **DAILY TELEGRAPH**

York patrol on Andy

Even Scholes and Cantona can't save United

MANCHESTER UNITED 1
MANCHESTER CITY 0

HOME TEAM

		RATING
1.	Peter Schmeichel	7
20.	Gary Neville	7
23.	Phil Neville	7
4.	Steve Bruce	7
6.	Gary Pallister	7
16.	Roy Keane	7
19.	Nicky Butt	7
24.	David Beckham	7
11.	Ryan Giggs	7
17.	Andy Cole	7
22.	Paul Scholes	8

SUBSTITUTES

2.	Paul Parker	
5.	Lee Sharpe	7
	Scholes	63 mins	
9.	Brian McClair	7
	Keane	76 mins	

SCORER

Scholes | 4 mins

REFEREE

L R Dilkes | Mossley

VISITORS

21.	Eike Immel
2.	Richard Edghill
3.	Terry Phelan
4.	Steve Lomas
5.	Keith Curle
7.	George Kinkladze
9.	Niall Quinn
10.	Gary Flitcroft
11.	Peter Beagrie
14.	Kit Symons
28.	Uwe Rosler

SUBSTITUTES

8.	Gerry Creaney
	Quinn	80 mins
15.	Alan Kernaghan
16.	Nicky Summerbee
	Beagrie	59 mins

MATCH REPORT

United fans were hoping for a repeat of their 5–0 drubbing of the Blues and, having seen City lose eight of their last nine, who could blame them?

When Scholes put the Reds up after just four minutes, it looked as if we could be seeing a repeat of that rout. However, wiser fans know that predicting a derby match is mission impossible. City, to their credit, didn't play like a team bedding in for a relegation battle. With Kinkladze spraying passes around, City created a couple of openings. Quinn was gifted with one such chance when he was put clear with only Schmeichel to beat. The lanky Irishman amazingly put the ball wide, and that summed up City's luck. Overall, the game reflected the dire Old Trafford atmosphere, which was partly due to the ban on away fans. But three points is three points.

Scholes euphoria

IN THE PAPERS

"Paul Scholes is turning into a baby-faced assassin. His early blow should have drained the last drop of confidence."
MANCHESTER EVENING NEWS

"Memories are certainly not made of stuff like this."
OBSERVER

"From a Ryan Giggs corner, Scholes nipped in to nod the ball past City keeper Eike Immel. City could have travelled back to Maine Road with a point and hope for the future. That they didn't was down to one man – striker Niall Quinn."
SUNDAY MIRROR

"United, parading their youngest team in memory, were poor by their own exalted standards, and missed the peerless Cantona in particular. But out-of-sorts or not, they still contrived to create the lion's share of the goalscoring chances, and therefore deserved a win which takes them up to second spot."
SUNDAY TIMES

"Middleton may be a long way from Marseille, but young Paul Scholes proved to Alex Ferguson that he can bridge the cultural gap with Eric Cantona. While Old Trafford's Gallic inspiration sat in the stand nursing his injured knee, his artistic understudy filled the void by scoring a crucial early winner."
NEWS OF THE WORLD

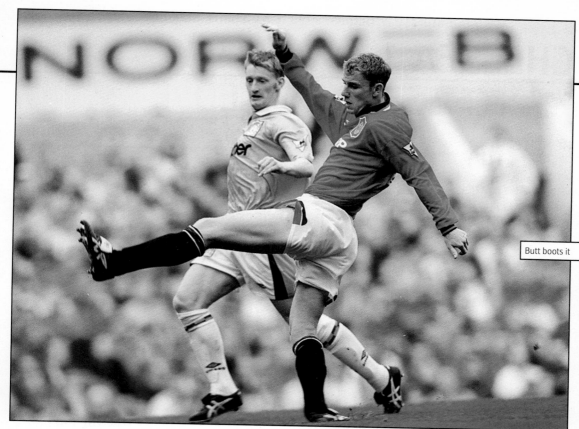

Butt boots it

Immel fix it

CHELSEA 1
MANCHESTER UNITED 4

HOME TEAM

1. Dmitri Kharine
2. Steve Clarke
4. Ruud Gullit
5. Erland Johnsen
6. Frank Sinclair
10. Gavin Peacock
11. Denis Wise
14. Paul Furlong
15. Andy Myers
18. Eddie Newton
8. Mark Hughes

SUBSTITUTES

7. John Spencer
   Peacock | 65 mins
12. Craig Burley
   Wise | 45 mins
13. Kevin Hitchcock

SCORER

Hughes | 75 mins

REFEREE

A Wilkie | Chester-le-Street

VISITORS

		RATING
1.	Peter Schmeichel	8
20.	Gary Neville	8
3.	Denis Irwin	8
4.	Steve Bruce	8
6.	Gary Pallister	8
11.	Ryan Giggs	8
16.	Roy Keane	8
17.	Andy Cole	8
19.	Nicky Butt	8
22.	Paul Scholes	9
7.	Eric Cantona	9

SUBSTITUTES

5.	Lee Sharpe	
9.	Brian McClair	8
	Scholes	80 mins	
24.	David Beckham	

SCORERS

Scholes | 3/9 mins
Giggs | 78 mins
McClair | 85 mins

MATCH REPORT

An exemplary display of fine, flowing football gained United three much-needed points on this trip to the capital. Scholes grabbed the headlines when most people were looking at Cantona, who was on his first trip back to London since his ban.

The youngster looked well above his tender age of 20, and two goals in 10 minutes proved it. Both goals set the pace for the game, but the scoreline stayed at 2–0 until the 76th minute. Mark Hughes gave Chelsea a glimmer of hope with a fine goal, but it only spurred United on to greater things.

Giggs, on top of his form, broke away and capped a magnificent display with a stunning solo goal. Then five minutes from time, Cole unselfishly gave a scoring chance to substitute McClair, who needed no invitation to hammer home the fourth. The match was marred when Sinclair was sent off for a scything tackle on McClair.

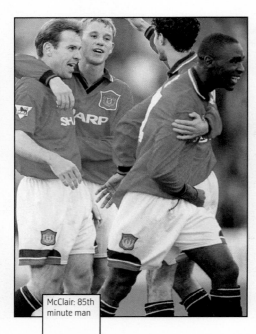

McClair: 85th minute man

IN THE PAPERS

"As on Cantona's comeback against Liverpool at Old Trafford (when he set up one goal and converted a penalty to rescue a point), the Frenchman demanded attention and, in a roving role, he was given so much space that Glenn Hoddle on the Chelsea bench might have pondered a bid for the only man to stay close to Cantona on the day: United's security officer Ned Kelly." **OBSERVER**

"Marvellous talent though he is, there are obvious pitfalls in allowing Gullit the licence to roam where he pleases from his sweeper's station. Defensive responsibility does not feature high on his list of priorities, and he was conspicuous by his absence on both occasions as United scored twice in the first 10 minutes." **SUNDAY TIMES**

"This time it was definitely the French Can-Can. He CAN behave himself. He CAN still play superb football. And he CAN inpsire United to win the title." **PEOPLE**

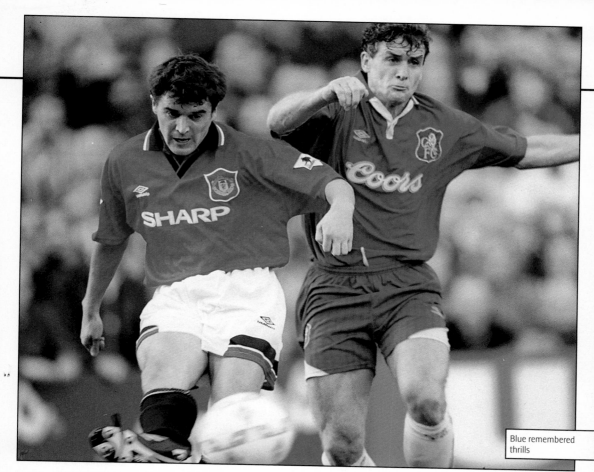

Blue remembered thrills

Eyes on the prize

MANCHESTER UNITED 2
MIDDLESBROUGH 0

HOME TEAM

		RATING
1.	Peter Schmeichel	8
20.	Gary Neville	7
3.	Denis Irwin	8
4.	Steve Bruce	7
6.	Gary Pallister	8
16.	Roy Keane	7
19.	Nicky Butt	8
11.	Ryan Giggs	9
7.	Eric Cantona	8
17.	Andy Cole	7
22.	Paul Scholes	7

SUBSTITUTES

5.	Lee Sharpe	
9.	Brian McClair	7
	Scholes	45 mins
24.	David Beckham	

SCORERS

Pallister | 43 mins
Cole | 87 mins

REFEREE

S J Lodge | Barnsley

VISITORS

13.	Gary Walsh
2.	Neil Cox
3.	Chris Morris
4.	Steve Vickers
5.	Nigel Pearson
7.	Nick Barmby
8.	Jamie Pollock
9.	Jan Aage Fjørtoft
11.	Robbie Mustoe
15.	Phil Whelan
21.	Craig Hignett

SUBSTITUTES

12.	Alan Moore	
	Morris	69 mins
19.	Jaime Moreno	
	Fjørtoft	69 mins
22.	Craig Liddle	

MATCH REPORT

United legend Bryan Robson lapped up the hero's welcome he received prior to this clash, but must have been dissappointed to go home with nothing.

The game always had a tough edge to it, which was to result in Keane being sent off on the half-hour mark. Fjørtoft for Boro challenged strongly and Keane reacted by punching the Norwegian.

As seen before, the 10 men of United reacted well. From a Giggs corner, Teesside-bred Pallister headed home his first of the season.

Boro felt they were unlucky not to have got a penalty when Moreno was brought down, but it was not to be their day. Despite continued pressure, United sealed the victory with three minutes remaining when Cantona switched on the style with a pass to Cole, who turned a defender and struck a powerful shot past Walsh.

Both players and fans were ecstatic at the end of Cole's lean spell and went home happy after a resounding win against the Premier League new boys.

Cole breaks his United duck

IN THE PAPERS

"Boro manager Bryan Robson was revered at Old Trafford for his snarling, passionate approach to the game during his 13 years of toil and triumph. And he would have required a heart of stone not to be moved by the tremendous reception he received." **SUNDAY EXPRESS**

"The United midfielder was sensationally sent off in the 29th minute for throwing a right-handed punch at Jan Fjørtoft, but 10-man United bounced back to scupper Robbo's return."
SUNDAY MIRROR

"United found the going tough against Robbo's well-drilled side with the meanest defensive record in all four divisions. But, ironically aided by Keane's departure and the inspiration of Cantona's pure brilliance, Fergie's men took the game by the throat and squeezed until Boro were choked." **PEOPLE**

"Boro's continuing lack of enterprise was punished again two minutes from the end when Cantona, the game's major creative influence and a model of restraint, released Cole with a perfect through-pass. Checking back inside Whelan, United's £7-million striker unleashed a shot that Walsh got his hands to but could not stop." **SUNDAY TELEGRAPH**

> "We did have one or two moments of worry about the result, but in the end it turned out OK."
> ALEX FERGUSON

Walsh closes down Irwin

4 Premiership games | 1 Coca Cola Cup game | **12 goals**

OCTOBER STATS

PLAYER RECORDS

home | away

■ PREMIERSHIP ■ UEFA CUP ■ COCA COLA CUP ■ FA CUP

FULL APPEARANCE CAME ON AS SUB

■■ SCORER SCORED AS SUB

Columns (opponents): Aston Villa, West Ham United, Wimbledon, Blackburn Rovers, Everton, Rotor Volgograd, Bolton Wanderers, York City, Sheffield Wednesday, Liverpool, Rotor Volgograd, York City, Manchester City, Chelsea, Middlesbrough

No.	Player	Full Appearances	Sub Appearances	Goals
1.	Peter Schmeichel	14	0	1
2.	Paul Parker	4	1	0
3.	Denis Irwin	10	0	0
4.	Steve Bruce	13	1	0
5.	Lee Sharpe	11	1	3
6.	Gary Pallister	15	0	1
7.	Eric Cantona	3	0	1
9.	Brian McClair	4	3	1
11.	Ryan Giggs	10	3	3
12.	David May	0	0	0
15.	Graeme Tomlinson	0	0	0
16.	Roy Keane	11	1	3
17.	Andy Cole	9	1	2
18.	Simon Davies	2	5	0
19.	Nicky Butt	13	0	1
20.	Gary Neville	11	0	0
21.	Patrick McGibbon	1	0	0
22.	Paul Scholes	12	2	9
23.	Philip Neville	6	1	0
24.	David Beckham	11	2	2
25.	Kevin Pilkington	1	0	0
26.	Chris Casper	0	0	0
27.	Terry Cooke	2	3	1
29.	Ben Thornley	0	1	0
30.	John O'Kane	1	1	0

PLAYER OF THE MONTH

PAUL SCHOLES

AVERAGE PERFORMANCE RATING: 8.0

FA CARLING PREMIERSHIP

as at 28 October 1995

	Pld	Home W	D	L	F	A	Away W	D	L	F	A	Pts	GD
▲ Newcastle United	10	5	0	0	15	2	4	0	1	11	5	27	+19
▼ Manchester United	11	5	1	0	13	4	3	1	1	10	7	26	+12
■ Liverpool	11	5	1	0	16	2	2	1	2	8	6	23	+16
▲ Arsenal	10	3	2	0	9	4	3	1	1	6	1	21	+10
▲ Nottingham Forest	11	3	2	0	10	5	2	4	0	9	7	21	+7
▲ Middlesbrough	11	4	1	0	7	1	2	2	2	4	5	21	+5
▼ Aston Villa	11	4	1	1	8	3	2	1	2	5	5	20	+5
▲ Leeds United	11	4	0	2	9	7	2	2	1	8	6	20	+4
▲ Tottenham Hotspur	10	2	0	3	6	7	2	3	0	9	6	15	+2
■ Chelsea	11	2	2	1	7	6	2	1	3	4	8	15	-3
▲ Blackburn Rovers	11	4	1	1	13	5	0	1	4	3	10	14	+1
▼ West Ham United	11	1	2	2	6	8	2	2	2	4	4	13	-2
▼ Sheffield Wednesday	11	1	1	4	3	8	2	1	2	6	5	11	-4
▲ Queens Park Rangers	11	1	1	4	6	13	2	0	3	4	4	10	-7
▼ Wimbledon	11	2	1	3	9	11	1	0	4	6	14	10	-10
▼ Everton	11	1	1	3	6	9	1	2	3	6	7	9	-4
▲ Southampton	11	1	2	2	6	8	1	1	4	5	12	9	-9
▼ Coventry City	11	1	2	2	3	6	0	2	4	5	15	7	-13
■ Bolton Wanderers	10	1	2	2	5	7	0	0	5	6	15	5	-15
■ Manchester City	11	0	2	3	1	5	0	0	6	2	16	2	-18

NOVEMBER

1 | 2 | 3 | 4 | 5 | 6 | 7 | 8 | 9 | 10 | 11 | 12 | 13 | 14 | 15 | 16 | 17 | 18 | 19 | 20 | 21 | 22 | 23 | 24 | 25 | 26 | 27 | 28 | 29 | 30

NOVEMBER

THE MONTH IN REVIEW

While Lady Di and some Brazilian bloke called Juninho grabbed most of the headlines in November, there was only one man making the news at Old Trafford.... Ryan Giggs.

Millions tuned in to see Lady Di pour her heart out on TV and sombrero-wearing Boro fans lined the streets to cheer the arrival of Juninho. But it was United's Welsh wing wizard who turned out to be the star of November. This was the month when Giggs spectacularly shook off all those injury nightmares and burst into form, swivelled and swerved back to his very best and prompted Alex Ferguson to claim boldly: "All those niggling injuries have gone. He is back to the way we know he can play and he's full of confidence."

Things didn't start well in November, however, for Giggs or United. On the 4th the Reds travelled to Highbury and, surprise, surprise, the match finished 1–0 to Arsenal. In fact, United turned in a cracking performance but came away with nothing thanks to a Dennis Bergkamp goal, some super-human Arsenal defending and a couple of misses Andy Cole will try to forget.

With Cole paid to hit the back of the net, he might have been just a tad embarrassed when it was revealed a few days later that he was reportedly the 15th highest-earning sportsman in Britain (his transfer to United helped him rake in a cool £1.25 million in 1995). But who says footballers are overpaid? Damon Hill pocketed £3 million for 16 races for Williams in Formula One!

The Southampton match on 18 November marked the return of away fans to Old Trafford after building work on the new stand entered a new phase. But after just 15 seconds, the Saints' supporters who made the journey north probably wished they hadn't. With the

kick-off barely taken and fans still settling in their seats, Paul Scholes dispossessed an unsuspecting Southampton player and found Cantona with his crossfield pass. Eric in turn laid it into the feet of Giggs and before you could say "stick it in the onion bag", the ball was nestling in the back of the net. It was 1–0 to United after 15 seconds and Giggs's strike was the third quickest goal in Premiership history. It finished 4–1 to United and, as the *Sunday People* said, "Had it been a boxing match the referee would have stepped in to stop it." Even out-of-luck striker Andy Cole scored.

With Giggs relishing his new attacking midfield role, it was on to Coventry three days later. Lady Di had just told the nation she wanted to be "Queen of

NOVEMBER
NUMBER ONES

SINGLE
I Believe/Up
on the Roof
**Robson &
Jerome**

ALBUM
Robson &
Jerome
**Robson &
Jerome**

FILM
Goldeneye

Damon can afford to splash out

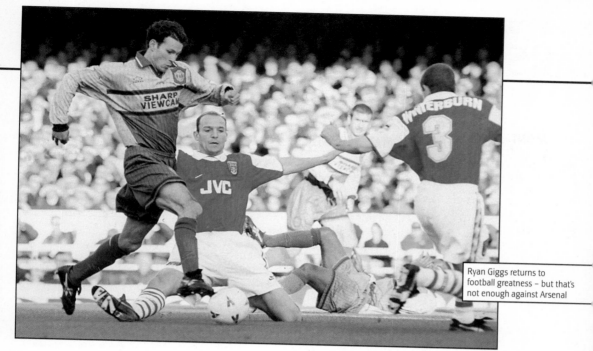

Ryan Giggs returns to football greatness – but that's not enough against Arsenal

people's hearts", but Giggs showed who was King of Highfield Road with an awesome display of attacking skills which brought Coventry to their knees and inspired United to a 4–0 win. The gap between Newcastle and United was down to three points and the Reds were on song. As for Blackburn, not only were they floundering in the League and positively sinking without trace in Europe, their own players were punching each other's lights out over in Poland.

For a chance to close the gap on pace-setters Newcastle on 27 November, United travelled to the City Ground to take on a Forest side that hadn't been beaten there in over a year. The record

Hats on to Brazilian star Juninho

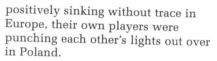

> ## "Giggsy was simply excellent, absolutely marvellous. This was an outstanding performance from him and he's having a great season."
>
> ALEX FERGUSON

remained intact – but only just. With Giggs and Cantona superb again, it was United v Mark Crossley after Eric had equalised from the spot, but the second goal wouldn't come. That made it two wins, a draw and a defeat... but the best result of all was Giggs' return to form.

ARSENAL 1
MANCHESTER UNITED 0

HOME TEAM

1. David Seaman
2. Lee Dixon
3. Nigel Winterburn
5. Steve Bould
6. Tony Adams
7. David Platt
8. Ian Wright
9. Paul Merson
10. Dennis Bergkamp
11. Glen Helder
14. Martin Keown

SUBSTITUTES

13. Vince Bartram
16. John Hartson
    Wright | 81 mins
19. John Jensen

SCORER

Bergkamp | 14 mins

REFEREE

P Durkin | Portland

VISITORS

		RATING
1.	Peter Schmeichel	8
20.	Gary Neville	7
3.	Denis Irwin	7
4.	Steve Bruce	7
6.	Gary Pallister	7
7.	Eric Cantona	7
11.	Ryan Giggs	8
16.	Roy Keane	7
17.	Andy Cole	7
19.	Nicky Butt	7
22.	Paul Scholes	7

SUBSTITUTES

5.	Lee Sharpe	7
	Scholes	64 mins	
9.	Brian McClair	7
	Irwin	82 mins	
24.	David Beckham	7
	Butt	64 mins	

MATCH REPORT

On a day when Alex Ferguson should have been celebrating his nine years at United, he must have been quietly cursing his luck. A display which would have normally secured a point at least resulted in United's second defeat this season.

It was a day for the men between the sticks, with Schmeichel and Seaman producing world-class displays, but it was another world-class performer who won the game.

After just 14 minutes, Bergkamp ran on to an uncharacteristic mistake from Irwin and coolly slotted the ball home.

Cole was having a frustrating day and felt his luck had changed when he appeared to have scored. However, a linesman disagreed and it was not to be.

United could rightly feel aggrieved at the result, but there was solace in another fine display.

IN THE PAPERS

"Typically, Arsenal absorbed the threats and, in the 15th minute, punished Ferguson's men for their profligacy by snatching the lead."
SUNDAY EXPRESS

"It was Bergkamp's tenacity which gave Arsenal their barely deserved victory. After just 15 minutes he gave hopeful chase to a deep ball from David Platt which being shepherded back to his goalkeeper by Denis Irwin."
MAIL ON SUNDAY

"Arsenal survived the most precise and relentless of attacks in the second half and, in the dying minutes, came close to putting even more space between themselves and their visitors. United had been disappointing in the first half, but they made far more use of their better possession in the second and, as Eric Cantona increasingly came into the game, they always seemed on the brink of an equaliser."
INDEPENDENT ON SUNDAY

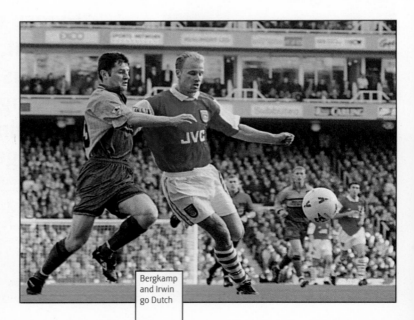

Bergkamp and Irwin go Dutch

Cantona foxes Bould

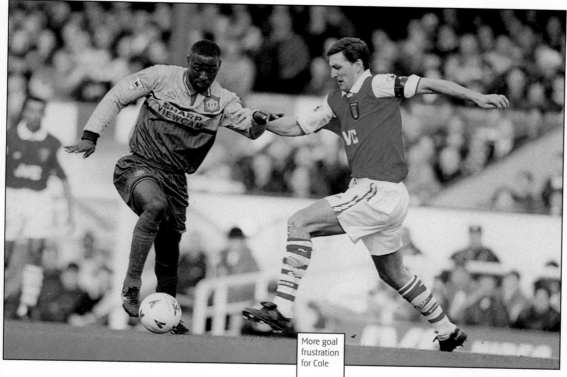

More goal frustration for Cole

MANCHESTER UNITED 4
SOUTHAMPTON 1

HOME TEAM

		RATING
1.	Peter Schmeichel	8
20.	Gary Neville	8
3.	Denis Irwin	8
4.	Steve Bruce	8
6.	Gary Pallister	8
19.	Nicky Butt	8
11.	Ryan Giggs	9
7.	Eric Cantona	8
17.	Andy Cole	8
22.	Paul Scholes	8
24.	David Beckham	8

SUBSTITUTES

5.	Lee Sharpe	8
	Giggs	67 mins	
9.	Brian McClair	8
	Scholes	49 mins	
23.	Phil Neville	8
	Irwin	45 mins	

SCORERS

Giggs | 1/4 mins
Scholes | 8 mins
Cole | 69 mins

REFEREE

P Danson | Leicester

VISITORS

13.	Dave Beasant
2.	Jason Dodd
3.	Francis Benali
4.	Jim Magilton
5.	Richard Hall
6.	Ken Monkou
8.	Gordon Watson
9.	Neil Shipperley
11.	Neil Heaney
12.	Tommy Widdrington
16.	David Hughes

SUBSTITUTES

1.	Bruce Grobbelaar
10.	Neil Maddison
	Watson	56 mins
21.	Frankie Bennett
	Heaney	56 mins

SCORER

Shipperley | 85 mins

MATCH REPORT

Old Trafford saw two exclusives in the Southampton match. First, away supporters were present for the first time in the season. Second was the new look of Eric Cantona.

Eric's new look matched his new temperament, and for 90 minutes there were 12 "saints" on the pitch – but only one who made any difference in the game.

Giggs, a thorn in Southampton's side, grabbed a couple of goals within four minutes, the first after only 16 seconds. Shell-shocked Southampton didn't know what had hit them and United proceeded to run riot.

In-favour Scholes continued his form with another on eight minutes and the scene was set for a rout. The pace slowed a little and United fans had to wait until Cole nodded one in with 68 minutes on the clock.

Shipperley managed a consolation for the Saints, but the night most definitely belonged to Eric.

IN THE PAPERS

"Initially energetic, ultimately economical, Manchester United effectively secured victory before 10 minutes had elapsed, enabling them to concentrate on conserving legs and lungs for more exacting afternoons."
SUNDAY TIMES

"Where's the sense in Manchester United completing a stadium of 55,000 seats when everyone keeps jumping out of them?"
OBSERVER

"On this form Giggs, scintillating in a new, free-ranging, attacking midfield role, will become one of the dominant players in this season's Championship chase." **SUNDAY EXPRESS**

"United mercilessly destroyed the Saints with a show of power football. Old Trafford hasn't seen such a tremendous opening to a match in years."
SUNDAY TELEGRAPH

Another four goals for United

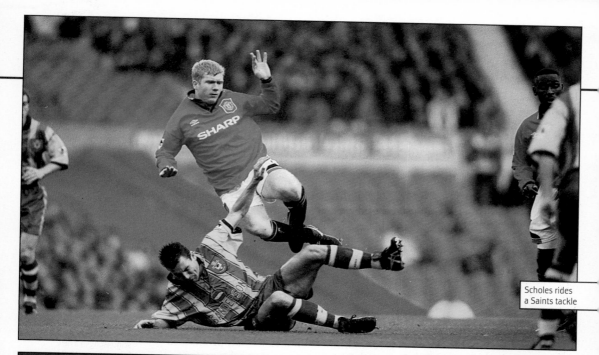

Scholes rides
a Saints tackle

Gary Neville, top 20

COVENTRY CITY 0
MANCHESTER UNITED 4

HOME TEAM

1. Steve Ogrizovic
24. Richard Shaw
18. Marcus Hall
4. Paul Williams
5. David Rennie
26. Gordon Strachan
6. Kevin Richardson
8. Isaias
9. Peter Ndlovu
10. Dion Dublin
11. John Salako

SUBSTITUTES

13. John Filan
15. Paul Cook
   Isaias | 70 mins
17. Ally Pickering

REFEREE

K W Burge | Tonypandy

VISITORS

		RATING
1.	Peter Schmeichel	8
20.	Gary Neville	8
3.	Denis Irwin	8
4.	Steve Bruce	8
6.	Gary Pallister	7
7.	Eric Cantona	8
11.	Ryan Giggs	9
9.	Brian McClair	8
17.	Andy Cole	7
19.	Nicky Butt	7
24.	David Beckham	7

SUBSTITUTES

5.	Lee Sharpe	7
	Butt	65 mins	
12.	David May	7
	Bruce	79 mins	
23.	Phil Neville	7
	Neville, G	48 mins	

SCORERS

Irwin | 27 mins
McClair | 47/76 mins
Beckham | 57 mins

MATCH REPORT

United sent a chilling warning to Newcastle with a clinical display that left the home side staring ominously at the Endsleigh League.

The scoreline suggests a walkover, but Coventry laid siege to United's goal early on. Schmeichel had to be alert and Bruce cleared a Dublin effort off the line.

United stayed calm under pressure and Coventry reeled after a fine goal from Irwin. This was the start of a United onslaught, with Cantona and Giggs both going close before half time.

Two minutes after the break, McClair weighed in with a goal set up by Giggs. Beckham controversially put United further in front, and Coventry were dead and buried. McClair rounded off an excellent performance with his second, which showed why the canny Scot is still on Old Trafford's books.

Leave it to Cantona

IN THE PAPERS

"Magnificent United, led by the trickery of Ryan Giggs, cut Newcastle's lead to a manageable three points – and dumped Big Ron to the bottom of the table."
DAILY EXPRESS

"Four goals – and there should have been more – told their own story of a dominant display. Two goals by Brian McClair and others by Denis Irwin and David Beckham guaranteed the three points.. But what was really impressive was the way United then strolled through the second half as if they were playing a testimonial game."
DAILY STAR

"Alex Ferguson's thoroughbreds showed exactly why the Premiership race could soon become simply Red by overpowering poor Coventry. With Ryan Giggs providing the inspiration through his sheer genius, this encounter became increasingly one-sided." **DAILY MIRROR**

PEUGEOT

Steve Bruce
crash lands

NOTTINGHAM FOREST 1
MANCHESTER UNITED 1

HOME TEAM

1. Mark Crossley
2. Des Lyttle
3. Stuart Pearce
4. Colin Cooper
5. Steve Chettle
8. Scott Gemmill
11. Steve Stone
14. Ian Woan
19. Stephen Howe
20. Paul McGregor
21. Chris Bart-Williams

SUBSTITUTES

7. David Phillips
18. Alf Inge Haaland
   McGregor | 73 mins
24. Richard Irving
   Howe | 88 mins

SCORER

McGregor | 19 mins

REFEREE

K Cooper | Pontypridd

VISITORS

		RATING
1.	Peter Schmeichel	7
20.	Gary Neville	8
3.	Denis Irwin	9
4.	Steve Bruce	8
6.	Gary Pallister	8
19.	Nicky Butt	7
11.	Ryan Giggs	8
7.	Eric Cantona	7
17.	Andy Cole	7
9.	Brian McClair	7
24.	David Beckham	7

SUBSTITUTES

5. Lee Sharpe
   Beckham | 81 mins
22. Paul Scholes   8
   McClair | 45 mins
23. Phil Neville

SCORER

Cantona | 66 mins (pen)

MATCH REPORT

United were in control at the City Ground, but wasted opportunities led to the spoils being shared. Cole, Cantona and Giggs all saw chances go begging on what was a frustrating night for United.

Young McGregor carried on from his UEFA Cup exploits and put Forest in the driving seat after 18 minutes. United then pummelled Forest's goal in search of an equalizer. Forest seemed content to sit back and soak up the pressure, but they paid when Chettle up-ended Cantona in the penalty area.

Cantona brushed himself down and coolly put away his 50th goal for the Reds. United pressed on to no avail, and had a scare at the end when Irving headed wide.

United fans travelled home knowing two points had been dropped. However, they could be satisfied with a good performance and the character shown by the Reds in recovering from going a goal down early in the game.

IN THE PAPERS

"Ryan Giggs bewitched the City Ground last night, but Nottingham Forest refused to be bound by his spells."
GUARDIAN

"Furious Forest fans chanted 'Cheat, cheat, cheat' after Cantona's penalty had rescued a point for United. They were convinced Cantona had dived when Steve Chettle challenged him in the 66th minute. From most angles, they seem right."
DAILY STAR

"The abiding memory will be of two teams trusting entirely in the finer arts, and of Mark Crossley's defiance."
INDEPENDENT

"Between Cantona and Giggs, these two cavalier performers were able to raise United to a standard high enough to convert all of their possession into a single point. All the possession in the world grants United nothing if Cole cannot fit more profitably into the passing shapes being woven around him."
DAILY MAIL

"He stamped and snorted for 90 minutes. But this was not the angry, maverick Cantona. It was a footballer full of frustration that victory was going to elude him."
PEOPLE

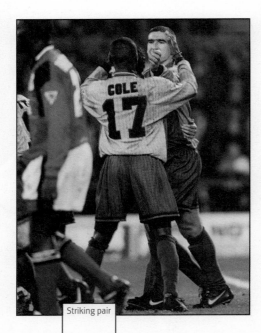

Striking pair

Gemmill blocks Beckham's shot

4 Premiership games | 9 goals

NOVEMBER STATS

PLAYER RECORDS

home | away

■ PREMIERSHIP ■ UEFA CUP ■ COCA COLA CUP ■ FA CUP

Opponent columns (left to right): Aston Villa, West Ham United, Wimbledon, Blackburn Rovers, Everton, Rotor Volgograd, Bolton Wanderers, Sheffield Wednesday, York City, Rotor Volgograd, Liverpool, York City, Chelsea, Manchester City, Middlesbrough, Arsenal, Southampton, Coventry City, Nottingham Forest

FULL APPEARANCE / CAME ON AS SUB / SCORER / SCORED AS SUB

#	Player	Full Appearances	Sub Appearances	Goals
1.	Peter Schmeichel	18	0	1
2.	Paul Parker	4	1	0
3.	Denis Irwin	14	0	1
4.	Steve Bruce	17	1	0
5.	Lee Sharpe	11	5	3
6.	Gary Pallister	19	0	1
7.	Eric Cantona	7	0	2
9.	Brian McClair	6	5	3
11.	Ryan Giggs	14	3	5
12.	David May	0	1	0
15.	Graeme Tomlinson	0	0	0
16.	Roy Keane	12	1	3
17.	Andy Cole	13	1	3
18.	Simon Davies	2	5	0
19.	Nicky Butt	17	0	1
20.	Gary Neville	15	0	0
21.	Patrick McGibbon	1	0	0
22.	Paul Scholes	14	3	10
23.	Philip Neville	6	3	0
24.	David Beckham	14	3	3
25.	Kevin Pilkington	1	0	0
26.	Chris Casper	0	0	0
27.	Terry Cooke	2	3	1
29.	Ben Thornley	0	1	0
30.	John O'Kane	1	1	0

PLAYER OF THE MONTH
RYAN GIGGS

AVERAGE PERFORMANCE RATING: 8.5

FA CARLING PREMIERSHIP

as at 27 November 1995

	Pld	Home W	D	L	F	A	Away W	D	L	F	A	Pts	GD
■ Newcastle United	14	7	0	0	18	3	4	2	1	13	7	35	+21
■ Manchester United	15	6	1	0	17	5	4	2	2	15	9	33	+18
▲ Arsenal	15	5	3	0	14	6	3	1	3	7	4	28	+11
▲ Aston Villa	14	4	2	1	9	4	4	1	2	10	6	27	+9
▲ Tottenham Hotspur	14	3	1	3	9	9	4	3	0	13	8	25	+5
▼ Nottingham Forest	14	4	3	0	15	7	2	4	1	9	14	25	+3
▼ Liverpool	14	5	1	1	17	4	2	2	3	9	8	24	+14
■ Leeds United	13	5	0	2	10	7	2	3	1	9	7	24	+5
▼ Middlesbrough	14	4	2	1	8	3	2	3	2	4	5	23	+4
■ Chelsea	14	3	3	1	10	8	2	1	4	4	9	19	+7
■ Blackburn Rovers	15	5	1	1	20	5	0	2	6	3	12	18	+6
▲ Everton	14	3	1	3	9	9	2	2	3	8	8	18	0
▼ West Ham United	14	1	3	3	7	12	3	2	2	7	4	17	-2
▼ Sheffield Wednesday	14	1	2	4	4	9	2	2	3	8	9	13	-6
▲ Southampton	14	2	2	3	8	9	1	1	5	6	16	12	-11
▼ Queens Park Rangers	14	1	2	4	7	14	2	0	5	4	8	11	-11
▼ Wimbledon	14	2	2	3	9	11	1	0	6	7	19	11	-14
▲ Manchester City	14	2	2	3	3	5	0	1	6	3	17	9	-16
■ Bolton Wanderers	14	2	2	3	6	10	0	0	7	8	19	8	-15
▼ Coventry City	14	1	2	4	5	13	0	3	4	6	16	8	-18

DECEMBER

1 | 2 | 3 | 4 | 5 | 6 | 7 | 8 | 9 | 10 | 11 | 12 | 13 | 14 | 15 | 16 | 17 | 18 | 19 | 20 | 21 | 22 | 23 | 24 | 25 | 26 | 27 | 28 | 29 | 30 | 31

DECEMBER

THE MONTH IN REVIEW

"As always, December is going to be the most important month. It's when the Championship always takes shape." So said Fergie at the end of November, and he was right. For as United slipped up on a couple of Premiership banana skins in the run up to the festive season, Newcastle soared into a 10-point lead in the Championship...

The month started badly. Cole wasn't scoring, Schmeichel and Keane were still injured, the England cricket team looked like losing every match they played out in South Africa and Mark Hughes was playing for Chelsea.

The return of Sparky brought a tear to many an eye when Chelsea visited Old Trafford – including the man himself. It also brought about the loss of vital home points. Maybe it was Sparky's return, but whatever the reason the Reds spluttered against the Blues and in the end a draw was probably a fair result, though Cole could have won it if he hadn't fired wide

from six yards. "In times like this Coley maybe feels he is never going to score again," said Hughes afterwards. "He just tries too hard."

In fact, just about the only United fan smiling after the Chelsea game was Mike Atherton, who saved the Second Test with a 10-hour unbeaten innings of 185. In the meantime Eric Cantona was voted the most hated man in football in a magazine poll (Alex Ferguson and Roy Keane came third and seventh respectively), although he was too busy launching his film career in France to notice. "Eric stands in front of that

Hello, Mr Magpie: Keane scores the second against Newcastle

Michael Atherton wonders how the Reds are doing

camera like he is about to take a penalty," said the director of *Le Bonheur est dans le Pré* (Happiness is in the Glade), in which Cantona has a part as a rugby player!

Maybe it was his film role, but in United's next match at home to Sheffield Wednesday Cantona was the star of the show. "He was marvellous," said Fergie, but it wasn't enough. The match finished 2–2, with another two home points washed down the drain, although all credit to Wednesday. Without Eric, we would have lost all three.

Next stop Liverpool, and with the mad cow disease scare forcing education authorities to ban beef in schools, maybe Fergie should have had extra rations sent to Anfield eight days later. If ever a team needed beefing up, it was the United side which lost so disappointingly to their arch rivals on 18 December. The score was 2–0 and, but for the return of Peter Schmeichel, it would have been worse. "When United go to Anfield, I expect them to fight," raged Fergie. "They didn't. That was the most lifeless performance from a United side in years." So Liverpool got their Christmas present early this year, and United still hadn't won a competitive match in their new grey away kit.

It may have been back to red shirts against arch-rivals Leeds on Christmas Eve, but United's festive generosity struck again. Andy Cole scored after being subbed at Anfield and Roy Keane

returned from injury, but apart from that, Reds fans had about as much to smile about as a freshly fattened turkey and Leeds – inspired by new signing Thomas Brolin – ran out 3–1 winners. The gap between United and Newcastle was now a Grand Canyon-like 10 points, but the geordies were coming to Old Trafford.

On the day after Boxing Day, all eyes turned to the televised top-of-the-table clash at Old Trafford... and what a day it turned out to be for Andy Cole. It was his superb sixth-minute strike that sank his former team mates, inspiring United's best performance of the season so far and their 2–0 victory. The Championship leaders were outclassed and victory over QPR three days later (with another goal from Cole) kept up the pressure.

"It's important we go on a run now," said Fergie. "If people think we reached the heights against Newcastle, they were wrong. We can play better than that."

I don't like Wednesday: Eric shone against Sheffield

MANCHESTER UNITED 1
CHELSEA 1

HOME TEAM

		RATING
25.	Kevin Pilkington	8
20.	Gary Neville	7
3.	Denis Irwin	7
4.	Steve Bruce	8
12.	David May	8
5.	Lee Sharpe	5
7.	Eric Cantona	8
9.	Brian McClair	8
17.	Andy Cole	6
22.	Paul Scholes	7
24.	David Beckham	9

SUBSTITUTES

18.	Simon Davies	
21.	Patrick McGibbon	
27.	Terry Cooke	7

Cole | 75 mins

SCORERS

Beckham | 60 mins

REFEREE

M Bodenham | East Looe

VISITORS

1.	Dmitri Kharine
7.	John Spencer
8.	Mark Hughes
11.	Denis Wise
12.	Craig Burley
15.	Andy Myers
18.	Eddie Newton
20.	David Lee
23.	Gareth Hall
24.	Dan Petrescu
26.	Michael Duberry

SUBSTITUTES

6.	Frank Sinclair
13.	Kevin Hitchcock
14.	Paul Furlong

Spencer | 81 mins

SCORERS

Wise | 53 mins

MATCH REPORT

Chelsea continued their impressive form at Old Trafford – just two defeats in 21 outings – with a well-earned draw. As expected, United legend Mark Hughes received a standing ovation from the dedicated ranks of the Red Army.

On a day when Cole and Sharpe were below par, Cantona and Beckham put in terrific performances to ensure United gained at least a point. Chelsea took the lead early in the second half with a goal from Wise, and this gave the Blues a much-needed boost.

United had plenty of chances and Cole was horrified when he saw an effort from five yards go agonisingly wide. After an hour of play, a drive from Cole was cleared to Beckham who rocketed a superb shot into the top corner.

Sensing the streak of bad luck cursing Cole, Ferguson sent on the ever-impressive Terry Cooke. United pressed for a winner but Chelsea held out. It was two points dropped for United.

Pilkington keeps busy

IN THE PAPERS

"Beckham struck a sweet equaliser just past the hour and, although United had chances to win it from there, the ball would not go in. Cole missed perhaps the best of those chances, side-footing wide from six yards."
SUNDAY TIMES

"The loss of five players – Ryan Giggs, Peter Schmeichel, Gary Pallister, Roy Keane and Nicky Butt – because of injury and suspension – offered some mitigation for the listlessness of United's play before the interval, but not for the poorness of their finishing in the second half."
SUNDAY TELEGRAPH

"Leytonstone-born Beckham, growing rapidly in maturity and confidence, saved his side with a goal of glittering quality."
NEWS OF THE WORLD

"An immediate solution for Andy Cole's desperate lack of self-belief must be found – or the title race is as good as dead." **SUNDAY EXPRESS**

David Beckham,
rocket man

"I have got to
give credit to
Chelsea for today's
performance."
ALEX FERGUSON

MANCHESTER UNITED 2
SHEFFIELD WEDNESDAY 2

HOME TEAM

		RATING
25.	Kevin Pilkington	7
20.	Gary Neville	7
12.	David May	7
4.	Steve Bruce	7
23.	Phil Neville	7
5.	Lee Sharpe	6
7.	Eric Cantona	8
9.	Brian McClair	7
17.	Andy Cole	7
22.	Paul Scholes	7
24.	David Beckham	7

SUBSTITUTES

2.	Paul Parker	
18.	Simon Davies	7
	Scholes | 53	
27.	Terry Cooke	7
	Sharpe | 83 mins	

SCORERS

Cantona | 17/83 mins

REFEREE

P Jones | Loughborough

VISITORS

13.	Kevin Pressman	
2.	Peter Atherton	
3.	Ian Nolan	
5.	Steve Nicol	
8.	Chris Waddle	
9.	David Hirst	
10.	Mark Bright	
14.	Marc Degryse	
17.	Des Walker	
19.	Guy Whittingham	
29.	Lee Briscoe	

SUBSTITUTES

11.	John Sheridan	
	Waddle | 75 mins	
15.	Andy Sinton	
16.	Graham Hyde	

SCORERS

Bright | 59 mins
Whittingham | 78 mins

MATCH REPORT

Eric Cantona provided a much-needed one man show when the Reds most definitely were in need of inspiration. As seen before this season, United were guilty of missing some gilt-edged chances and, without Cantona, a defeat was surely on the cards.

Six first-teamers were missing from United's line-up, but the rest started well. Cantona created plenty of chances, culminating in his goal: a neat shot lifted over the body of Pressman. United then attacked with a flourish, but chances usually tucked away with ease were thrown away.

Wednesday got back into the game through Bright, then Whittingham got a second to put the visitors in front. Only one man was capable of saving United and seven minutes from time Cantona spared United's blushes with a cracking volley, signalling his timely return to form.

Eric chips in number one

IN THE PAPERS

"Forget the youthful cavalry, Manchester United send for the French Foreign Legion when they need saving from an embarrassing scrape. Cantona performed throughout like a man possessed. His work rate was outstanding and he displayed a single-minded conviction that defeat would not be tolerated." **DAILY MAIL**

"Alex Ferguson knows his asset-stripped team looked a gift-horse in the mouth... and then played like donkeys." **DAILY STAR**

"Eric Cantona turned babysitter to help Manchester United's kids through a crisis and keep Old Trafford dreams of another Championship success alive. It needed Cantona's wit, arrogance and new maturity to save a point." **NEWS OF THE WORLD**

"Fergie's babes suffered an attack of the nursery wobbles and were in danger of toppling from their pram with a real crash – until big brother Eric came riding to the rescue against slick Wednesday." **PEOPLE**

Cole's wings
clipped by the
Owls' defence

"Cantona was the best
player in our team today.
He was marvellous."

ALEX FERGUSON

LIVERPOOL 2
MANCHESTER UNITED 0

HOME TEAM

1. David James
2. Rob Jones
4. Jason McAteer
5. Mark Wright
8. Stan Collymore
10. John Barnes
12. John Scales
16. Michael Thomas
17. Steve McManaman
22. Steve Harkness
23. Robbie Fowler

SUBSTITUTES

19. Mark Kennedy
21. Dominic Matteo
26. Tommy Warner

SCORER

Fowler | 45/87 mins

REFEREE

G Poll | Berkhamsted

VISITORS

		RATING
1.	Peter Schmeichel	8
20.	Gary Neville	5
3.	Denis Irwin	5
4.	Steve Bruce	6
12.	David May	6
5.	Lee Sharpe	5
7.	Eric Cantona	6
9.	Brian McClair	6
17.	Andy Cole	5
11.	Ryan Giggs	7
24.	David Beckham	5

SUBSTITUTES

22.	Paul Scholes	5
	Cole | 53 mins	
23.	Phil Neville	
25.	Kevin Pilkington	

MATCH REPORT

United were outclassed and outplayed by a superior Liverpool side, and title hopes were given a severe denting. Rivals off the pitch for years gone by, United's players weren't up for the challenge set out by the Scousers from the wrong end of the East Lancs Road.

United looked average without the fire normally induced by the likes of Keane and Butt, and this showed in a dire performance.

Luckily for United, Schmeichel was on form, but even he couldn't stop a Fowler free-kick launched straight into the top corner a minute before half time. Cole was substituted seven minutes into the second half, continuing a rough patch that had seen him go four matches without a goal.

Schmeichel continued with the heroics, denying Collymore an astonishing 13 times, but Fowler finished it off with an 87th minute winner.

Schmeichel takes charge at the back

IN THE PAPERS

"Eric Cantona was, inevitably enough, booed whenever he came within an acre of the ball, but the Danish goalkeeper revelled in his capacity to induce apoplexy. He could even be forgiven for the barrage of abuse he directed at his defenders."
DAILY TELEGRAPH

"Rarely can a United team have been so comprehensively out-fought, out-run and outplayed by their most bitter rivals. Too many of their players appeared to lack the necessary passion for this highly charged fixture. But for a string of superb saves by Schmeichel, the scoreline could have been embarrassing for furious Fergie… "
DAILY MIRROR

"The United challenge was so weak that they deserved the public rebuke hurled at his players by incensed manager Alex Ferguson." **DAILY MAIL**

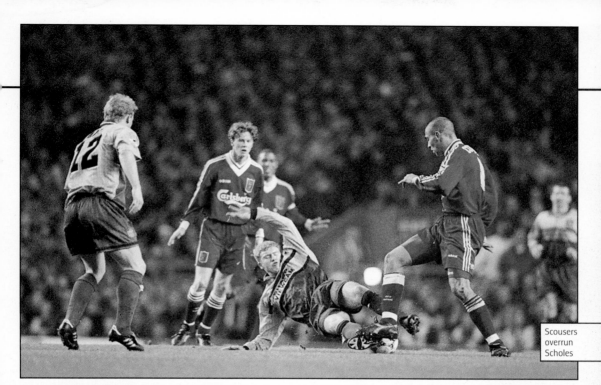

Scousers overrun Scholes

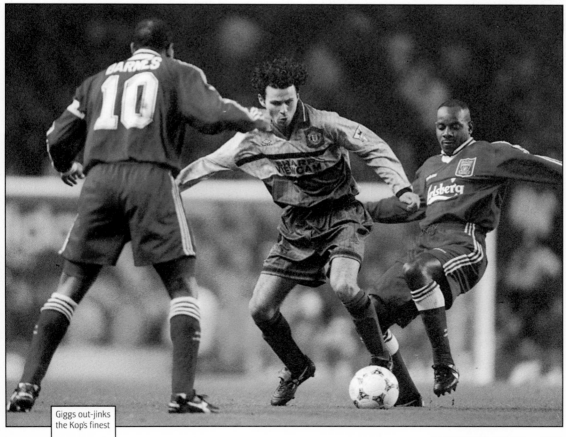

Giggs out-jinks the Kop's finest

LEEDS UNITED 3
MANCHESTER UNITED 1

HOME TEAM

13. Mark Beeney
2. Gary Kelly
3. Tony Dorigo
4. Carlton Palmer
6. David Wetheral
9. Brian Deane
10. Gary McAllister
11. Gary Speed
16. Richard Jobson
18. Tomas Brolin
21. Anthony Yeboah

SUBSTITUTES

5. Lucas Radebe
8. Rod Wallace
   Yeboah | 86 mins
15. Nigel Worthington

SCORERS

McAllister | 6 mins (pen)
Yeboah | 35 mins
Deane | 78 mins

REFEREE

D J Gallagher | Banbury

VISITORS

		RATING
1.	Peter Schmeichel	7
2.	Paul Parker	6
3.	Denis Irwin	7
4.	Steve Bruce	7
7.	Eric Cantona	7
9.	Brian McClair	6
16.	Roy Keane	8
17.	Andy Cole	7
19.	Nicky Butt	7
20.	Gary Neville	6
24.	David Beckham	6

SUBSTITUTES

12.	David May	7
	Parker	71 mins	
22.	Paul Scholes	7
	Beckham	74 mins	
23.	Phil Neville	7
	Bruce	74 mins	

SCORER

Cole | 28 mins

MATCH REPORT

United turned out to be the Christmas turkey at the party held at Elland Road. The game might have taken an entirely different pattern if it weren't for a sixth-minute penalty for Leeds.

Butt was judged to have handled during an aerial tussle, and McAllister put Leeds ahead. Cole got the goal everyone had been waiting for half an hour into play. Butt worked well on the right, and Cole finished with clinical precision.

Parker made an untimely slip to let Yeboah thunder a shot past Schmeichel and, to add insult to injury, Deane nodded in a Brolin cross late in the game.

Unlike the Liverpool game, where United didn't perform, Keane and Butt brought back some fighting spirit to the midfield, but nothing came of it.

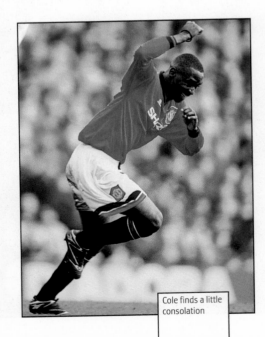

Cole finds a little consolation

IN THE PAPERS

"Ferguson must have felt like joining in with Peter Schmeichel's constant chastising."
DAILY TELEGRAPH

"In the space of eight days, the Manchester United manager has seen his team's title credentials look as tatty as last year's tinsel."
INDEPENDENT

"This was the stage during which Schmeichel blew kisses to the Leeds Kop."
DAILY MAIL

"He was really having a go at his team mates during the game. That shows how much he cares about winning. He's an emotional guy and he wears his heart on his sleeve."
GARY McALLISTER ON PETER SCHMEICHEL

"The skill and awareness of Tomas Brolin, the power and strength of Tony Yeboah and the giant presence of Brian Deane were United's undoing. Poor Parker was out-paced and overpowered and United didn't have the strength of character or concentration to cope in this frightening atmosphere." **DAILY STAR**

"United were forced to play central midfielders Nicky Butt and David Beckham on the flanks. And that left the supply line for Andy Cole desperately thin." **SUN**

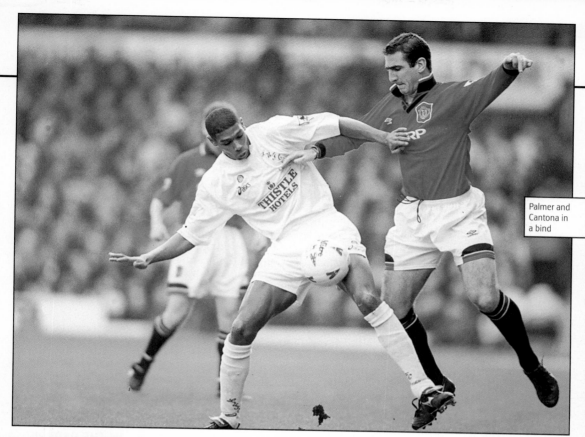

Palmer and Cantona in a bind

Rock 'n' Brolin

MANCHESTER UNITED 2
NEWCASTLE UNITED 0

HOME TEAM

		RATING
1.	Peter Schmeichel	7
23.	Phil Neville	8
3.	Denis Irwin	7
20.	Gary Neville	9
12.	David May	7
7.	Eric Cantona	7
16.	Roy Keane	9
19.	Nicky Butt	8
11.	Ryan Giggs	8
17.	Andy Cole	8
24.	David Beckham	6

SUBSTITUTES

9.	Brian McClair	7
	May	45 mins	
21.	Pat McGibbon	
22.	Paul Scholes	

SCORERS

Cole | 6 mins
Keane | 53 mins

REFEREE

P E Alcock | Redhill

VISITORS

1.	Pavel Srnicek
2.	Warren Barton
3.	John Beresford
4.	Darren Peacock
6.	Steve Howey
7.	Robert Lee
8.	Peter Beardsley
10.	Lee Clark
14.	David Ginola
9.	Les Ferdinand
18.	Keith Gillespie

SUBSTITUTES

19.	Steve Watson	
	Gillespie	15 mins	
26.	Robbie Elliott	
28.	Paul Kitson	
	Clark	75 mins	

MATCH REPORT

Cole v Ferdinand, Cantona v Ginola: it was billed as the Championship decider by many, but come 90 minutes there was only one United at Old Trafford.

Cantona was made captain by Ferguson and his mature play was enhanced by superb performances around him. After only five minutes, Cole got the goal he must have been dreaming about – a sweet strike guided past Srnicek.

Newcastle hit back; Ferdinand and Ginola both missed goalscoring opportunities. In the 53rd minute, Phil Neville cleverly found Keane who had all the time in the world to hammer home the second.

A magnificent display from the team and the personal success of Andy Cole made it a choice game to remember.

Give the man a big hand

IN THE PAPERS

"A goal in each half from Cole and Roy Keane cut Newcastle's lead in the Premiership to seven points, and the sweep and zest of much of the winners' football eventually reduced the visitors' defence to damage limitation."
GUARDIAN

"Manchester United had heroes all over the park, but Roy Keane was the king. Eric Cantona, skipper for the night, was a driving inspiration, totally overshadowing Ginola's flickering display."
DAILY STAR

"Manchester United unfurled the full, glorious expanse of their football at Old Trafford last night to bite harder into Newcastle's spirit than the frost into the ground. If a 10-point lead seemed like a luxury yesterday afternoon, by the middle of the evening it had been trimmed to seven and the leaders suddenly looked eminently catchable."
DAILY MAIL

Keane makes it two

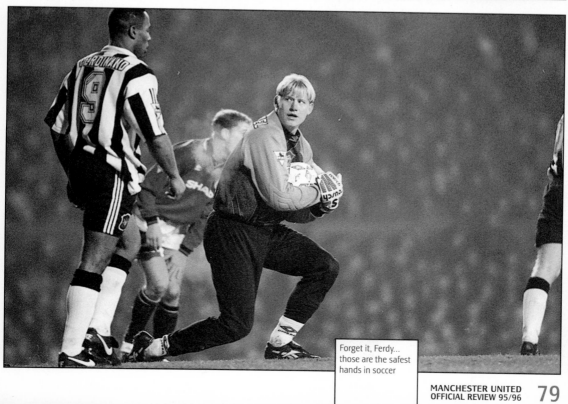

Forget it, Ferdy... those are the safest hands in soccer

MANCHESTER UNITED 2
QUEENS PARK RANGERS 1

HOME TEAM

		RATING
1.	Peter Schmeichel	7
3.	Denis Irwin	7
20.	Gary Neville	8
31.	William Prunier	8
23.	Phil Neville	7
16.	Roy Keane	9
19.	Nicky Butt	8
7.	Eric Cantona	8
11.	Ryan Giggs	8
17.	Andy Cole	7
24.	David Beckham	7

SUBSTITUTES

		RATING
2.	Paul Parker	7
	Neville, P	55 mins	
5.	Lee Sharpe	
	Beckham	88 mins	
9.	Brian McClair	7
	Cole	55 mins	

SCORERS

Cole | 44 mins
Giggs | 52 mins

REFEREE

R Hart | Darlington

VISITORS

25.	Juergen Sommer
2.	David Bardsley
3.	Rufus Brevett
21.	Steve Yates
6.	Danny Maddix
7.	Andrew Impey
8.	Ian Holloway
19.	Steve Hodge
27.	Matthew Brazier
17.	Bradley Allen
11.	Trevor Sinclair

SUBSTITUTES

1.	Tony Roberts
9.	Daniele Dichio
	Allen	47 mins
14.	Karl Ready
	Bardsley	71 mins

SCORERS

Dichio | 68 mins

MATCH REPORT

French débutant William Prunier turned in a sterling performance to provide United with three vital Championship points.

Ferguson said United needed to win this game, and win it they did. Butt was superb in midfield and Cole showed the critics his true form. However, it was not all good for Cole: he limped off with a suspected hamstring strain.

Both teams started well and Rangers were unfazed by the gap in League placings, going close a couple of times. United broke the deadlock through Cole in first-half injury time with a simple header yards from goal.

Soon after the break, Giggs collected a pass from Irwin to finish with ease. The two-goal cushion allowed United to cruise for a while, but a rare mistake from Schmeichel let the visitors get back in the game courtesy of Dichio.

IN THE PAPERS

"A nugget of coal carried across the threshold has long been regarded as a lucky omen. Ferguson's very own nugget of Cole – £7-million Andy – has given him the perfect 54th birthday gift." **SUNDAY EXPRESS**

"Inspired by Cole's third goal in successive festive games, United ground out a crucial win. They brushed aside gallant QPR, condemning Wilkins to a relegation dogfight." **SUNDAY MIRROR**

"The 'Glory, Glory Man United' anthem blaring out at the end of the game was correct in stressing that the 'Reds go marching on'. Alex Ferguson's side are striding out so well they are only four points behind Newcastle, the Premier League leaders, whose game at West Ham was frozen off." **SUNDAY TIMES**

Gary Neville denies Rangers' Dichio

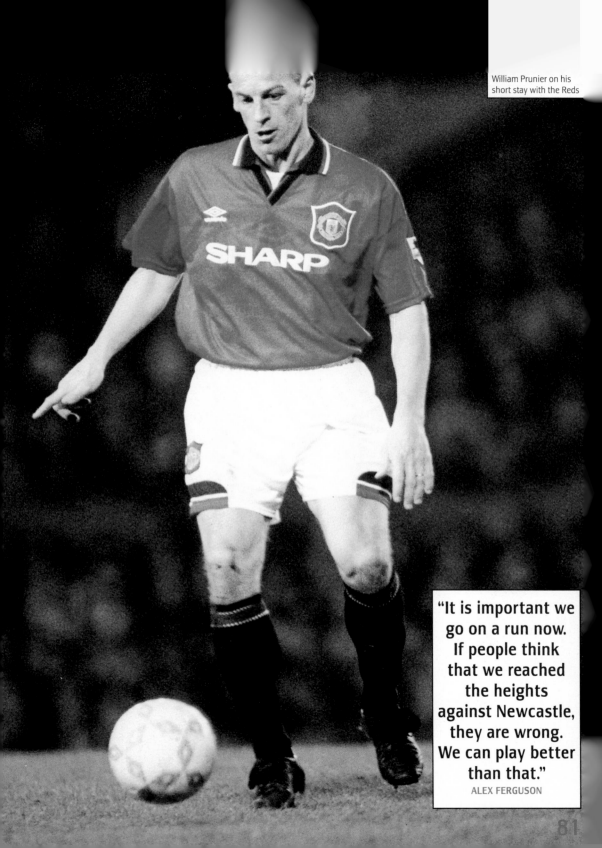

William Prunier on his short stay with the Reds

"It is important we go on a run now. If people think that we reached the heights against Newcastle, they are wrong. We can play better than that."

ALEX FERGUSON

81

DECEMBER STATS

PLAYER RECORDS

home | away

■ PREMIERSHIP ■ UEFA CUP ■ COCA COLA CUP ■ FA CUP

■▮ FULL APPEARANCE / CAME ON AS SUB

■▮ SCORER / SCORED AS SUB

Column headers (opponents): Aston Villa, West Ham United, Wimbledon, Blackburn Rovers, Everton, Bolton Wanderers, Rotor Volgograd, York City, Rotor Volgograd, York City, Sheffield Wednesday, Liverpool, Manchester City, Middlesbrough, Southampton, Coventry City, Nottingham Forest, Chelsea, Sheffield Wednesday, Liverpool, Newcastle United, Queens Park Rangers

No.	Player	Full Appearances	Sub Appearances	Goals
1.	Peter Schmeichel	22	0	1
2.	Paul Parker	5	2	0
3.	Denis Irwin	19	0	1
4.	Steve Bruce	21	1	0
5.	Lee Sharpe	14	6	3
6.	Gary Pallister	19	0	1
7.	Eric Cantona	13	0	4
9.	Brian McClair	10	7	3
11.	Ryan Giggs	17	3	6
12.	David May	4	2	0
15.	Graeme Tomlinson	0	0	0
16.	Roy Keane	15	1	4
17.	Andy Cole	19	1	6
18.	Simon Davies	2	6	0
19.	Nicky Butt	20	0	1
20.	Gary Neville	21	0	0
21.	Patrick McGibbon	1	0	0
22.	Paul Scholes	16	5	10
23.	Philip Neville	6	3	0
24.	David Beckham	20	3	4
25.	Kevin Pilkington	3	0	0
26.	Chris Casper	0	0	0
27.	Terry Cooke	2	4	1
29.	Ben Thornley	0	1	0
30.	John O'Kane	1	1	0
31.	William Prunier	1	0	0

PLAYER OF THE MONTH

ERIC CANTONA

AVERAGE PERFORMANCE RATING: 7.3

FA CARLING PREMIERSHIP

as at 30 December 1995

	Pld	Home					Away					Pts	GD
		W	D	L	F	A	W	D	L	F	A		
■ Newcastle United	20	10	0	0	24	5	4	3	3	16	13	45	+22
■ Manchester United	21	8	3	0	24	9	4	2	4	16	14	41	+17
▲ Liverpool	20	7	2	1	23	6	3	3	4	13	12	35	+18
▲ Tottenham Hotspur	21	4	3	3	12	11	5	5	1	15	10	35	+6
▼ Arsenal	21	6	4	1	19	10	3	3	4	9	8	34	+10
■ Nottingham Forest	20	6	4	0	18	8	2	6	2	12	19	34	+3
▲ Middlesbrough	21	7	2	1	18	7	2	4	5	5	12	33	+4
▼ Aston Villa	19	5	3	1	14	6	4	2	4	11	9	32	+6
▲ Blackburn Rovers	21	9	1	1	29	8	0	3	7	4	18	31	+7
▼ Leeds United	20	6	1	3	14	10	3	3	4	14	17	31	+1
▲ Everton	21	6	2	3	21	11	2	3	5	9	11	29	8
▼ Chelsea	21	4	5	2	14	12	3	3	4	7	11	29	-2
■ West Ham United	19	3	3	3	10	13	3	2	5	11	15	23	-7
■ Sheffield Wednesday	20	3	3	4	16	16	2	4	4	12	14	22	-2
▲ Wimbledon	21	2	4	4	13	16	3	2	6	16	25	21	-12
▼ Southampton	20	3	4	3	9	9	1	3	6	10	21	19	-11
▲ Coventry City	20	3	3	4	15	17	1	3	6	12	25	18	-15
▼ Queens Park Rangers	21	3	3	4	11	16	2	0	9	5	15	18	-15
▼ Manchester City	20	3	3	4	5	7	1	1	8	5	23	16	-20
▼ Bolton Wanderers	21	2	3	6	8	16	0	1	9	11	24	10	-21

JANUARY

1 | 2 | 3 | 4 | 5 | 6 | 7 | 8 | 9 | 10 | 11 | 12 | 13 | 14 | 15 | 16 | 17 | 18 | 19 | 20 | 21 | 22 | 23 | 24 | 25 | 26 | 27 | 28 | 29 | 30 | 31

JANUARY

THE MONTH AHEAD

Happy New Year? You must be joking. 1996 was only a few hours old when United went to White Hart Lane and got stuffed by Spurs. If the boys had been up all night seeing in the year, the result might have been understandable. But the decision to play Peter Schmeichel even though he'd injured himself in the warm-up was probably more to blame. "Every time Spurs crossed into the box you thought they'd score," said Fergie after the 4–1 defeat. "A fully fit Peter Schmeichel would've claimed those crosses."

In the same month, William Prunier's ghostly appearance in the first team came to an end. He first played on 28 December against QPR and he left after the encounter with Spurs, his tryout with the Reds coming to nothing.

The team was lifted, however, by news from Europe that because of the Bosman ruling, UEFA was set to scrap the limits on the number of foreign players in European competitions... surely the only reason United hadn't won the European Cup for the last three seasons in succession. The squad was also buoyed by revelations that blonde bombshell TV presenter Ulrika Johnston has an inch-high tattoo of a red devil on her bottom. Whether this is in support of the Reds, who knows; but it's certainly something worth thinking about! Maybe Ulrika's backside was in the players' thoughts when they faced Sunderland in the Third Round of the FA Cup at Old Trafford. Certainly, for much of the game it looked like their minds were elsewhere. Credit to Sunderland and their raucous fans though; if it hadn't been for Eric's 80th minute equaliser, they'd have made it through to the next round and no one could have complained.

Fergie had problems. Not only was the United team struggling, but with her personal debts of £3 million, the Queen was said to be furious with her and the future of Budgie the Helicopter was in serious doubt. Fortunately, this had nothing to do with the real Fergie (the good looking one!), who was getting on with preparations for the next game, at home to Aston Villa.

Unfortunately, things didn't pick up. Villa came to Old Trafford for a 0–0 draw, which is exactly what they got. Newcastle found themselves six points clear with two games in hand. Andy Cole, who was no doubt pleased that

Ghosting through
OT: William Prunier

Andy Cole gets the sole Red goal in the wipe-out by Spurs

FIFA was still considering widening the goals, had his critics roaring again... but he answered them in the best possible way three days later at Roker Park. With the scores locked at 1–1 and extra time looming in the Third Round Sunderland replay, Cole rose at the far post and headed United into the next round. You could say he was quite happy.

The same could not be said for Terry Venables, who announced he was quitting the England job after Euro '96 and suggested a certain Bryan Robson as his replacement. Robbo would have relished United's next Premiership match, a real blood-and-thunder battle at Upton Park against West Ham. It ended with another away victory and another controversy involving Julian Dicks.

The Reds ran the game and should have been three or four up by half time. Instead, they went in 1–0 up, thanks to the shaven-headed Cantona who'd had his hair cut especially to match Julian Dicks. The pair would meet later. With United hanging on, Dicks lunged at Cole, the referee missed it and Butt lunged at Dicks. It was the United man who received his marching orders (although TV showed Dicks's challenge on Cole had been as bad if not worse) and, as all hell threatened to break out, who was there to keep the peace? A certain Frenchman called Eric.

> ## "Had Cole not taken his leg away, he would have carried it off the pitch himself."
>
> ANDY GRAY ON SKY SPORTS

It seemed like foreign players were pouring into England from every direction at the end of January to join Cantona: even Millwall signed a couple of Russian internationals. The balance was redressed somewhat when schoolgirl Sarah Cooke, 13, made a shock move to Turkey. But for United it was off to the less exotic climes of Reading for the last stop of the month in the FA Cup, and a third away win on the trot. Things were improving fast. Even though they seemed like the only club in the Premiership who hadn't signed a Croatian defender, the team was starting to click.

Roker stonker: Cole scores the second against Sunderland

TOTTENHAM HOTSPUR 4
MANCHESTER UNITED 1

HOME TEAM

1. Ian Walker
2. Dean Austin
3. Justin Edinburgh
5. Colin Calderwood
8. Ilie Dumitrescu
10. Teddy Sheringham
11. Chris Armstrong
14. Stuart Nethercott
16. Ronny Rosenthal
20. Darren Caskey
23. Sol Campbell

SUBSTITUTES

18. **Gerry McMahon**
   Dumitrescu | 81 mins
29. **Steve Slade**
30. **Chris Day**

SCORERS
Sheringham | 36 mins
Campbell | 45 mins
Armstrong | 47/65 mins

REFEREE
G Ashby | Worcestershire

VISITORS   RATING

1. Peter Schmeichel   5
2. Paul Parker   5
20. Gary Neville   6
23. Phil Neville   6
31. William Prunier   5
7. Eric Cantona   5
16. Roy Keane   6
19. Nicky Butt   7
11. Ryan Giggs   5
17. Andy Cole   7
24. David Beckham   6

SUBSTITUTES

5. **Lee Sharpe**   5
   Neville, P | 70 mins
9. **Brian McClair**   6
   Keane | 70 mins
25. **Kevin Pilkington**   5
   Schmeichel | 45 mins

SCORER
Cole | 36 mins

MATCH REPORT

A disastrous start to the New Year. United played well down at Tottenham, but some slack defending coupled with missed opportunities resulted in United's biggest defeat of the season.

Sheringham and Armstrong were on top form for Spurs, and it was Sheringham who put them in the lead. United saw a glimmer of hope when Cole equalised, but Sol Campbell made sure Spurs were ahead at half time.

The second half was a lively affair, with Armstrong scoring twice.

United tried to get back into it and Cole was desperately unlucky to see an overhead-kick goal ruled out. There were a few last minute chances but the scoreline stayed at a hugely disappointing 4–1.

Gendarme in lilywhite traffic

IN THE PAPERS

"Manchester United were left well and truly stuffed by a Teddy." **DAILY STAR**

"Ferguson fielded a makeshift defence that was slipshod when confronted by a Spurs side with their own New Year aspirations of at least a place in Europe. United didn't have a prayer of coming back from three goals down, yet Cole had a goal disallowed – his scissor-kick deemed dangerous – and it was inevitable that United would slump to their fifth defeat of the season." **DAILY MIRROR**

"United's problem is that their injuries are mostly defensive, and covering for the loss of Steve Bruce and Gary Pallister is difficult enough without losing Denis Irwin as well. Sheringham's immense power in the air was always a problem for Gary Neville, while Frenchman William Prunier looked like a gendarme asked to do traffic duty in Piccadilly Circus." **DAILY MAIL**

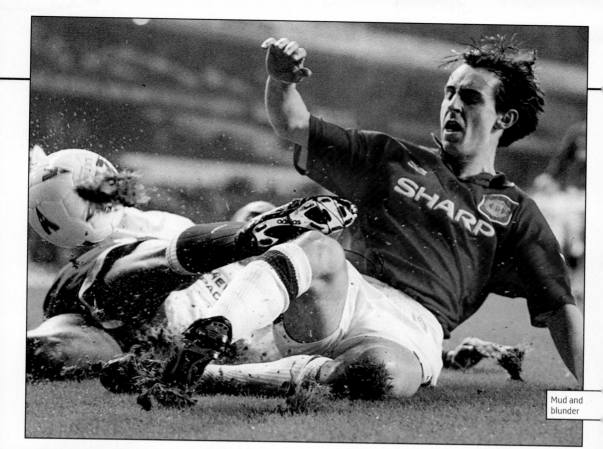

Mud and blunder

Walker on the wild side

MANCHESTER UNITED 2
SUNDERLAND 2

HOME TEAM

		RATING
1.	Kevin Pilkington	7
2.	Gary Neville	7
3.	Denis Irwin	8
4.	Steve Bruce	6
5.	Roy Keane	8
6.	Gary Pallister	7
7.	Eric Cantona	7
8.	Nicky Butt	9
9.	Andy Cole	7
10.	David Beckham	7
11.	Ryan Giggs	8

SUBSTITUTES

12.	Brian McClair	
14.	Lee Sharpe	7
	Beckham	59 mins	
15.	Phil Neville	7
	Gary Neville	65 mins	

SCORERS

Butt | 12 mins
Cantona | 80 mins

REFEREE

M D Reed | Birmingham

VISITORS

1.	Alec Chamberlain
2.	Dariuz Kubucki
3.	Martin Stott
4.	Paul Bracewell
5.	Kevin Ball
6.	Andy Melville
7.	Michael Gray
8.	Richard Ord
9.	Craig Russell
10.	Phil Gray
11.	David Kelly

SUBSTITUTES

12.	Lee Howey	
13.	Steve Agnew	
	Ball	25 mins	
14.	Martin Smith	
	Kelly	82 mins	

SCORERS

Agnew | 61 mins
Russell | 64 mins

MATCH REPORT

Alex Ferguson admitted that he thought United were on their way out of the Cup, and it definitely looked that way for 79 minutes.

Sunderland didn't come to Old Trafford to lie down and were backed well by their 8,000 supporters from the North East. United went in front through Cole, and the move leading up to it was a testament to United's flair: 14 passes paved the way for Butt and Cantona to let Cole in.

Sunderland were jolted into life. Immediately, Gary Neville was clearing off his goal line and Gray saw his thunderous shot hit the upright.

With an hour gone, Agnew steered a right-footed shot under Pilkington and, three minutes later, Agnew played to provider Russell who finished off the move.

Sunderland's second provoked passion in United's game and, with 11 minutes left, Sharpe's free-kick was headed into the roof of the net by Cantona.

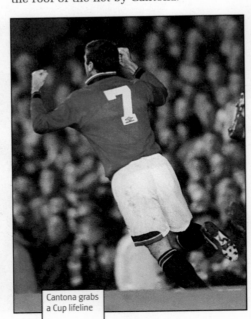

Cantona grabs a Cup lifeline

IN THE PAPERS

"Ferguson praised Sunderland for their enterprise and quality. Would other managers have shown such generosity? 'They outplayed us for most of the game. There is no substitute for what Sunderland provided: desire. It was a terrific effort.'" **TIMES**

"He rescued them from defeat and the Old Trafford faithful bowed in homage. Eric the King had saved his subjects from humiliation with a late goal." **DAILY MAIL**

"Backed by thousands of roaring fans, Sunderland were a real handful. Sunderland upstaged Ferguson's superstars with a lack of reverence that suggests United are in for a night of football terror on Wearside." **PEOPLE**

"Cantona salvaged a replay with a headed goal 10 minutes from time in a 2–2 draw, and even United manager Alex Ferguson admitted: 'I couldn't see us getting out of trouble.'" **SUNDAY EXPRESS**

"Peter Reid's team were caught out in the end only by tiredness and an understandable but unwise decision to defend their advantage from too deep." **OBSERVER**

> "The problem was that they came out for a Cup tie and we were ready for a normal game. We were lucky to get a second chance – which just illustrates what the FA Cup is about."
>
> ALEX FERGUSON

Cole fades to Gray

89

MANCHESTER UNITED 0
ASTON VILLA 0

HOME TEAM

		RATING
1.	Peter Schmeichel	8
3.	Denis Irwin	8
4.	Steve Bruce	7
23.	Phil Neville	8
20.	Gary Neville	7
5.	Lee Sharpe	6
16.	Roy Keane	8
19.	Nicky Butt	7
7.	Eric Cantona	7
11.	Ryan Giggs	8
17.	Andy Cole	7

SUBSTITUTES

2.	Paul Parker	
9.	Brian McClair	
22.	Paul Scholes	5
	Sharpe I 78 mins	

REFEREE

G Willard I Worthing

VISITORS

1.	Mark Bosnich
16.	Ugo Ehiogu
5.	Paul McGrath
4.	Gareth Southgate
2.	Gary Charles
7.	Ian Taylor
8.	Mark Draper
11.	Andy Townsend
14.	Alan Wright
9.	Savo Milosevic
10.	Tommy Johnson

SUBSTITUTES

17.	Fanz Carr	
20.	Riccardo Scimeca	
	Johnson I 90 mins	
13.	Nigel Spink	

MATCH REPORT

United continued a series of draws with a dour 0–0 against a Villa side determined to defend.

Every United attack was thwarted by hordes of blue shirts gathering behind the ball. Cole had a good chance in the 28th minute but couldn't direct his header goalwards. Phil Neville was instrumental to United's attacks, darting down the flank.

Sadly, no one could break the deadlock, and towards the end chances were sparse. Scholes replaced Sharpe but nothing was to come of it. A definite stumble in the steeplechase that is the Championship race.

Eric stays in front

IN THE PAPERS

"Villa made it difficult for United with an almost perfect defensive display."
DAILY TELEGRAPH

"Chances were few and far between. An aerodynamically cropped Eric Cantona must have wished he'd left some hair to tear out as his frustration mounted."
MANCHESTER EVENING NEWS

"The suggestion is that taming Eric Cantona's fiery temperament has left a town crier without his bell. Cantona's co-ordination with Andy Cole is not what he enjoyed with Mark Hughes."
DAILY EXPRESS

"Eric Cantona's barber ran riot with the clippers, giving the Frenchman a menacing, convict-style look that suggested he wouldn't be taking any prisoners."
DAILY MIRROR

"In the end the outcome suited only Premiership leaders Newcastle. And former Magpie Andy Cole made the biggest contribution to the stalemate."
MAIL ON SUNDAY

Lob prospect

Overhead projection

SUNDERLAND 1
MANCHESTER UNITED 2

HOME TEAM

1. Alec Chamberlain
2. Dariuz Kubucki
3. Andy Melville
4. Richard Ord
5. Martin Scott
6. Michael Gray
7. Paul Bracewell
8. Steve Agnew
9. Martin Smith
10. Phil Gray
11. Craig Russell

SUBSTITUTES

12. Lee Howey
    Bracewell | 89 mins
14. John Mullin
    Smith | 50 mins
15. Martin Gray
    Agnew | 70 mins

SCORER

Gray | 24 mins

REFEREE

M D Reed | Birmingham

VISITORS

		RATING
1.	Peter Schmeichel	8
2.	Paul Parker	6
3.	Denis Irwin	7
4.	Steve Bruce	7
5.	Gary Neville	8
6.	Phil Neville	7
7.	Eric Cantona	7
8.	Andy Cole	7
9.	Nicky Butt	7
10.	Roy Keane	7
11.	Ryan Giggs	9

SUBSTITUTES

12.	Lee Sharpe	7

Parker | 46 mins

14.	Paul Scholes	8

Butt | 62 mins

15. Brian McClair

SCORERS

Scholes | 69 mins
Cole | 89 mins

MATCH REPORT

Cole delivered the goods on a night where United left it very late.

The match was most definitely a game of two halves, with Sunderland dominating the first half and United taking control of the last 45.

The impressive Gray opened the scoring, due partly to slick attacking, partly due to slack defending. The ball came over and Gray prodded it home through a mass of legs.

The second half saw a tactical change from United which worked for the better. Sharpe was a threat on the wing and Scholes a hive of activity upfront. With 70 minutes gone, United equalised, ginger wonder-kid Scholes firing home from 18 yards.

As fans were preparing for extra time, Sharpe centred a deep cross and who else was there to send United into the Fourth Round draw but Andy Cole?

United reach the Fourth Round

IN THE PAPERS

"They taunted him for his Newcastle United background and chortled when things went wrong for him, but Andy Cole had the last laugh on Sunderland's supporters with almost the last touch of the match." **DAILY MAIL**

"It wasn't until Ferguson's inspired substitution that United got back into this blood-and-thunder battle." **DAILY MIRROR**

"United took advantage of Sunderland's heavy legs to pour forward and Ferguson strengthened his attacking options by bringing on leading scorer Paul Scholes for Nicky Butt in the 62nd minute." **DAILY TELEGRAPH**

"The Roker roar was reduced to a stunned silence as Andy Cole rammed the taunts back down poor Sunderland's throats. North East fans had taunted the Manchester United striker on a night when he seemed destined once again to be labelled a £7-million flop. But he struck with chilling accuracy 30 seconds from the end to wipe out all the hard work that Peter Reid's men had put into two breathtaking Cup ties." **DAILY EXPRESS**

Brother beyond

Andy Cole scores a classic headed winner

WEST HAM UNITED 0
MANCHESTER UNITED 1

HOME TEAM

1.	Ludek Miklosko
4.	Steve Potts
15.	Kenny Brown
8.	Marc Rieper
3.	Julian Dicks
7.	Ian Bishop
20.	Danny Williamson
9.	Tony Cottee
14.	Iain Dowie
10.	John Moncur
19.	Robbie Slater

SUBSTITUTES

12.	Kevin Rowland
	Slater I mins
21.	Peter Shilton
27.	Chris Whyte

REFEREE

S Lodge I Barnsley

VISITORS

		RATING
1.	Peter Schmeichel	8
3.	Denis Irwin	8
4.	Steve Bruce	7
23.	Phil Neville	7
20.	Gary Neville	7
5.	Lee Sharpe	7
16.	Roy Keane	9
19.	Nicky Butt	8
7.	Eric Cantona	8
11.	Ryan Giggs	8
17.	Andy Cole	7

SUBSTITUTES

2.	Paul Parker	
22.	Paul Scholes	
24.	David Beckham	6
	Cole I 77 mins	

SCORER

Cantona I 8 mins

MATCH REPORT

West Ham failed to repeat the party spoiling antics which have been their trademark in recent times.

A 10-man United side turned in a fiery display to snatch the points. Butt was given his marching orders for two bookable offences, and many Reds felt aggrieved that Dicks wasn't given the same for a two-footed challenge on Cole. That challenge brought protests from United players and an unlikely peacemaker in the shape of Cantona.

Both sides created chances but United capitalised on theirs early on, with a Sharpe cross missed by all but man of the moment Cantona, who coolly stroked the ball home.

United's 10 men held out at the end, despite a West Ham siege on goal, and can look back on a solid performance.

"Does this hurt?"

IN THE PAPERS

"West Ham, always fevered competitors against United, went for the men in blood-red shirts in a Premiership match of high tempo and higher temperatures."
DAILY TELEGRAPH

"A vigorous victory, at a venue that has seen them endure so much disappointment in recent years." **MANCHESTER EVENING NEWS**

"With Butt and Roy Keane mastering the midfield against the lightweight Ian Bishop and John Moncur, it seemed as if all the past ghosts Manchester have seen here would be exorcised."
DAILY EXPRESS

"Eric Cantona proved that he is more genius than jerk. Cantona's touch, technique and range of passing was one reason for United's domination, despite the thrilling and dramatic way West Ham came back at them." **DAILY MIRROR**

"In the middle of the flying boots and fury of Upton Park, Cantona turned into Daddy Cool. He even acted as peacemaker at one stage."
MAIL ON SUNDAY

Neville gets that Dowie feeling

"Upton Park is an emotional place, and so many expected us to drop points here again. We are well pleased."
ALEX FERGUSON

READING 0
MANCHESTER UNITED 3

HOME TEAM

1. Nicky Hammond
2. Tom Jones
3. Andy Bernal
4. Adrian Williams
5. Michael Gilkes
6. Mick Gooding
7. Phil Parkinson
8. Lee Nogan
9. Paul Holsgrove
10. Jimmy Quinn
11. Trevor Morley

SUBSTITUTES

12. Michael Meaker
13. Stuart Lovell
14. James Lambert

REFEREE

J Winter | Stockton-on-Tees

VISITORS

		RATING
1.	Peter Schmeichel	8
23.	Phil Neville	8
3.	Denis Irwin	8
4.	Steve Bruce	8
20.	Gary Neville	8
5.	Lee Sharpe	8
7.	Eric Cantona	9
17.	Andy Cole	8
19.	Nicky Butt	8
16.	Roy Keane	8
11.	Ryan Giggs	9

SUBSTITUTES

2.	Paul Parker	8
	P Neville	53 mins	
19.	Brian McClair	
22.	Paul Scholes	

SCORERS

Giggs | 36 mins
Parker | 56 mins
Cantona | 89 mins

MATCH REPORT

The pundits had a Cup upset in their sights, but in the end class shone through and United ran out comfortable winners against Berkshire's finest.

Is was not all United though. Quinn should have scored from at least one of his three first-half chances as Reading put on the pressure. Giggs and Sharpe combined to bring about the Reds' first goal, and United began to settle down and play football.

Parker replaced Phil Neville early on in the second half and, with his second touch, found the net with what can only be described as a fluke. The defender celebrated the second United goal of his career with a mixture of ecstasy and bemusement.

The two-goal advantage proved too much for Reading and, in the last minute, Cantona slotted home a third. On a freezing day the biggest cheers were reserved for a glaring miss from Steve Bruce, who otherwise had a solid game as skipper.

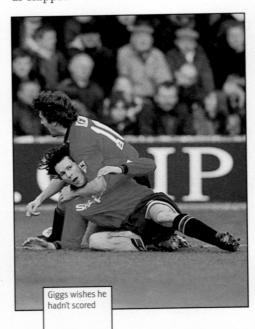

Giggs wishes he hadn't scored

IN THE PAPERS

"It was the story of the banana skin that wasn't. Manchester United's sure-footed progress into the Fifth Round was conspicuous, not only for Eric Cantona's polite return of the half-eaten banana some ignoramus threw at him in the second half." **DAILY MAIL**

"Now, slow but most definitely sure, Cantona is getting back to the level of expected brilliance." **DAILY STAR**

"Wooden stands, a sandy pitch, a park bench for the Manchester United management. So this was FA Cup heaven. Until the three goals went in, a linesman was hit by a coin and Reading and romance froze over." **DAILY TELEGRAPH**

"Reading are a side with one or two wily old owls, who might have sprung a surprise for the United youngsters suffering the claustrophobia of a tightly packed little ground." **DAILY EXPRESS**

Sharpe springs

Parker pretends he meant to shoot

JANUARY STATS

PLAYER RECORDS

home | away

■ PREMIERSHIP ■ UEFA CUP ■ COCA COLA CUP ■ FA CUP

FULL APPEARANCE CAME ON AS SUB

SCORER SCORED AS SUB

#	Player	Full Appearances	Sub Appearances	Goals
1.	Peter Schmeichel	27	0	1
2.	Paul Parker	7	3	1
3.	Denis Irwin	24	0	1
4.	Steve Bruce	26	1	0
5.	Lee Sharpe	17	9	3
6.	Gary Pallister	20	0	1
7.	Eric Cantona	19	0	7
9.	Brian McClair	10	8	3
11.	Ryan Giggs	23	3	7
12.	David May	4	2	0
15.	Graeme Tomlinson	0	0	0
16.	Roy Keane	21	1	4
17.	Andy Cole	25	1	8
18.	Simon Davies	2	6	0
19.	Nicky Butt	26	0	2
20.	Gary Neville	27	0	0
21.	Patrick McGibbon	1	0	0
22.	Paul Scholes	16	7	11
23.	Philip Neville	11	4	0
24.	David Beckham	22	4	4
25.	Kevin Pilkington	4	1	0
26.	Chris Casper	0	0	0
27.	Terry Cooke	2	4	1
29.	Ben Thornley	0	1	0
30.	John O'Kane	1	1	0
31.	William Prunier	2	0	0

PLAYER OF THE MONTH

ROY KEANE

AVERAGE PERFORMANCE RATING: 7.7

FA CARLING PREMIERSHIP

as at 22 January 1996

	Pld	Home					Away					Pts	GD
		W	D	L	F	A	W	D	L	F	A		
■ Newcastle United	23	12	0	0	28	6	5	3	3	17	13	54	+26
■ Manchester United	24	8	4	0	24	9	5	2	5	18	18	45	+15
■ Liverpool	23	9	2	1	32	8	3	4	4	14	13	42	+25
■ Tottenham Hotspur	24	6	3	3	17	12	5	5	2	16	12	41	+9
▲ Aston Villa	22	6	3	1	16	7	5	3	4	13	9	39	+13
▲ Blackburn Rovers	24	10	1	1	32	8	1	4	7	5	18	38	+11
▼ Arsenal	24	6	4	2	20	12	4	3	5	12	12	37	+8
▼ Nottingham Forest	23	7	4	0	19	8	2	6	4	14	24	37	+1
▼ Everton	24	6	3	3	21	12	4	3	5	14	14	36	+9
▲ Chelsea	24	5	5	2	15	12	4	4	4	10	13	36	0
▼ Leeds United	23	7	2	3	16	10	3	3	5	14	22	35	-2
▼ Middlesbrough	24	7	2	3	20	12	2	4	6	14	14	33	0
▼ Sheffield Wednesday	23	4	4	4	21	19	2	4	5	12	17	26	-3
▲ Wimbledon	24	3	4	5	17	20	3	2	7	16	26	24	-13
▼ West Ham United	22	3	3	4	10	14	3	2	7	12	19	23	-11
■ Southampton	23	4	4	3	11	10	1	4	7	11	23	23	-11
▲ Coventry City	23	3	4	5	16	19	1	4	6	13	26	20	-16
▲ Manchester City	23	4	4	4	8	9	1	1	9	5	24	20	-20
▼ Queens Park Rangers	24	3	3	6	12	19	2	0	10	6	17	18	-18
■ Bolton Wanderers	24	3	3	6	9	16	0	1	11	14	30	13	-23

FEBRUARY

1 | 2 | 3 | 4 | 5 | 6 | 7 | 8 | 9 | 10 | 11 | 12 | 13 | 14 | 15 | 16 | 17 | 18 | 19 | 20 | 21 | 22 | 23 | 24 | 25 | 26 | 27 | 28 | 29

FEBRUARY

THE MONTH IN REVIEW

Even with February turning out to be the month of the break-up (Manchester's second most popular bunch of lads Take That announced they were to split; Charles and Di finally agreed to a divorce), United managed to hold together their good run. The Reds made it five wins out of five in fabulous February, and by the end of the month Newcastle would know that the pressure was really on...

When you're on a roll, however, the one thing that's guaranteed to bring you back to earth is a trip to face Wimbledon at Selhurst Park. As it was Eric's first match back at the scene of his crime, security was stepped up around the ground. Fortunately the security measures didn't extend to the Wimbledon goal, and in the end Fergie's Fledglings cruised it, running out 4–2 winners. With Eric in fine form and three quarters of the 25,000 crowd cheering on United, even without Steve Bruce (injured during a first-half clash of heads with Dean Holdsworth) it only ever looked like United would win it.

Next up was Blackburn, and there was a point to make against last season's champions. In a bad-tempered match, the closest Alan Shearer got to upsetting United was when he lunged unnecessarily at Peter Schmeichel. The Reds kept up their run with a narrow 1–0 win inspired by Roy Keane and back-in-form star Lee Sharpe. It was getting tighter at the top, but fading champs Blackburn were well and truly out of it. Shame!

In the middle of February, Britain was rocked by news of a dreadful oil slick disaster in Wales. Welsh dragon Giggsy, meanwhile, was making big news of his own after signing a massive £1.8 million boot deal with Reebok. Still only 22,

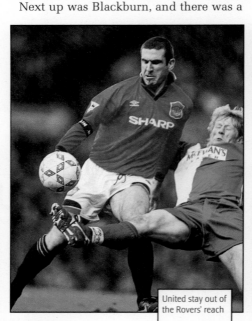

United stay out of the Rovers' reach

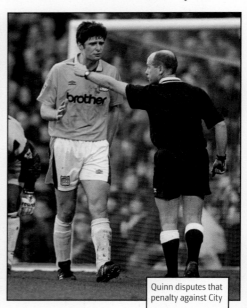

Quinn disputes that penalty against City

Giggsy was in awesome form: good news for Reebok but bad for the next visitors to Old Trafford, arch-rivals City, there for the FA Cup Fifth Round.

With the match beamed live across the world and one end of the ground heaving with City fans, it was the blue half (or should that be quarter) of Manchester which celebrated first after Uwe Rösler put the visitors ahead. Even United fans were mystified by the penalty that brought the Reds back into contention, though Cantona insisted he'd been pulled in the box. When Lee Sharpe scored the winner right in front of the City fans, United had Wembley back in their sights.

This was the month in which the IRA broke the ceasefire. The two bombs that went off in February may have exploded in the capital but their impact was felt all over the world. In football, Mick McCarthy was installed as the new Republic of Ireland manager (a job that Fergie turned down), and Colombian live-wire Faustino Asprilla's on-off transfer to Newcastle was now definitely on. The geordies were hoping that Asprilla would be the final piece in their jigsaw, but United were piecing together a run of their own and closing on Newcastle fast. And a 2–0 Old Trafford victory over Everton kept the heat on Kevin Keegan's men.

With Jarvis Cocker in the news for jumping on stage when Michael Jackson was in flow, United went into their next match and (sorry about this one) crushed Bolton to a pulp. Before the match, the local police announced a £10,000 reward had been put up by local hooligans for

> ## "When Cantona went into the Selhurst Park crowd this time, it was to celebrate with Manchester United fans."
>
> THE SUN AFTER THE 4–2 WIN OVER WIMBLEDON.

anyone who could "get" Eric Cantona. In the end, no one got anywhere near the Frenchman – and that includes the Bolton players. Even Keith Gillespie wouldn't have bet on United winning 6–0 away from home, but thanks to Beckham, Cole, Scholes and Butt, that was the final score at Burnden Park.

As the geordies spluttered, the Red machine was cranking into top gear. Newcastle's name was next on Fergie's fixture list.

Reds invade and conquer Burnden Park

WIMBLEDON 2
MANCHESTER UNITED 4

HOME TEAM

- 23. Neil Sullivan
- 21. Chris Perry
- 2. Kenny Cunningham
- 3. Alan Kimble
- 7. Oyvind Leonhardsen
- 10. Dean Holdsworth
- 11. Marcus Gayle
- 15. Alan Reeves
- 18. Neil Ardley
- 22. Andy Clarke
- 28. Steve Talboys

SUBSTITUTES

- 14. Jon Goodman
  Clarke | 77 mins
- 34. Jason Euell
  Holdsworth | 73 mins
- 35. Andy Pearce

SCORERS

Gayle | 68 mins
Euell | 76 mins

REFEREE

P Durkin | Portland

VISITORS

		RATING
1.	Peter Schmeichel	8
3.	Denis Irwin	8
4.	Steve Bruce	8
20.	Gary Neville	8
23.	Phil Neville	9
5.	Lee Sharpe	8
16.	Roy Keane	9
19.	Nicky Butt	8
7.	Eric Cantona	9
11.	Ryan Giggs	9
17.	Andy Cole	8

SUBSTITUTES

- 13. Tony Coton
- 22. Paul Scholes
- 24. David Beckham | 9
  Bruce | 15 mins

SCORERS

Cole | 41 mins
Perry | 45 mins o.g.
Cantona | 71 (pen) /81 mins

MATCH REPORT

Eric Cantona returned to Selhurst Park for the first time since that fateful night on 25 January, but today it was his footballing ability that made the headlines as he helped United to a 4–2 victory over the London side.

The game began at a lightening pace but it wasn't until the minutes preceding half time that the deadlock was broken with a cracking header from Andy Cole, shortly followed by a David Beckham effort that came back off the bar for Roy Keane to force home.

As United sat back, Wimbledon were allowed to re-enter the game after the break. But with the score at 2–1, the Reds were awarded a penalty and the inevitable followed. Once more, United slackened and allowed their hosts to get within a goal again, before Eric finally killed the game off with his second, a close-range header.

Keane points the way to victory

IN THE PAPERS

"Cantona gave another of those detached, dispassionate performances which have left some wondering if his determination not to become involved in more controversy has reduced his effectiveness. As he scored twice, first with a header and then through another of those penalties he keeps in the ice-box, there would appear to be no case to answer." **GUARDIAN**

"The hordes of lenses directed at him at Selhurst Park were waiting for a few sardines to be scattered. All they could catch, however, were his feet doing what they do best." **DAILY EXPRESS**

"Few experts have given United the praise they deserve for sticking to home-grown players and largely ignoring foreign imports. Lads like Gary Neville, who saved his side a couple of times with outstanding tackles, have the loyalty and comradeship that good teams need to foster to become great teams." **DAILY MAIL**

Cantona coolly
slots home
the penalty

"When Steve
Bruce was
stretchered off
we were left with
an extremely
young team.
But I think
they coped
remarkably well."
ALEX FERGUSON

MANCHESTER UNITED 1
BLACKBURN ROVERS 0

HOME TEAM

		RATING
1.	Peter Schmeichel	8
3.	Denis Irwin	7
6.	Gary Pallister	7
12.	David May	8
23.	Phil Neville	8
5.	Lee Sharpe	8
7.	Eric Cantona	7
16.	Roy Keane	9
11.	Ryan Giggs	7
17.	Andy Cole	8
24.	David Beckham	8

SUBSTITUTES

2. Paul Parker
9. Brian McClair
22. Paul Scholes

SCORER

Sharpe | 14 mins

REFEREE

K Burge | Tonypandy

VISITORS

1. Tim Flowers
2. Chris Coleman
3. Jeff Kenna
4. Tim Sherwood
5. Colin Hendry
8. Kevin Gallagher
9. Alan Shearer
10. Mike Newell
11. Jason Wilcox
17. Billy McKinlay
20. Henning Berg

SUBSTITUTES

12. Nicky Marker
    Coleman | 83 mins
14. Graham Fenton
    Newell | 65 mins
18. Nicky Gudmundsson
    Wilcox | 72 mins

MATCH REPORT

After three difficult away games, it was back to Old Trafford to face current champions Blackburn Rovers — a contest which is always hotly contested.

The Reds started brightly and after only 14 minutes found themselves a goal up courtesy of Lee Sharpe: Eric Cantona and Andy Cole had skilfully interchanged passes to give Cole a clear run on goal. His shot eluded Tim Flowers, only to bounce off the far post where Sharpe hammered home a left-footed volley.

From that point on, United dominated the game and it looked as if they would completely overwhelm Rovers, who certainly played some delightful football but couldn't finish the moves off with the goals that they deserved. The points would have been shared had the visitors' substitute Nicky Gudmundsson not wildly overshot when put clean through in the closing stages of the game.

Fergie is thrilled at victory over the Champions

IN THE PAPERS

"Sharpe was a revelation on the left flank and tortured Rovers all afternoon. Sharpe has feared his days at Old Trafford were numbered as he failed to find his best form. But there was proof enough here that he's back to the player the fans had worshipped when he was a talented teenager."
SUNDAY MIRROR

"Arguably for the first time in his life, England's Mr Clean Alan Shearer was wearing a tarnished crown. And didn't Old Trafford let him know it. His late, stud-flashing lunge was not just a serious health warning for Peter Schmeichel. It was also the worst kind of body language, telling the world all is not well at Rovers." **SUN**

"It did not require vintage stuff from United, but at times there were some heady moments before a delighted Old Trafford crowd. Although United's football was in the main both cohesive and incisive, it was the solitary strike which was to determine the outcome."
MAIL ON SUNDAY

"United were magical at times." **OBSERVER**

David
May
flies

Sharpe sews
up three points

MANCHESTER UNITED 2
MANCHESTER CITY 1

HOME TEAM

		RATING
1.	Peter Schmeichel	7
3.	Denis Irwin	7
4.	Steve Bruce	7
6.	Gary Pallister	7
23.	Phil Neville	7
5.	Lee Sharpe	8
16.	Roy Keane	8
19.	Nicky Butt	9
7.	Eric Cantona	7
11.	Ryan Giggs	7
17.	Andy Cole	7

SUBSTITUTES

22. **Paul Scholes**
12. **David May**
13. **Tony Coton**

SCORERS

Cantona | 38 mins
Sharpe | 77 mins

REFEREE

A Wilkie | Chester-Le-Street

VISITORS

21. Eike Immel
3. Michael Frontzech
4. Steve Lomas
5. Keith Curle
7. Georgiou Kinkladze
9. Niall Quinn
14. Kit Symons
16. Nicky Summerbee
17. Michael Brown
18. Nigel Clough
28. Uwë Rosler

SUBSTITUTES

8. **Gerry Creaney**
   Quinn | 80 mins
32. **Edwards Abajaz**
13. **Martin Margetson**

SCORER

Rosler | 11 mins

MATCH REPORT

This was the game Manchester had been waiting for. City started the brighter: the United defence looked vulnerable and Lomas and Brown were winning the midfield battle. City's dominance was rewarded after 11 minutes when Uwe Rosler lofted the ball over Schmeichel and the Reds inside Old Trafford were stunned into silence by the visitors' dominance. But then in the 38th minute, United were awarded an extremely controversial penalty after Frontzeck was judged to have held down Cantona. The Frenchman sent Immel the wrong way with the spot kick and levelled the scores.

After the interval United dominated, but chance after chance was spurned until Giggs went down the left flank releasing Phil Neville, whose precise pull-back was volleyed in by Lee Sharpe. The winning goal kept United on course for their third consecutive FA Cup final appearance.

IN THE PAPERS

"With a wave of his arm, Alan Wilkie yesterday lifted himself out of Manchester United's chamber of horrors and into their hall of fame. Wilkie, the man whose red card preceeded Eric Cantona's kung-fu kick and eight-month ban, redeemed himself in the eyes of the Old Trafford faithful in the most dramatic manner." **INDEPENDENT**

"United knew they were lucky to get back into the tie after a miserable start, but Cantona converted the spot kick and Lee Sharpe's superbly taken winner settled a match that at times threatened to boil over." **DAILY EXPRESS**

"The United boss praised his side's quality – before the bout with Manchester City – of overturning deficits... But in the Cup derby, it was referee Alan Wilkie who stepped in to provide bewildering assistance." **MANCHESTER EVENING NEWS**

Sharpe gets the high fives

Butt and Pallister climb for the ball

Cantona keeps his feet

MANCHESTER UNITED 2

EVERTON 0

HOME TEAM

		RATING
1.	Peter Schmeichel	8
3.	Denis Irwin	7
6.	Gary Pallister	7
4.	Steve Bruce	7
23.	Phil Neville	9
19.	Nicky Butt	8
16.	Roy Keane	8
5.	Lee Sharpe	7
11.	Ryan Giggs	7
7.	Eric Cantona	7
17.	Andy Cole	7

SUBSTITUTES

20.	Gary Neville	
22.	Paul Scholes	
24.	David Beckham	6
	Sharpe	83 mins	

SCORERS

Keane | 30 mins
Giggs | 81 mins

REFEREE

M Bodenham | East Loe

VISITORS

1.	Neville Southall
3.	Andy Hinchcliffe
4.	David Unsworth
5.	Dave Watson
7.	Graham Stuart
10.	Barry Horne
12.	Daniel Amokachi
14.	John Ebbrell
17.	Andrei Kanchelskis
20.	Tony Grant
24.	John O'Connor

SUBSTITUTES

21.	Craig Short
13.	Jason Kearton
23.	Michael Branch
	Grant	72 mins

MATCH REPORT

The visit of Joe Royle's Everton to Old Trafford saw United looking to make it seven succesive victories and close the gap on leaders Newcastle.

On a night as cold as Kanchelskis' reception, neither side was particularly lively in the opening stages. But if one team seemed more likely to score, it was Everton. However United came more and more into the game as the half progressed, and Sharpe and Phil Neville had both gone close before Roy Keane made the breakthrough on the half hour. After a one-two with Nicky Butt he ran on to fire into the net for his fifth of the season.

As the snow came down in the second half, Schmeichel was forced into a magnificent save by Ebbrell's shot as the visitors went in search of an equaliser. Their hopes were finally killed off in the 82nd minute, when Cole sent over a delightful cross for Ryan Giggs to casually chip over Neville Southall. That made it seven wins from seven games for the Reds.

The famous Giggs ball control in action

IN THE PAPERS

"The craftsmanship and execution of the brace that sank Everton's stubborn resistance belonged to another, more majestic performance. But if United can continue to dig in while still creating moments of breathtaking goalscoring, then there will be few complaints around Old Trafford and they'll be getting increasingly edgy at Newcastle." **MANCHESTER EVENING NEWS**

"The Merseysiders had looked the more threatening before Keane's breakthrough on the half hour, and they were probing, albeit unconvincingly, in search of an equaliser before Giggs spectacularly put the game beyond them. " **DAILY TELEGRAPH**

"The fans who packed Old Trafford saw Roy Keane and Ryan Giggs strike fine goals, and left convinced that the title won in 1993 and 1994 can be recaptured." **DAILY MAIL**

"Just as the pressure mounted and almost destroyed Blackburn last season, United are once again staging an ominous onslaught." **DAILY STAR**

Southall comes out to block Cantona's shot

Bruce wins the aerial battle

BOLTON WANDERERS 0
MANCHESTER UNITED 6

HOME TEAM

1. Keith Branagan
2. Scott Green
3. Jimmy Phillips
17. Simon Coleman
21. Chris Fairclough
7. David Lee
4. Sasa Curcic
11. Alan Thompson
12. Scott Sellars
20. Nathan Blake
14. Fabian De Freitas

SUBSTITUTES

6. Alan Stubbs
10. John McGinlay
   Lee | 74 mins
9. Mixu Paatelainen

REFEREE

D Gallagher | Banbury

VISITORS
RATING

1. Peter Schmeichel — 8
3. Denis Irwin — 8
4. Steve Bruce — 8
6. Gary Pallister — 8
23. Phil Neville — 8
24. David Beckham — 8
16. Roy Keane — 9
19. Nicky Butt — 9
7. Eric Cantona — 7
11. Ryan Giggs — 8
17. Andy Cole — 7

SUBSTITUTES

9. Brian McClair — 7
   Giggs | 57 mins
22. Paul Scholes — 9
   Cantona | 73 mins
20. Gary Neville

SCORERS

Beckham | 5 mins
Bruce | 15 mins
Cole | 70 mins
Scholes | 75/78 mins
Butt | 89 mins

MATCH REPORT

With United second in the table and making serious progress on leaders Newcastle, they were clear favourites to dispose of relegation-haunted Wanderers.

It took the Reds only five minutes to gain the initiative through Beckham, who was first to react to a Giggs shot which came back off the bar. The advantage was doubled after 16 minutes when Steve Bruce headed home from a corner.

Despite United's dominance, the destiny of the three points wasn't conclusively decided until the 70th minute when Andy Cole smashed the ball home off the underside of the bar. With the game won, Fergie took Eric off for a deserved rest. Paul Scholes came on and within five made it 5–0 with two typical striker's goals. To further the humiliation, Nicky Butt scored a sixth to ensure United's biggest victory since their 9–0 thrashing of Ipswich at Old Trafford in March 1995.

Keane takes it on the cheek

IN THE PAPERS

"Bolton Wanderers, their optimism revived after winning at Middlesbrough, were re-acquainted with reality. The chasm between top and bottom was vividly demonstrated and Colin Todd's side are surely destined for an instant return to the Endsleigh League after all." **INDEPENDENT**

"United took just 15 minutes at Burnden Park to prise open the Championship race with a victory that was like nipping next door and taking away your neighbour's furniture – although to be honest there is not a lot worth taking from Bolton." **DAILY EXPRESS**

"This 6–0 win was United's best victory since they beat Ipswich 9–0 in March 1995 and their best away victory in the League since they won 6–0 at Blackpool in the 1959/60 season." **TELEGRAPH**

The beginning: Beckham takes the first...

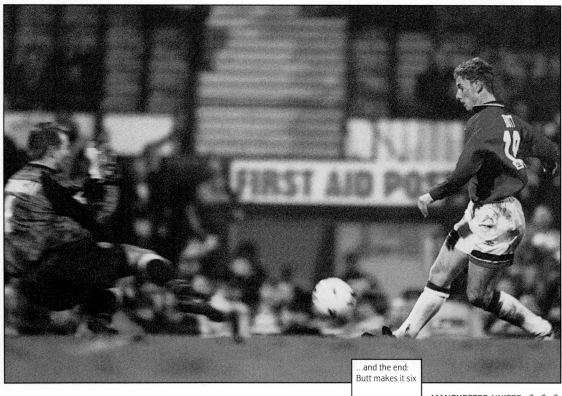

...and the end: Butt makes it six

4 Premiership games | 1 FA Cup game | 15 goals

FEBRUARY STATS

PLAYER RECORDS

home | away

■ PREMIERSHIP ■ UEFA CUP ■ COCA COLA CUP ■ FA CUP

■ FULL APPEARANCE
■ CAME ON AS SUB
■ SCORER
■ SCORED AS SUB

#	Player	FULL APPEARANCES	SUB APPEARANCES	GOALS
1.	Peter Schmeichel	32	0	1
2.	Paul Parker	7	3	1
3.	Denis Irwin	29	0	1
4.	Steve Bruce	30	1	1
5.	Lee Sharpe	21	9	5
6.	Gary Pallister	24	0	1
7.	Eric Cantona	24	0	10
9.	Brian McClair	10	9	3
11.	Ryan Giggs	28	3	8
12.	David May	5	2	0
15.	Graeme Tomlinson	0	0	0
16.	Roy Keane	26	1	5
17.	Andy Cole	30	1	10
18.	Simon Davies	2	6	0
19.	Nicky Butt	30	0	3
20.	Gary Neville	28	0	0
21.	Patrick McGibbon	1	0	0
22.	Paul Scholes	16	8	13
23.	Philip Neville	16	4	0
24.	David Beckham	24	6	5
25.	Kevin Pilkington	4	1	0
26.	Chris Casper	0	0	0
27.	Terry Cooke	2	4	1
29.	Ben Thornley	0	1	0
30.	John O'Kane	1	1	0
31.	William Prunier	2	0	0

PLAYER OF THE MONTH

ROY KEANE

AVERAGE PERFORMANCE RATING: 8.6

FA CARLING PREMIERSHIP

as at 25 February 1996

	Pld	Home					Away					Pts	GD
		W	D	L	F	A	W	D	L	F	A		
■ Newcastle United	27	13	0	0	30	6	6	4	4	22	19	61	+27
■ Manchester United	28	10	4	0	27	9	7	2	5	28	20	57	+26
■ Liverpool	27	7	3	2	19	9	6	4	4	18	12	52	+29
■ Aston Villa	26	7	3	2	19	9	6	4	4	18	12	46	+16
■ Tottenham Hotspur	27	7	3	4	18	13	5	6	2	16	12	45	+9
▲ Arsenal	27	6	5	2	21	13	6	3	5	14	12	44	+10
▲ Everton	28	8	3	3	26	12	4	4	6	16	18	43	+12
▲ Chelsea	28	6	5	3	21	14	4	5	5	13	16	42	+4
■ Blackburn Rovers	27	11	1	2	37	12	1	4	8	5	19	41	+11
▼ Nottingham Forest	27	8	4	1	21	10	2	6	6	14	28	40	+3
▲ West Ham United	28	6	3	5	16	17	5	2	7	15	20	38	-6
▼ Leeds United	25	7	2	3	16	10	3	3	7	15	27	35	-6
▼ Middlesbrough	28	7	2	5	22	18	2	5	7	6	19	34	-9
■ Sheffield Wednesday	27	5	4	5	24	23	2	4	7	12	20	29	-7
■ Southampton	26	4	6	4	16	16	1	4	7	11	23	25	-12
■ Wimbledon	27	3	5	6	22	27	3	2	8	17	28	25	-16
■ Coventry City	27	4	5	5	17	19	1	7	5	16	30	25	-16
▼ Manchester City	25	5	5	4	13	12	1	2	10	6	27	25	-20
■ Queens Park Rangers	27	3	3	7	13	21	3	0	11	9	20	21	-19
■ Bolton Wanderers	28	3	3	8	9	24	1	1	12	19	34	16	-30

1 | 2 | 3 | 4 | 5 | 6 | 7 | 8 | 9 | 10 | 11 | 12 | 13 | 14 | 15 | 16 | 17 | 18 | 19 | 20 | 21 | 22 | 23 | 24 | 25 | 26 | 27 | 28 | 29 | 30 | 31

MARCH

THE MONTH IN REVIEW

March 1996 will be remembered the world over for the Dunblane massacre. Sixteen Scottish schoolchildren and their teacher were shot dead by gunman Thomas Hamilton, and suddenly soccer seemed rather trivial. A minute's silence was kept country-wide to honour the memory of the dead, and the government had a good hard look at its gun laws.

British beef took a bashing as the Mad Cow disease scare reached fever pitch and the rest of Europe gave our exports a wide berth. For a few days, McDonald's stopped serving Big Macs until they managed to get some Dutch beef in their stockrooms.

Aston Villa took no beef from Leeds in the Coca-Cola Cup final, thrashing them 3–0 at Wembley. Frank Bruno lasted just three rounds against Iron Mike Tyson, and announced afterwards that he was to retire. Thousands payed nearly 10 quid each to Sky under the controversial new pay-per-view scheme, then waited up until the middle of the night for less than 10 minutes of action. Anxious football fans wondered when they would have to start paying per match to watch soccer on the box.

United started the month off four points behind leaders Newcastle, but had the chance to close the gap with what was billed as the match of the season at St James' Park. Nobody would have minded paying Sky Sports for this one. Newcastle started the match like they were 1–0 down with five minutes to go, pouring into the United goalmouth like a pack of Hitchcockian magpies. In the first half, only profligate finishing by the usually deadly Ferdinand and fine goalkeeping by Schmeichel kept United in the game. But a Cantona volley in the 51st minute completely changed the shape of the match and moved Fergie's Fledglings to within a point of the leaders. The points were vital, but the crushing blow to Newcastle's morale was just as important. It was the first time this season they hadn't won at fortress St James'.

No peace for the Red Devils: next up were the quarter finals of the FA Cup. Southampton came to Old Trafford looking for a famous victory, but they didn't account for Eric Cantona, who scored the first early in the second half and laid the second on a plate for Lee Sharpe. Not only did the Saints put up a fight, they actually created more chances than United. But Schmeichel looked 10 feet wide in the United goal.

A trip to Loftus Road five days later didn't look too daunting a proposition, with former United star Ray Wilkins' men seemingly down and out of the

Cole equalises in the semi final: he's in there somewhere!

**MARCH
NUMBER ONES**

SINGLE
How Deep is
Your Love?
Take That

ALBUM
What's the
Story
(Morning
Glory)?
Oasis

FILM
Toy Story

Premiership. Denis Irwin headed into the net on the half hour – but it was the wrong net and QPR looked to have stolen the points. Then up popped – guess who? – Eric Cantona in injury time to rob QPR of two points and put United ahead of Newcastle on goal difference. But in Sky's Monday game, the Geordies countered with a 3–0 drubbing of West Ham and leapfrogged back into their accustomed position.

A crowd of 50,020 fans (United's biggest for 10 years) witnessed another piece of magic from *Le Roi* in the midweek clash with Bruce Rioch's hot-and-cold Arsenal side. United were at their mesmerising best, but Andy Cole had put his boots on the wrong feet and missed chance after chance. Arsenal were defending like heroes, but one clearance fell to the wrong man on 66 minutes. Eric chested down the ball, took a couple of giant strides and volleyed it past Seaman to give United the points – and the lead in the title race on goal difference.

Newcastle's defeat at Arsenal the following Saturday gave Fergie's boys the chance to put a bit of daylight between the two sides when Tottenham came to Old Trafford. United were nervous and didn't play at all well. In the end we had to thank the referee for awarding a goal-kick instead of a Tottenham corner

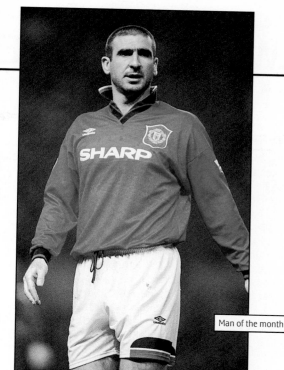

Man of the month

on 51 minutes. From the subsequent move, Cantona scored a sublime winning goal. Having missed out on the Championship run-in last year, he looked like he wanted to bring the title back to Manchester single-handedly.

The last day of the month was FA Cup semi-final day. Wembley looked a long

> # "Eric has scored a lot of important goals. His record is fantastic."
> ALEX FERGUSON

way away when Gullit put Chelsea ahead. But this stoked up the United fire and an equaliser looked inevitable. Cole obliged, poking in Cantona's looping header. Within two minutes we had the winner: David Beckham picked up an errant Burley backpass and coolly slotted it past the onrushing Hitchcock. Liverpool piled three past Villa in the other tie to set up a mouthwatering final. Suddenly, another Double looked on the cards.

Dugout delirium as Eric saves United at Loftus Road

NEWCASTLE UNITED 0
MANCHESTER UNITED 1

HOME TEAM

1. Pavel Srnicek
2. Warren Barton
3. John Beresford
6. Steve Howey
22. David Batty
27. Philippe Albert
7. Robert Lee
14. David Ginola
8. Peter Beardsley
11. Faustino Asprilla
9. Les Ferdinand

SUBSTITUTES

10. Lee Clarke
18. Keith Gillespie
15. Steve Watson

REFEREE

D Elleray | Harrow

VISITORS

		RATING
1.	Peter Schmeichel	10
3.	Denis Irwin	7
20.	Gary Neville	7
4.	Steve Bruce	8
23.	Phil Neville	8
19.	Nicky Butt	8
7.	Eric Cantona	7
16.	Roy Keane	9
11.	Ryan Giggs	8
17.	Andy Cole	7
5.	Lee Sharpe	7

SUBSTITUTES

12. David May
24. David Beckham
22. Paul Scholes

SCORER

Cantona | 51 mins

MATCH REPORT

United travelled to the North East hoping to do what no other team had done so far this season: win at St James's Park. The game was billed as a title decider. In truth, it wasn't quite that, but it would give the winners initiative in the final stages of the Premiership race.

The opening exchanges saw United camped in their own half – and often their own penalty area – as they struggled to deal with the ingenuity of Asprilla (making his home debut) and the power of Les Ferdinand. Fortunately for the Reds, they survived the early onslaught and the closest the home side came to a goal was when Philippe Albert crashed a 25-yard free kick against the bar.

After the break, United gradually came back into the game and, in the 51st minute, Cole twisted on the edge of the box and released Phil Neville, whose cross was met by Cantona and volleyed home at the far post. Though the stunned Geordies poured forward in the latter stages, they could not beat "Peter the Great" in the United goal. A truly great victory had been won.

Beardsley races to stop Cantona

IN THE PAPERS

"Billed the game of the season, it lived up to it. This was heartstopping football on a stage fit for kings. The one who wore the crown last night was Eric Cantona."
DAILY EXPRESS

"In the event, the chances – most of which fell to Les Ferdinand – were wasted. Manchester United were not so profligate: Cantona finished with deadly accuracy after 51 minutes. The goal changed the match irrevocably, raising questions about Newcastle's self-belief."
INDEPENDENT

"They were singing in Geordieland last night, but the words were a death-knell to the Toon Army. One of their beloved anthems was suddenly taken over by Manchester United fans, who sang 'Frog on the Tyne's all mine all mine' in celebration of Eric Cantona."
DAILY MIRROR

"What had appeared to be a one-horse race now involves three thoroughbreds travelling at different speeds towards the wire." **TELEGRAPH**

Cole's face tells the story

Sharpe fights for possession

MANCHESTER UNITED 2
SOUTHAMPTON 0

HOME TEAM

		RATING
1.	Peter Schmeichel	9
3.	Dennis Irwin	7
4.	Steve Bruce	8
20.	Gary Neville	7
23.	Philip Neville	8
5.	Lee Sharpe	7
16.	Roy Keane	7
19.	Nicky Butt	7
11.	Ryan Giggs	7
7.	Eric Cantona	9
17.	Andy Cole	7

SUBSTITUTES

12.	David May
22.	Paul Scholes
24.	David Beckham

SCORERS

Cantona | 49 mins
Sharpe | 90 mins

REFEREE

S Dunn | Bristol

VISITORS

13.	Dave Beasant
2.	Jason Dodd
5.	Richard Hall
6.	Ken Monkou
14.	Simon Charlton
27.	Mathew Oakley
4.	Jim Magilton
12.	Tommy Widdrington
19.	Mark Walters
7.	Mathew Le Tissier
9.	Neil Shipperley

SUBSTITUTES

1.	Bruce Grobbelaar
16.	David Hughes
26.	Mathew Robinson

Mark Walters | 89

MATCH REPORT

The largest crowd in four years made light of the miserable weather as they witnessed United become the first semi finalists of this year's FA Cup. However, it was anything but the stroll into the next round that had been predicted.

Strangely ineffective against a team in perilous danger of relegation, United found it difficult to dominate the proceedings, thanks largely to an inspired performance by the Saints, who attacked with flair and determination. Indeed, they were unlucky not to be rewarded with the lead when Shipperley was dubiously judged to have pushed Lee Sharpe in the aerial tussle that led to a disallowed Southampton goal.

But in the second half Cantona took control of things and, with a 49th minute goal created out of a lovely break down the left by Giggsy, the Frenchman boosted his team's confidence. United finished on a high, with Eric this time acting as provider hitting a perfectly placed pass across the face of the goal for Lee Sharpe to score one of the easiest goals he will ever be asked to finish.

Butt makes it look easy

IN THE PAPERS

"Eric Cantona clearly likes Mondays. Last week the Frenchman scored the winner at Newcastle to put United one point behind the Premiership leaders. Last night he scored the first goal in the 49th minute and laid on the second for Lee Sharpe in stoppage time." **TELEGRAPH**

"The Frenchman with a fuse as notoriously short as his shaven hair would not be everyone's obvious choice for the calm head in a storm. But on a night when United were forced to navigate through choppy waters to reach the FA Cup semi finals, King Eric proved his side's leader of men." **DAILY EXPRESS**

"Alex Ferguson proudly proclaimed new-look Old Trafford would be a stadium fit for kings. Last night, more than 45,000 loyal subjects once again paid homage to the man they anointed as King Eric long ago." **SUN**

Cole looks for space

Irwin set to strike

QUEENS PARK RANGERS 1
MANCHESTER UNITED 1

HOME TEAM

- 25. **Juergen Sommer**
- 2. **David Bardsley**
- 3. **Rufus Brevett**
- 5. **Alan McDonald**
- 21. **Steve Yates**
- 4. **Simon Barker**
- 8. **Ian Holloway**
- 19. **Nigel Quashie**
- 9. **Daniel Dichio**
- 10. **Kevin Gallen**
- 11. **Trevor Sinclair**

SUBSTITUTES

- 7. **Andrew Impey**
  Quashie | 46 mins
- 14. **Karl Ready**
  Gallen | 85 mins
- 26. **Mark Hately**
  Dichio | 81 mins

SCORER

Irwin o.g. | 64 mins

REFEREE

R Hart | Darlington

VISITORS

		RATING
1.	**Peter Schmeichel**	7
3.	**Denis Irwin**	6
4.	**Steve Bruce**	7
12.	**David May**	7
20.	**Gary Neville**	7
9.	**Brian McClair**	5
16.	**Roy Keane**	7
11.	**Ryan Giggs**	7
17.	**Andy Cole**	7
7.	**Eric Cantona**	7
24.	**David Beckham**	6

SUBSTITUTES

5.	**Lee Sharpe**	7
	David Beckham	74 mins
19.	**Nicky Butt**	7
	May	74 mins
22.	**Paul Scholes**	7
	McClair	59 mins

SCORER

Cantona | 90 mins

MATCH REPORT

Rangers were never going to be a pushover. You can rely on Ray Wilkins to instil an element of common sense in his team, and the threat of relegation will always prompt a side to play with passion. Rangers duly exhibited these qualities and, with a healthy dose of luck, managed to go ahead through a Denis Irwin own goal.

An embarrassing loss to a team 18 positions below them looked on the cards for United and, come the 90th minute, the Rangers fans were delirious in their excitement at the prospect of a win. But in added time, their joy turned to tears as Eric once again saved his side's blushes when he latched on to a cross by Giggs and headed in his 10th goal of the season. It was a strike which put United at the top of the table, and could have sealed the relegation fate of QPR.

QPR get shirty

IN THE PAPERS

"So the game finished even. But at the start, United wove bewildering patterns with Cantona masterminding much of it from a static position, rather like a circus ringmaster signalling each entertainer to perform." **OBSERVER**

"The brave and adventurous approach of Ray Wilkins was so nearly granted vindication. His team, gravely threatened with relegation, were only seconds from what would have been an invigorating first home victory of the year, when Eric Cantona's equaliser put Manchester United back on top of the Premiership." **SUNDAY TELEGRAPH**

"Danny Dichio's shot – headed in by Denis Irwin – seemed to have earned them three crucial points in their survival fight... Eric Cantona was the man for the moment again, grabbing that injury-time equaliser." **DAILY STAR**

Giggs fires in a shot

Schmeichel jumps proud in the crowd

MANCHESTER UNITED 1

ARSENAL 0

HOME TEAM

		RATING
1.	Peter Schmeichel	9
12.	David May	7
4.	Steve Bruce	7
20.	Gary Neville	7
23.	Phil Neville	7
5.	Lee Sharpe	7
16.	Roy Keane	8
19.	Nicky Butt	8
7.	Eric Cantona	9
11.	Ryan Giggs	7
17.	Andy Cole	7

SUBSTITUTES

9.	Brian McClair	
22.	Paul Scholes	7
	Cole	59 mins	
24.	David Beckham	

SCORERS

Cantona | 66 mins

REFEREE

G Willard | Worthing

VISITORS

1.	David Seaman
2.	Lee Dixon
3.	Nigel Winterburn
7.	David Platt
8.	Ian Wright
9.	Paul Merson
10.	Dennis Bergkamp
12.	Andy Linighan
14.	Martin Keown
16.	John Hartson
25.	Scott Marshall

SUBSTITUTES

11.	Glenn Helder	
	Merson	69 mins	
17.	David Hillier	
	Bergkamp	45 mins	
31.	Matthew Rose	

MATCH REPORT

Arsenal came to Old Trafford on the back of a six-game unbeaten run and promised to provide a difficult hurdle for United to overcome in their quest for the Championship.

United took command of the game early on. In the 10th minute, a Roy Keane shot came back off the post only for the luckless Andy Cole to be denied by the legs of David Seaman. The onslaught continued for the duration of the first half with shots and headers raining in on the Arsenal goal, but at half time the game was still goalless.

Thirteen minutes into the second period, Fergie pulled off Andy Cole to give Paul Scholes the chance to break the deadlock. In the event, it was Old Trafford's favourite Frenchman who controlled an Andy Linighan clearance magnificently and volleyed home from 25 yards out. One goal was always going to be enough and the vast majority of the 50,028 crowd went home happy – very happy indeed.

IN THE PAPERS

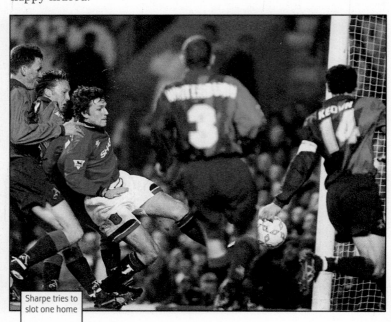

Sharpe tries to slot one home

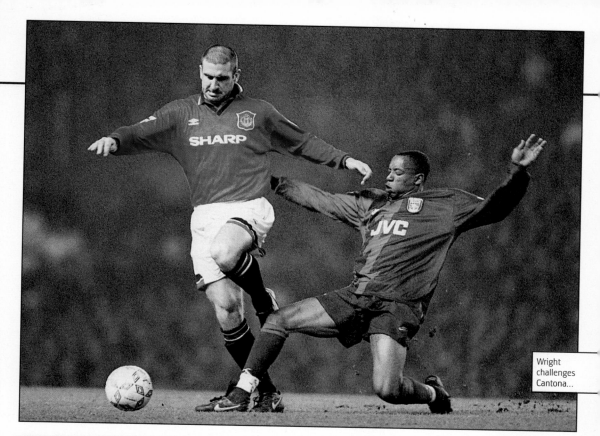

Wright
challenges
Cantona...

Cantona
prevails

MANCHESTER UNITED 1
TOTTENHAM HOTSPUR 0

HOME TEAM

		RATING
1.	Peter Schmeichel	8
4.	Steve Bruce	6
12.	David May	9
20.	Gary Neville	7
23.	Phil Neville	7
5.	Lee Sharpe	7
16.	Roy Keane	7
19.	Nicky Butt	7
7.	Eric Cantona	8
11.	Ryan Giggs	7
17.	Andy Cole	8

SUBSTITUTES

9.	Brian McClair	8
	Cole	72 mins	
22.	Paul Scholes	
24.	David Beckham	8
	Neville, P	63 mins	

SCORER

Cantona | 51 mins

REFEREE

G Ashby | Worcester

VISITORS

1.	Ian Walker
2.	Dean Austin
4.	David Howells
6.	Gary Mabbutt
7.	Ruel Fox
10.	Teddy Sheringham
11.	Chris Armstrong
12.	Jason Dozzell
15.	Clive Wilson
23.	Sol Campbell
27.	Andy Sinton

SUBSTITUTES

3.	Justin Edinburgh
13.	Erik Thorstvedt
14.	Stuart Nethercott
	Mabbutt	51 mins

MATCH REPORT

On their arrival at Old Trafford, Spurs were the last team to beat United in any competition – 4–1 in the League on New Year's Day – and their confidence was evident during the game's early stages.

Schmeichel was twice called upon to make good saves from Sheringham (a fierce shot and a far-post header) as the visitors looked to find an opening. Perhaps their best chance fell to Chris Armstrong after a defensive mix-up involving Bruce and Schmeichel; the striker was given a clear run at goal but could only shoot weakly into the body of the big Dane.

As United came more into the game, again it was Cole who suffered cruel luck in front of goal, but in the 50th minute the breakthrough came. Cantona picked the ball up midway inside the Spurs half, ran at the defence and unleashed a low drive from the edge of the area which beat Ian Walker and nestled in the bottom corner. The man had done it again.

Tottenham still pushed forward and Sheringham was always a threat, but once more a single Cantona goal was enough to win it for the Reds.

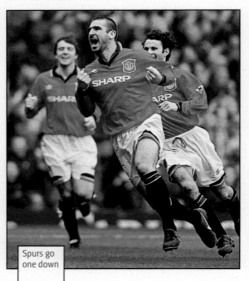

Spurs go one down

IN THE PAPERS

"Francis was furious when Eric Cantona scored his 51st minute Premiership match winner at Old Trafford. It came from a move which began when the referee awarded United a goal kick instead of a corner to Spurs." **DAILY MAIL**

"Compared with the speed and flair against Arsenal on Wednesday, this was a lean-footed Cantona with his fifth goal in five games – goals that have earned United 10 points from a possible 12 – who rescued them with his strike five minutes into the second half." **GUARDIAN**

"Day by day, piece by piece, the picture is becoming clearer. When the Championship jigsaw is complete, it will surely reveal a central image. Eric Cantona of course, for this brilliant Frenchman seems determined to bring the trophy back to Old Trafford on his own." **TIMES**

Eric carries his success lightly

CHELSEA 1
MANCHESTER UNITED 2

HOME TEAM

13. Kevin Hitchcock
2. Steve Clarke
12. Craig Burley
15. Andy Myers
25. Terry Phelan
20. David Lee
7. John Spencer
8. Mark Hughes
26. Michael Duberry
4. Ruud Gullit
11. Dennis Wise

SUBSTITUTES

5. **Erland Johnsen**
   Clarke | 38 mins
10. **Gavin Peacock**
    Phelan | 64 mins
14. **Paul Furlong**
    Lee | 86 mins

SCORER

Gullit | 35 mins

REFEREE

S Lodge | Barnsley

VISITORS   RATING

1. Peter Schmeichel
23. Phil Neville
20. Gary Neville
12. David May
5. Lee Sharpe
16. Roy Keane
19. Nicky Butt
11. Ryan Giggs
7. Eric Cantona
17. Andy Cole
24. David Beckham

SUBSTITUTES

2. Paul Parker
9. Brian McClair
22. Paul Scholes

SCORERS

Cole | 55 mins
Beckham | 59 mins

MATCH REPORT

A near-capacity crowd descended on Villa Park on a dreary Birmingham day for this eagerly anticipated semi final. Why wasn't the ground full to capacity? Well, at £30 and £38 for the majority of tickets, could *you* afford to attend this game? An adult and two kids would have to pay an extortionate £114 for the only tickets left on sale – hardly cheap, even for the quality football that followed.

Gullit has been a revelation for Chelsea this season. From the first whistle, he made his presence felt on a below-par pitch. His vision and passing left the crowd gasping at times and, for the first half at least, even Eric Cantona was overshadowed by his brilliance. After 35 minutes, ex-United legend Mark Hughes crossed for the flying Dutchman to put Glen Hoddle's side a goal up to the delight of the 20,000 fans decked out in blue and white.

Chelsea may have gone into the break with a deserved lead, but in the second half things were very different. Enter the real United: solid, enterprising and full of spirit. It was the turn of the Frenchman to take centre stage and he obliged by feeding a cross to Cole who knocked the ball in. Just three minutes later, with the United fans still dancing on their seats, David Beckham burst through to score. Chelsea had no answer. Cantona was now the man controlling the game and United kept their lead to reach our third consecutive FA Cup final. You did us proud, boys. Now bring on the scousers.

United's first goal goes to Cole

IN THE PAPERS

"Having dominated large areas of the first half on a ploughman's lunch of a pitch, Chelsea looked well worth the lead the head of Gullit had given them in the 34th minute. They were then undone by goals from Cole and Beckham in the space of six minutes early in the second half, the winner coming after a basic error by Burley." **GUARDIAN**

"The jubilant Manchester United boss cuddled his hero Eric Cantona then wrapped his arms round Ruud Gullit. They say no one remembers semi-final losers, but no one will forget the Dutchman's FA Cup campaign." **DAILY MIRROR**

"When United were standing behind the guillotine at Villa Park yesterday Eric Cantona, as straightbacked as General De Gaulle, strode forward to win them a pardon, then led them to ultimate victory." **DAILY EXPRESS**

Keane and Hughes go back to back

Gary Neville, high flyer

4 Premiership games | 2 FA Cup games | 8 goals

MARCH STATS

PLAYER RECORDS

home | away

■ PREMIERSHIP ■ UEFA CUP ■ COCA COLA CUP ■ FA CUP

■ ■ FULL APPEARANCE / CAME ON AS SUB

■ ■ SCORER / SCORED AS SUB

		Full Appearances	Sub Appearances	Goals
1.	Peter Schmeichel	38	0	1
2.	Paul Parker	7	3	1
3.	Denis Irwin	32	0	1
4.	Steve Bruce	35	1	1
5.	Lee Sharpe	26	10	6
6.	Gary Pallister	24	0	1
7.	Eric Cantona	30	0	15
9.	Brian McClair	11	10	3
11.	Ryan Giggs	34	3	8
12.	David May	9	2	0
15.	Graeme Tomlinson	0	0	0
16.	Roy Keane	32	1	5
17.	Andy Cole	36	1	11
18.	Simon Davies	2	6	0
19.	Nicky Butt	35	1	3
20.	Gary Neville	34	0	0
21.	Patrick McGibbon	1	0	0
22.	Paul Scholes	16	11	13
23.	Philip Neville	21	4	0
24.	David Beckham	25	9	6
25.	Kevin Pilkington	4	1	0
26.	Chris Casper	0	0	0
27.	Terry Cooke	2	4	1
29.	Ben Thornley	0	1	0
30.	John O'Kane	1	1	0
31.	William Prunier	2	0	0

PLAYER OF THE MONTH

PETER SCHMEICHEL

AVERAGE PERFORMANCE RATING: 8.5

FA CARLING PREMIERSHIP

as at 24 March 1996

	Pld	Home					Away					Pts	GD
		W	D	L	F	A	W	D	L	F	A		
▲ Manchester United	32	12	4	0	29	9	8	3	5	30	21	67	+29
▼ Newcastle United	30	14	0	1	33	7	6	4	5	22	21	64	+27
■ Liverpool	31	11	4	1	39	10	6	4	5	21	17	59	+33
■ Aston Villa	32	10	4	2	28	13	6	4	6	18	17	56	+16
▲ Arsenal	32	8	5	2	26	14	7	4	6	18	14	54	+16
▼ Tottenham Hotspur	32	9	3	5	24	17	6	6	3	19	15	54	+11
▼ Everton	33	8	4	4	30	18	6	5	6	23	20	51	+15
▲ Blackburn Rovers	32	12	1	3	38	15	2	5	9	9	24	48	+8
▲ Nottingham Forest	31	9	4	1	22	10	3	7	7	18	31	47	-1
▼ Chelsea	32	6	7	3	23	16	5	5	6	14	19	45	-2
■ West Ham United	32	8	3	5	22	19	5	3	8	17	25	45	-5
■ Leeds United	30	7	3	5	18	14	3	6	8	17	29	39	-8
■ Middlesbrough	33	7	3	6	23	21	3	6	8	7	21	39	-12
▲ Sheffield Wednesday	32	6	4	6	27	26	3	4	9	16	25	35	-8
▲ Wimbledon	32	4	6	7	24	31	4	3	8	23	32	33	-16
▲ Manchester City	33	6	6	4	16	14	1	4	12	11	36	31	-23
▲ Southampton	31	5	6	5	17	17	1	4	10	12	29	28	-17
▲ Queens Park Rangers	33	4	5	8	19	25	3	1	12	12	25	27	-19
▼ Coventry City	32	4	6	6	19	23	1	6	9	19	36	27	-21
■ Bolton Wanderers	33	4	4	9	14	29	3	1	12	22	34	26	-27

APRIL

APRIL

THE MONTH AHEAD

If you hadn't seen the Premiership table since December, you'd have thought someone was playing an April fool if you saw it again on 1 April. United were sitting pretty right at the top and pundits all over the country were munching away at large helpings of humble pie, having seen Newcastle's lead slowly whittled away by Fergie's flyers. And when Liverpool snatched another three points from the Geordies' grasp in a 4–3 "match of the decade" thriller at Anfield, the Reds from Manchester moved over into the title-race driving seat.

If United kept up this streak of winning form, the title was surely in the bag. Nevertheless, they say that the form book goes out of the window in a local derby, and when United play City at Maine Road and the Blues are fighting for their Premiership lives, it might as well never have existed. So when the two teams met on 6 April it was no surprise that City's performance made a mockery of their League position. It was a typical cut-and-thrust derby, but United eventually triumphed despite being overrun at times by their near neighbours. Goals from Cole, Cantona and a Giggs special gave the red half of Manchester three reasons to party the night away. "Five chances, three goals," moaned City keeper Eike Immel after the match. "That's the important thing with this United team. They are so good. They are a better team than Newcastle."

Newcastle themselves had struggled to beat relegation-threatened QPR at home, but they'd got the three points. And while all this was going on, the football-loving public just scoffed Easter eggs and wondered what was going to happen next.

And so it went on. Against Coventry on Easter Monday, United spluttered to a 1–0 victory, although the result was overshadowed by a horrific injury to Coventry's David Busst. The following night there was a shock of a different kind. With Newcastle cruising to a 1–0 win over champions Blackburn, born-and-bred Geordie Graham Fenton (with his entire Newcastle-supporting family in the crowd) came on as sub and scored twice. "I won't be going home for a while," said the young Blackburn forward, who might just have etched United's name on the Premiership trophy. In fact the title race was getting so interesting that hardly anyone noticed Prince Andrew and Fergie were to divorce... and even fewer cared.

APRIL
NUMBER ONES

SINGLE
Firestarter
The Prodigy

ALBUM
Greatest Hits
Take That

FILM
Toy Story

Giggs takes his chances against City

A sad departure from Old Trafford by David Busst

For United it was down to struggling Southampton next... but what a grey day it turned out to be. Sporting the grey strip in which they'd never won a competitive match, United were 3–0 down by half-time. "We can't see each other," the players told Fergie. "Who said that?" replied the manager, before ordering the team to change into blue and white. Giggs got one back, but the title race was wide open again. Newcastle saw off Villa the next day and in midweek United just scraped past arch-rivals Leeds, who played valiantly. But how would they play against Newcastle? That was the question on everyone's lips...

If Newcastle and United won all their final games they'd be level on points and goal difference would be the key. But as the FA prepared for the possibility of a play-off, United went out of their way to make that scenario an unlikely one by slamming five past poor Mark Crossley

in their last home match of the season against Forest. The players did a lap of honour at Old Trafford and the bookies made Man United 7-1 on favourites for the title. But was there to be yet another twist in the tail of the Championship?

"The players prefer the blue and so do I."

ALEX FERGUSON

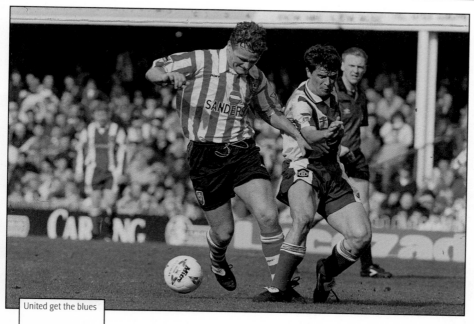
United get the blues

MANCHESTER CITY 2
MANCHESTER UNITED 3

HOME TEAM

RATING

21.	Eike Immel	
3.	Michael Frontzeck	
5.	Keith Curle	
7.	Georgiou Kinkladze	
9.	Niall Quinn	
12.	Ian Brightwell	
14.	Kit Symons	
17.	Michael Brown	
16.	Nicky Summerbee	
18.	Nigel Clough	
32.	Mikhail Kavelashvili	

SUBSTITUTES

28. Uwe Rosler
Kavelashvili | 68 mins

13. Martyn Margetson

19. Martin Phillips
Frontzeck | 45 mins

SCORERS

Kavelashvili | 40 mins
Rosler | 71 mins

REFEREE

M Reed | Birmingham

VISITORS

1.	Peter Schmeichel	8
3.	Denis Irwin	8
4.	Steve Bruce	7
20.	Gary Neville	7
23.	Phil Neville	7
16.	Roy Keane	8
19.	Nicky Butt	9
7.	Eric Cantona	8
11.	Ryan Giggs	8
17.	Andy Cole	8
24.	David Beckham	7

SUBSTITUTES

5. Lee Sharpe 7
Cole | 75 mins

12. David May 8
Bruce | 75 mins

22. Paul Scholes

SCORERS

Cantona | 7 mins
Cole | 41 mins
Giggs | 77 mins

MATCH REPORT

United eroded the meaning of the cliché that anything can happen in derby games with yet another win at Maine Road. City haven't beaten the Reds once since 1989 and, prior to today's game, hadn't scored a single League goal against us in over 450 minutes of football.

United set about confirming their claim to be the "Pride of Manchester" when Eric knocked in his 16th goal of the season, in the form of a penalty after six minutes.

To their credit, City began to battle and equalised five minutes before the interval through new Georgian striker Kavelashvili. But United were back in the lead just 60 seconds later, when Andy Cole raced through on to a Cantona pass and knocked the ball past Immel.

City, in desperate need of points to avoid the drop, came out a different side in the second half and deserved it when they levelled the scores through Rosler. However, the game had one final, brilliant twist. Ryan Giggs, who had played an uncharacteristically subdued role, stole through the City defence and lashed the ball into the top corner of the net. The 2,000 Reds in the United end joined Giggs in his nonchalant jig of joy. The three points earned opened up a six-point gap at the top of the table.

IN THE PAPERS

"The haunting impression from a derby with more than ever riding on it was not the demonstration of Manchester United's worthiness as probable champions, but whether Manchester City have it in them to be saved from the Endsleigh abyss." **DAILY MAIL**

"City have not beaten United for nearly seven years. They might have ended that record on Saturday, as they battered the FA Carling Premiership leaders for long periods in the second half, with Peter Schmeichel much the busier keeper." **TIMES**

"Manchester United may have bagged the points but if there can ever truly be glory in defeat, it went to Manchester City ." **MANCHESTER EVENING NEWS**

Beckham blocked by Immel

He shoots...

...he scores!

MANCHESTER UNITED 1
COVENTRY CITY 0

HOME TEAM

		RATING
1.	Peter Schmeichel	8
3.	Denis Irwin	7
20.	Gary Neville	7
12.	David May	8
5.	Lee Sharpe	7
19.	Nicky Butt	8
7.	Eric Cantona	9
9.	Brian McClair	7
11.	Ryan Giggs	8
17.	Andy Cole	7
24.	David Beckham	7

SUBSTITUTES

2.	Paul Parker
4.	Steve Bruce
22.	Paul Scholes

SCORER

Cantona | 47 mins

REFEREE

D Gallagher | Banbury

VISITORS

1.	Steve Ogrizovic
12.	David Busst
4.	Paul Williams
7.	Paul Telfer
17.	Ally Pickering
30.	Liam Daish
6.	Kevin Richardson
11.	John Salako
9.	Peter Ndlovu
10.	Dion Dublin
14.	Noel Whelan

SUBSTITUTES

22.	Willie Boland
	Busst	4 mins
13.	John Filan
16.	Eion Jess
	Telfer	70 mins

MATCH REPORT

Eric Cantona continued his one-man crusade to win the Premiership for United with another crucial goal, his seventh in eight matches.

United made hard work of beating a willing Coventry side determined to avoid the drop. Despite having the territorial advantage, the Reds' attacks usually ended with the ball being cleared by the Coventry defence. Giggs, Beckham and Cole (twice) should all have scored, but Ogrizovic wasn't forced to make any world-class saves.

In the 47th minute, the biggest League crowd in Britain for nine years heaved a huge sigh of relief when Eric (who else?) broke the deadlock. The goal was no classic, but it didn't matter one bit as United fans round the ground waved their French *tricolores* as part of the fan-inspired flag day. Three significant points were what was needed to pressure Newcastle even further, on a day overshadowed by the horrific injury sustained by Coventry defender David Busst in the second minute of the match.

IN THE PAPERS

"Far from marching to victory, Manchester United were often too inclined to stroll around in the manner of men assuming that the points were theirs for the taking." **GUARDIAN**

"In the end, one goal was all they needed, and Eric Cantona scored it at Old Trafford yesterday to make composed amends for the kind of afternoon Manchester United have endured in the Championship past." **DAILY MAIL**

"Cantona's gilt-edged performance lifted the whole of Old Trafford after the horror of the opening seconds, when Coventry's Dave Busst suffered a compound fracture of the right leg." **DAILY MIRROR**

"You knew from the blaze of the waving *tricolores* among a baying, swaying crowd just who had scored the critical winning goal at Old Trafford." **DAILY EXPRESS**

Cole stretches to disposses

Cantona floats by the Coventry defence

SOUTHAMPTON 3
MANCHESTER UNITED 1

HOME TEAM

13. Dave Beasant
2. Jason Dodd
14. Simon Charlton
4. Jim Magilton
6. Ken Monkou
3. Francis Benali
7. Matthew Le Tissier
22. Barry Venison
9. Neil Shipperley
11. Neil Heaney
15. Alan Neilson

SUBSTITUTES

21. Frank Bennett
12. Tom Widdrington
19. Mark Walters

SCORERS

Shipperley | 23 mins
Monkou | 35 mins
Le Tissier | 43 mins

REFEREE

G Poll | Tring

VISITORS

		RATING
1.	Peter Schmeichel	6
3.	Denis Irwin	7
20.	Gary Neville	6
4.	Steve Bruce	6
5.	Lee Sharpe	5
16.	Roy Keane	6
19.	Nicky Butt	5
11.	Ryan Giggs	5
7.	Eric Cantona	6
17.	Andy Cole	6
24.	David Beckham	5

SUBSTITUTES

12.	David May	7
	Sharpe	55 mins	
13.	Tony Coton	
22.	Paul Scholes	6
	Butt	45 mins	

SCORER

Giggs | 69 mins

MATCH REPORT

A dreadful result. Southampton, like Coventry six days before, were desperate to avoid relegation. They came out looking like a side of world-beaters and inflicted United's first defeat in 19 games.

Alarmingly, United had no response to this super-charged Southampton side. In the unlucky grey kit, United were mere bystanders as Monkou put the Saints up after 11 minutes. Shipperley scored at 12 minutes later and Le Tissier made it 3–0 a couple of minutes before half-time. 3–0 down at half-time: it was just like Villa Park on the opening day of the season, when the grey kit made its debut.

Time for change, literally; as United emerged for the second half, they had changed into the blue third kit. Fortunes did improve – they could hardly have got worse – and United steadied their sinking ship. Chances were still few and far between, although Giggs grabbed what could only be a goal-difference consolation prize with a minute to play. It was going to be another nail-biting end to the season, but the players had been there before and hopefully their experience would count when it was really needed.

That's better... now we can see you

IN THE PAPERS

"Alex Ferguson was left seething last night at a Manchester United defence which may have thrown away the Premiership title. United did not just get it wrong, they got it desperately wrong, at a mad afternoon at The Dell." **NEWS OF THE WORLD**

Old Trafford manager Alex Ferguson, sick of the sight of the grey side after the most inept 45 minutes of their season, hauled his players into the dressing room at half time and ordered them to change." **SUNDAY EXPRESS**

"This was not just defeat for United. It was total demoralisation... sheer destruction." SUNDAY MIRROR

While there may be justification for the fact that United's grey second kit is a visual nightmare in match action, and there's an understandable superstitious argument against its use, Saturday's disaster can't simply be down to a change of strip." **SUNDAY MIRROR**

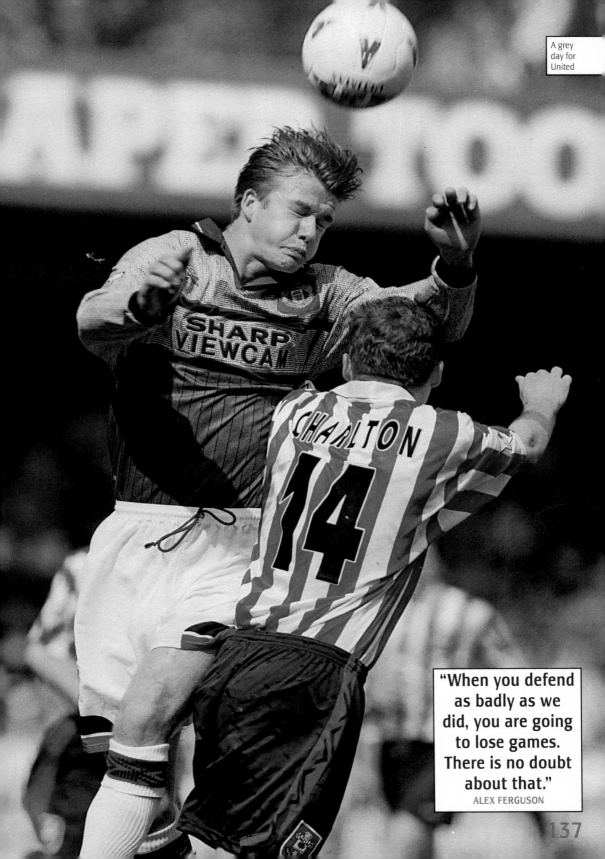

"When you defend as badly as we did, you are going to lose games. There is no doubt about that."

ALEX FERGUSON

MANCHESTER UNITED 1
LEEDS UNITED 0

HOME TEAM
RATING

1.	Peter Schmeichel	8
3.	Denis Irwin	7
6.	Gary Pallister	7
4.	Steve Bruce	6
23.	Phil Neville	7
9.	Brian McClair	7
7.	Eric Cantona	7
16.	Roy Keane	9
11.	Ryan Giggs	7
17.	Andy Cole	7
24.	David Beckham	7

SUBSTITUTES

12.	David May	9
	Bruce	17 mins	
5.	Lee Sharpe	7
	Cole	71 mins	
22.	Paul Scholes	7
	McClair	45 mins	

SCORER

Keane | 72 mins

REFEREE

K Cooper | Pontypridd

VISITORS

13.	Mark Beeney
2.	Gary Kelly
26.	Paul Beesley
15.	Nigel Worthington
6.	David Wetherall
27.	Andy Gray
22.	Mark Ford
4.	Carlton Palmer
10.	Gary McAllister
11.	Gary Speed
9.	Brian Deane

SUBSTITUTES

5.	Lucas Radebe
	Ford	17 mins
17.	Mark Tinkler
	Gray	83 mins
7.	Philemon Masinga
	Deane	83 mins

MATCH REPORT

With United and Newcastle playing on the same night, United were desperately in need of three points. Leeds, on a bad run of form, were looking for some pride from a game that stirs a lot of feelings in both sets of supporters. The game got off to a flying start and United had a few chances early on, Cantona forcing a save from Beeney straight from the kick-off.

Proceedings took a drastic twist after 10 minutes when keeper Beeney handled the ball outside the area and was shown the compulsory red card. Lucas Radebe donned the number one jersey and proved a noteworthy stand-in, frustrating United several times. Chances for both sides came and went, and Scholes and Sharpe were brought into the game to inject some sparkle to United's front line.

Just as the tension was reaching boiling point at Old Trafford, the United faithful were duly rewarded when Keane rocketed in the only goal of the night. A workmanlike performance from United against a grafting Leeds side ensured that United kept a three-point mantle at the top of the League.

Bad luck, old Beeney!

IN THE PAPERS

"It was a nail-biting, nerve fraying, scrambled victory... but only just. Manchester United came up against Lucas Radebe, the defender-turned-goalkeeper for a night, and only managed to squeeze a narrow victory that keeps them in the title driving-seat." **DAILY STAR**

"There may have been a few leprechauns creating their mischief around Old Trafford last night, but from somewhere Roy Keane found a Blarney stone to kiss." **DAILY EXPRESS**

"Stride for stride they galloped on, the thoroughbreds in red, black and white racing for the line with nothing to choose between them. If United's display was edged with haste, Leeds was riven with desire and intelligence." **DAILY TELEGRAPH**

"The word prolific could not be attached to Roy Keane's prowess as a goalscorer, but Old Trafford could not have cared a fig for that last night." **DAILY MAIL**

The long legs of Carlton Palmer

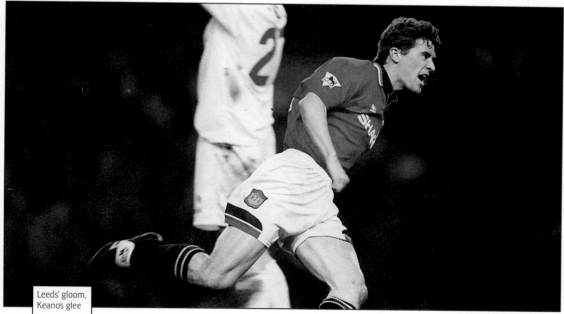

Leeds' gloom, Keano's glee

MANCHESTER UNITED 5
NOTTINGHAM FOREST 0

HOME TEAM

		RATING
1.	Peter Schmeichel	9
3.	Denis Irwin	9
6.	Gary Pallister	9
12.	David May	9
23.	Phil Neville	9
16.	Roy Keane	9
5.	Lee Sharpe	8
11.	Ryan Giggs	9
7.	Eric Cantona	9
22.	Paul Scholes	9
24.	David Beckham	10

SUBSTITUTES

9.	Brian McClair	
17.	Andy Cole	
20.	Gary Neville	6
	Phil Neville | 81 mins	

SCORERS

Scholes | 41 mins
Beckham | 44 /54 mins
Giggs | 69 mins
Cantona | 90 mins

REFEREE

J Winter | Stockton-on-Tees

VISITORS

1.	Mark Crossley
3.	Stuart Pearce
4.	Colin Cooper
5.	Steve Chettle
8.	Scott Gemmill
21.	Chris Bart-Williams
14.	Ian Woan
18.	Alf Inge Haaland
11.	Steve Stone
12.	Jason Lee
22.	Bryan Roy

SUBSTITUTES

2.	Des Lyttle
19.	Steven Howe
20.	Paul McGregor

MATCH REPORT

The most fervent Red fan couldn't have imagined a more emphatic victory in the final home game of the season. With the new stand fully open for the first time, an expectant crowd of 53,926 provided the ideal ambience for the Champions-elect to perform.

Paul Scholes had been given the starting place he deserved in favour of the luckless Cole, and it was Scholes who eased the growing tension with United's first goal on 41 minutes. Giggs, once again the provider, crossed for him to stab the ball past Crossley.

Old Trafford was still in a state of elation when Beckham added a second three minutes later. The young Londoner drove a free-kick goal-bound, but Crossley punched it away into the path of Cantona. The Frenchman miscued a volley across the goal which Beckham instinctively headed home. Brilliant Beckham steered home a third 10 minutes after half-time, after Irwin and Cantona combined well.

Playing classic football, the red shirts pounded the Forest defence in search of vital goals to boost goal difference. They didn't have to wait long. With 20 minutes left, Cantona advanced and released Giggs to his left. The dazzling winger appeared to play the ball through to Scholes but it rolled straight past and into the net: 4–0.

The final goal was fittingly scored by perhaps the most influential figure in United's glorious season, Eric Cantona. The King showed what his goal meant to him with a celebration more befitting the winning goal in a European Cup Final. As the players performed a lap of honour to rapturous adulation, there was just one thing missing: the Premiership trophy. Bring on Boro.

"I don't believe it!"

IN THE PAPERS

"A performance of growing confidence, verve replacing early nerve, blossomed three minutes before half-time with Paul Scholes and David Beckham changing the face of the game and probably the Championship." **DAILY TELEGRAPH**

"The Footballer of the Year showed why he deserved those votes from his biggest critics with another gem of a display as sparkling as the silverware presented before the game to United's Reserve and A teams' Championships." **DAILY MIRROR**

"It is not Cantona's title of course. There have been many ingredients, not least the classic values of Old Trafford football. But it's hard to believe it could have been won without him." **DAILY EXPRESS**

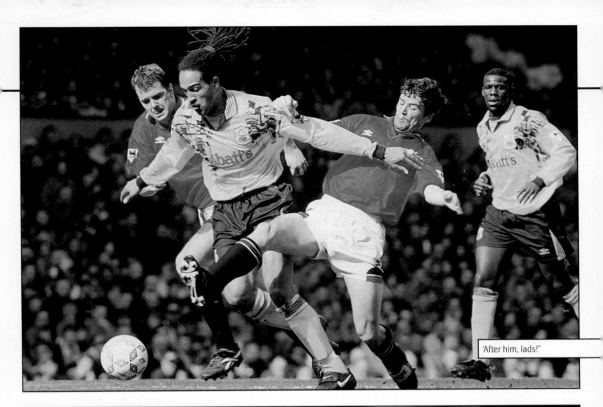

'After him, lads!'

Mark Crossley despairs

APRIL STATS

PLAYER RECORDS

home | away
■ PREMIERSHIP ■ UEFA CUP ■ COCA COLA CUP ■ FA CUP

■ ■ FULL APPEARANCE / CAME ON AS SUB
■ ■ SCORER / SCORED AS SUB

Column headers (opponents): Aston Villa, West Ham United, Wimbledon, Blackburn Rovers, Everton, Rotor Volgograd, Bolton Wanderers, York City, Sheffield Wednesday, Rotor Volgograd, Liverpool, Manchester City, York City, Chelsea, Arsenal, Middlesbrough, Southampton, Coventry City, Nottingham Forest, Chelsea, Sheffield Wednesday, Liverpool, Leeds United, Newcastle United, Queens Park Rangers, Tottenham Hotspur, Sunderland, Aston Villa, West Ham United, Reading, Wimbledon, Blackburn Rovers, Manchester City, Everton, Newcastle United, Bolton Wanderers, Queens Park Rangers, Arsenal, Tottenham Hotspur, Chelsea, Manchester City, Coventry City, Southampton, Leeds United, Nottingham Forest

Player	FULL APPEARANCES	SUB APPEARANCES	GOALS
1. Peter Schmeichel	43	0	1
2. Paul Parker	7	3	1
3. Denis Irwin	38	0	1
4. Steve Bruce	38	1	1
5. Lee Sharpe	29	12	6
6. Gary Pallister	26	0	1
7. Eric Cantona	29	0	18
9. Brian McClair	13	10	3
11. Ryan Giggs	39	3	11
12. David May	11	5	0
15. Graeme Tomlinson	0	0	0
16. Roy Keane	36	1	6
17. Andy Cole	39	1	12
18. Simon Davies	2	6	0
19. Nicky Butt	38	1	3
20. Gary Neville	36	1	0
21. Patrick McGibbon	1	0	0
22. Paul Scholes	17	12	14
23. Philip Neville	27	5	0
24. David Beckham	31	7	8
25. Kevin Pilkington	4	1	0
26. Chris Casper	0	0	0
27. Terry Cooke	2	5	1
29. Ben Thornley	0	1	0
30. John O'Kane	1	1	0
31. William Prunier	2	0	0

PLAYER OF THE MONTH

DAVID MAY

AVERAGE PERFORMANCE RATING: 8.6

FA CARLING PREMIERSHIP

as at 28 April 1996

	Pld	Home					Away					Pts	GD
		W	D	L	F	A	W	D	L	F	A		
▲ Manchester United	37	15	4	0	36	9	9	3	6	34	26	79	+35
▼ Newcastle United	35	17	0	1	37	8	6	4	7	26	27	73	+28
■ Liverpool	36	14	4	1	46	13	6	5	6	22	19	69	+36
▲ Aston Villa	37	11	5	3	32	15	7	4	7	20	19	63	+18
▲ Arsenal	36	9	6	2	28	15	7	5	7	19	16	59	+16
▼ Everton	37	9	5	4	34	19	7	5	7	29	25	58	+19
▼ Blackburn Rovers	37	14	2	3	44	19	3	5	10	14	26	58	+13
▲ Tottenham Hotspur	36	9	5	5	26	19	6	7	4	20	17	57	+10
▲ Nottingham Forest	36	10	5	2	29	16	4	7	8	21	37	54	-7
▼ Chelsea	37	7	7	4	28	19	5	7	7	16	22	50	+3
■ West Ham United	37	9	4	5	24	20	5	4	10	18	31	50	-9
■ Middlesbrough	37	8	3	7	27	24	3	7	9	8	23	43	-12
■ Leeds United	35	8	3	6	20	17	4	3	11	19	36	42	-14
■ Wimbledon	37	5	6	8	27	33	5	4	9	28	37	40	-15
▲ Sheffield Wednesday	37	7	5	7	30	31	3	4	11	17	29	39	-13
▲ Coventry City	37	6	6	6	21	23	2	7	10	21	37	37	-18
▲ Southampton	37	7	6	5	21	18	2	4	13	13	34	37	-18
▲ Manchester City	37	7	6	5	19	17	2	4	13	12	39	37	-25
▼ Queens Park Rangers	37	6	5	8	25	26	3	1	14	13	28	33	-16
■ Bolton Wanderers	37	5	4	10	16	31	3	1	14	22	38	29	-31

MAY

1 | 2 | 3 | 4 | 5 | 6 | 7 | 8 | 9 | 10 | 11 | 12 | 13 | 14 | 15 | 16 | 17 | 18 | 19 | 20 | 21 | 22 | 23 | 24 | 25 | 26 | 27 | 28 | 29 | 30 | 31

MAY

THE MONTH AHEAD

Alan Hansen sits back with that "been there, done that" look in his eyes and gives it to the nation straight. "You can't win things with kids," he tells the watching millions glued to the first *Match of the Day* of the season and that, it seems, is that.

With no Ince, Hughes or Kanchelskis, United had just been stuffed 3–1 by Aston Villa. Callers to Manchester radio stations had screamed for Alex Ferguson to resign over the controversial transfers and, after the Villa result, the chance of the United boss landing any silverware seemed about as likely as the Faroe Islands winning the World Cup.

Just eight months later and, incredibly, Fergie's second Double was in the bag. A phenomenal run of 16 wins in 17 games in the League and a glorious moment of pure genius from a certain Frenchman in the FA Cup Final had proved what the United boss had known all along... "The kids are all right".

In the space of less than a year, Fergie's Fledglings had earned their wings. The likes of Nicky Butt, David Beckham, the Nevilles and Paul Scholes had gone from little known youngsters to acclaimed, trophy-winning stars.

"I'm just so proud of them," said an emotional Fergie on the Wembley pitch, of an achievement which England boss Terry Venables described as "so stunning it's almost unbelievable" started to sink in.

It was the merry, merry month of May for United alright. As Glenn Hoddle landed the England job and talked of the "wealth of young talent" in English football, the richest source of that talent – Manchester United – was getting back to the business of winning trophies after a barren 1994/95 season. With just one League game left to play – at Middlesbrough – the Reds already had one hand on the Premiership trophy. But Newcastle weren't going to give up the fight that easily.

The Geordies went to Leeds and won, then they went to Forest and got just one point when they deserved the three which it would have taken to bring them level with United on points. It was enough to stretch the drama out to the last day of the season, and United knew that any slip-ups at the Riverside Stadium could send the Premiership trophy just down the road to St James' Park. But there were no mistakes.

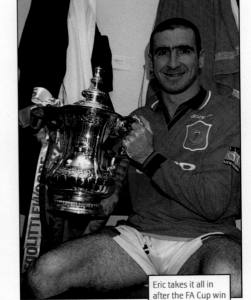

Eric takes it all in after the FA Cup win

"I'm just so proud of them!"

ALEX FERGUSON

David May, so long a United player but only now – playing in his favoured centre back role – truly seeming like one, got things rolling with a devastating far-post header that sent the normally calm and collected defender and his blue and white striped team-mates into delirium. With Newcastle only managing a draw at home to Spurs, in the end the statistics will say what happened next was irrelevent. But with Andy Cole scoring with a deft overhead flick and Ryan Giggs practically bursting the net with a scorcher, there was plenty more to cheer about. At the end of the match, even the Middlesbrough supporters stuck around to pay tribute to England's new Premiership Champions.

"Bring on the Double" cheered the travelling hordes, and at Wembley the team duly obliged. Billed as a classic, the FA Cup Final turned out to be a strangely subdued affair lit only by one moment of brilliance from Cantona. Earlier, in a TV interview in which he became the first person ever to out-smooth Des Lynam, he'd pledged his future to United. Of his own abililty, he said: "I am not arrogant like people say, just confident in myself. I think I can win a game on my own against 11 players."

A few hours after the interview was screened, he hit the winning goal with five minutes left on the clock and the match drifting towards extra time. David Beckham swung in a corner that David James could only punch to the edge of the area. Unfortunately for him, it fell to Le Dieu. Stepping back and steadying himself, Cantona struck a sweet first-time volley that rifled through a horde of players and flew into the famous Wembley net. Magnifique... or, as one newspaper exclaimed, "Formi-double!" The Double was won and Cantona – despite trying to hand the honour to club captain Steve Bruce – went up the Wembley steps to lift the cup. Halfway up he was spat on by Liverpool fans, but Eric just shrugged sadly. Nothing would spoil this moment, not even dropping the lid of the cup and seeing it roll past the Duchess of Kent and down the steps.

Now Fergie and the team could sit back on their laurels and enjoy the moment, relaxing in the magnitude of their achievements. But before the champagne had even started to flow, thoughts were turning to next season. "We owe it to ourselves and English football to do better in Europe next year," said Fergie. "Maybe this is a starting point for this club. We're going to do better, I'll tell you that right now."

MIDDLESBROUGH 0
MANCHESTER UNITED 3

HOME TEAM

- 13. **Gary Walsh**
- 2. **Neil Cox**
- 4. **Steve Vickers**
- 5. **Nigel Pearson**
- 6. **Derek Whyte**
- 7. **Nick Barmby**
- 8. **Jamie Pollock**
- 9. **Jan Fjortoft**
- 11. **Robbie Mustoe**
- 25. **Juninho**
- 30. **Branco**

SUBSTITUTES

- 12. **Alan Moore**
  Branco | 73 mins
- 15. **Phil Whelan**
  Sharpe | 16 mins
- 20. **Phil Stamp**
  Pollock | 57 mins

REFEREE

Paul Durkin | Portland

VISITORS

		RATING
1.	Peter Schmeichel	7
3.	Denis Irwin	7
6.	Gary Pallister	7
7.	Eric Cantona	7
11.	Ryan Giggs	8
12.	David May	8
16.	Roy Keane	7
19.	Nicky Butt	7
22.	Paul Scholes	7
23.	Philip Neville	7
24.	David Beckham	7

SUBSTITUTES

4.	Steve Bruce	
20.	Gary Neville	
17.	Andy Cole	7
	Scholes	53 mins	

SCORERS

May | 13 mins
Cole | 54 mins
Giggs | 80 mins

MATCH REPORT

Champions again! For the third time in four memorable years, Manchester United lifted the Championship trophy after an accomplished 3–0 victory over Middlesbrough at their new stadium.

The carnival atmosphere from the 2,700 United fans lucky enough to have tickets was in evidence well before kick-off, as they launched into their new anthem: "We're gonna win the football League again, down by the Riverside."

Only a United defeat, combined with Newcastle 30 miles up the road beating Tottenham, could prevent it. That was always an unlikely proposition – still more so after 13 minutes, when David May, a 66–1 shot to score the first goal, headed the ball home unimpeded from a Giggs cross.

Nine minutes after the interval Andy Cole, fresh from the substitutes bench to replace Scholes, grabbed a crucial second goal to put the game out of Boro's reach.

By now the United fans were in full voice, with "Are you crying, Newcastle?" and "Just like a team that's gonna win the football League." Encouraged by the news that Manchester City were quickly sinking out of the Premier League and that Newcastle were losing, some even started a conga at the front of the stand... only to be interrupted by yet another United goal.

It came from Giggs. 35 yards out, he skipped past one tackle and advanced towards the box before using the outside of his left foot to swerve the ball past Gary Walsh. Such was the quality of the goal that the entire 30,000-strong crowd gave a standing ovation.

The final whistle saw scenes of ecstasy among players and fans alike. Benched captain Bruce lifted the trophy, followed by the other heroes of this great side. Positioned in front of the travelling fans, the players joy was clear to see as they started celebrations that would last long into the night. Who was it said you don't win League Championships with kids?

May gets the first...

IN THE PAPERS

Cole gets the second...

...and Giggs gets the last goal of the League

MANCHESTER UNITED 1
LIVERPOOL 0

HOME TEAM	RATING
1. Peter Schmeichel	7
3. Denis Irwin	8
6. Gary Pallister	8
12. David May	8
23. Phil Neville	7
16. Roy Keane	9
19. Nicky Butt	8
11. Ryan Giggs	8
7. Eric Cantona	8
17. Andy Cole	6
24. David Beckham	8

SUBSTITUTES

5. Lee Sharpe	
22. Paul Scholes	7
Andy Cole	65 mins	
20. Gary Neville	
David Beckham	89 mins	

SCORER

Eric Cantona | 85 mins

REFEREE

D J Gallagher | Banbury

VISITORS

1. David James	
4. Jason McAteer	
12. John Scales	
5. Mark Wright	
6. Phil Babb	
2. Rob Jones	
15. Jamie Redknapp	
17. Steve McManaman	
10. John Barnes	
23. Robbie Fowler	
8. Stan Collymore	

SUBSTITUTES

9. Ian Rush	
Collymore	74 mins	
10. Michael Thomas	
Jones	85 mins	
3. Tony Warner	

MATCH REPORT

It was billed as the perfect match between two of the finest footballing sides in the country. To the neutral observer the reality may have been a damp squib, but United supporters couldn't have cared less when King Cantona clinched an unprecedented double Double with an astonishing 85th minute goal. General de Goals, the man who had secured 21 Premiership points during the title run-in with his equalising and winning goals, struck again to send 50,000 of his footsoldiers into ecstasy.

United dictated the play in the first half and didn't allow Liverpool to settle into their usual passing rhythm. Early half-chances fell to Cole, whose instinctive eye for goal was replaced by nervous indecision. United's best chance came when the impressive Beckham hit a powerful 20-yard shot that was parried by James. Liverpool's only clear-cut chance fell to Redknapp who blazed over.

Liverpool raised their game several notches in the second half, inspired by the ceaseless running of McManaman, but Schmeichel was rarely troubled. Fowler and Collymore failed to fire – mainly due to poor service – and Rush eventually came on for Collymore following United's substitution of Scholes for Cole.

The game appeared to be slipping aimlessly into extra time, when David James fumbled an out-swinging Beckham corner. The ball fell awkwardly to Cantona who won the Cup with an exquisite volley of inimitable precision and power. "You'll never win the Double with kids" sang the exultant Red fans with heavy irony at the final whistle, emphasising the enormity of what Alex Ferguson and his squad had achieved.

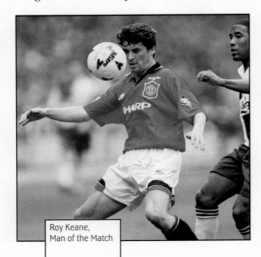

Roy Keane,
Man of the Match

IN THE PAPERS

"If ever an FA Cup Final needed some sort of sublime intervention it was this one – and only someone as uniquely accomplished as Cantona, hitting a wonder winner five minutes from time, could have pulled it off."
NEWS OF THE WORLD

"Ferguson, of Clydeside shipbuilding stock, plainly retains his affection for items which are functional and built to last. And in the moment of his greatest achievement, he may reflect that his ability to infuse Cantona with his own Protestant work-ethic is at the heart of his success."
INDEPENDENT ON SUNDAY

"Getting the Double for the second time in three years – a feat no other manager has achieved – will surely propel Ferguson into the elite of Scottish managers (Busby, Shankly, Stein) whose greatness is undisputed."
OBSERVER

Eric brings
joy to all Reds

DOUBLE DOUBLE WINNERS

The team that won the 1995/96 Premiership...

...goes on to win the FA Cup too

END OF SEASON STATS

PLAYER RECORDS

home | away

- PREMIERSHIP ■ UEFA CUP ■ COCA COLA CUP ■ FA CUP

FULL APPEARANCE / CAME ON AS SUB

SCORER / SCORED AS SUB

	Player	Full Appearances	Sub Appearances	Goals
1.	Peter Schmeichel	45	0	1
2.	Paul Parker	7	3	1
3.	Denis Irwin	39	0	1
4.	Steve Bruce	38	1	1
5.	Lee Sharpe	29	12	6
6.	Gary Pallister	28	0	1
7.	Eric Cantona	37	0	19
9.	Brian McClair	13	10	3
11.	Ryan Giggs	41	3	12
12.	David May	13	5	1
15.	Graeme Tomlinson	0	0	0
16.	Roy Keane	38	1	6
17.	Andy Cole	41	2	13
18.	Simon Davies	2	6	0
19.	Nicky Butt	40	1	3
20.	Gary Neville	37	2	0
21.	Patrick McGibbon	1	0	0
22.	Paul Scholes	18	13	14
23.	Philip Neville	29	5	0
24.	David Beckham	32	9	8
25.	Kevin Pilkington	4	1	0
26.	Chris Casper	0	0	0
27.	Terry Cooke	2	4	1
29.	Ben Thornley	0	1	0
30.	John O'Kane	1	1	0
31.	William Prunier	2	0	0

PLAYER OF THE MONTH

ROY KEANE

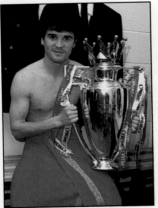

AVERAGE PERFORMANCE RATING: 8

FA CARLING PREMIERSHIP

Final League table

		Pld	Home W	D	L	F	A	Away W	D	L	F	A	Pts	GD
■	Manchester United	38	15	4	0	36	9	10	3	6	37	26	82	+38
■	Newcastle United	38	17	1	1	38	9	7	5	7	28	28	78	+29
■	Liverpool	38	14	4	1	46	13	6	7	6	24	21	71	+33
■	Aston Villa	38	11	5	3	32	15	7	4	8	20	20	63	+17
■	Arsenal	38	10	7	2	30	16	7	5	7	19	16	63	+17
■	Everton	38	10	5	4	35	19	7	5	7	29	25	61	+20
■	Blackburn Rovers	38	14	2	3	44	19	4	5	10	17	28	61	+14
■	Tottenham Hotspur	38	9	5	5	26	19	7	8	4	24	19	61	+12
■	Nottingham Forest	38	11	6	2	29	17	4	7	8	21	37	58	-4
▲	West Ham United	38	9	5	5	25	21	5	4	10	18	31	51	-9
▼	Chelsea	38	7	7	5	30	22	5	7	7	16	22	50	+2
■	Middlesbrough	38	8	3	8	27	27	3	7	9	8	23	43	-15
■	Leeds United	38	8	3	8	21	21	4	4	11	19	36	43	-17
■	Wimbledon	38	5	6	8	27	33	5	5	9	28	37	41	-15
■	Sheffield Wednesday	38	7	5	7	30	31	3	5	11	18	30	40	-13
■	Coventry	38	6	7	6	21	23	2	7	10	21	37	38	-18
■	Southampton	38	7	7	5	21	18	2	4	13	13	34	38	-18
■	Manchester City	38	7	7	5	21	19	2	4	13	12	39	38	-25
■	Queens Park Rangers	38	6	5	8	25	26	3	1	15	13	31	33	-19
■	Bolton Wanderers	38	8	4	10	16	31	3	1	15	23	40	29	-32

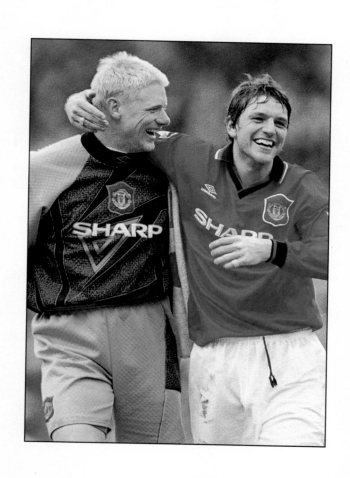

THE TEAM

DAVID BECKHAM

DAVID BECKHAM

PROFILE

Along with Ryan Giggs *et al*, David Beckham stands out as a shining example of how well Alex Ferguson's youth development policy can work at its best.

Born in Leytonstone, David moved to join as a Manchester United trainee when he was just 16 years old. He made his name as a member of Manchester United's trophy-trawling FA Youth Cup team with a winners' medal in 1992 and a runners' up medal in 1993. He is also an accomplished England Youth and Under-21 international with international caps from games in 1992 and 1993 against France, Switzerland, Spain and Denmark.

> **"Dave has got tremendous talent. In terms of pure technique – that is control, passing, shooting and taking free-kicks – Dave Beckham is as good as anyone here."**
>
> ERIC HARRISON

David's United first-team debut came when he was brought on as sub for Andrei Kanchelskis in a Coca-Cola Cup tie against Brighton on 23 September 1992. When Alex Ferguson put him in the starting line-up against Galatasaray in the Champions' League in December 1994, the boy David rose to the challenge with a magnificent goal in the 37th minute.

In the 1995/96 season, United's young lion went from strength to strength. As United trailed 0–3 in September's first game at Villa Park, David came on at half time for Phil Neville and produced the first League goal of the season: a missile in the 84th minute. It didn't go unnoticed. David got a "Goal of the Month" nomination and United's form lifted soon after.

Beckham has a good temperament and, in a midfield vacated by Ince and Kanchelskis, is finding room to show off his skills. He is more comfortable playing in a central role, though he's taken over Kan-kan's role wide on the right due to overcrowding in the midfield. His future contribution to United will surely be lethal.

FACT FILE

Born:
2 May 1975 | Leytonstone

Height: **6' 0"**

Weight: **11st 2lb**

Signed for United:
23 January 1993

Signed as trainee:
8 July 1991

United League debut:
2 April 1995 | Leeds United (h)

Previous clubs:
None

1995/96 RECORD

32(7) apps | 8 goals

MANCHESTER UNITED RECORD

39(11) apps | 9 goals

BEST MOMENT OF 95/96

Scoring the winner against Chelsea in the FA Cup semi final, 31 March 1996

Beckham call

STEVE BRUCE

STEVE BRUCE

PROFILE

Along with the usual array of bruises, black eyes and general sporting injuries that Brucey collects throughout the season, there was one in 1995/96 that threatened to challenge his title as Captain Invincible. It was in the game against Wimbledon at Selhurst Park, in which a sickening clash left Brucey prostrate on the floor. He was stretchered off the pitch for 10 stitches to a huge head-wound – the kind that provokes the fans' worst fears. Just two matches later, in the epic 2–2 FA Cup derby against City, the enduring image was of the skipper ripping off his bandages and striding towards the opposition box to get in on the action from a corner kick. It is this kind of courage and commitment that makes Steve Bruce one of the most respected players in the country.

> ## "Steve is irreplaceable... He's won everything there is to win in this country."
> #### ALEX FERGUSON

He's an inspirational club captain, always prepared to lead by example – though he can organise his troops in other ways as well, of course. Even Schmikes, not afraid of a bit of shouting himself, admits to being scared of his skipper. Just like Bryan Robson before him, Brucey has to earn his place in the first team, but even though he's getting on a bit now he still has as strong a hold on his place as any other player at Old Trafford.

His experience and footballing intelligence is worth at least a yard of pace and his determination and pride in the club are invaluable. With Pallister by Bruce's side, United have a formidable central defensive duo: a foundation strong enough to give confidence to the glamour players in front and allow them to play their exciting brand of attacking football.

Brucey's a big man at the biggest club, and a fine ambassador for United. Not bad... for a geordie!

Red ambassador at the airport

FACT FILE

Born:
31 December 1960 | Newcastle

Height: **6' 0"**

Weight: **13st 0lb**

Signed for United:
17 December 1987

Transfer fee:
£800,000

United League debut:
19 December 1987 | Portsmouth (a)

Previous clubs:
Gillingham | Norwich City

1995/96 RECORD

38(1) apps | 1 goal

MANCHESTER UNITED RECORD

407(3) apps | 51 goals

BEST MOMENT OF 95/96

Scoring his first goal of the season against Bolton, 25 February 1996.

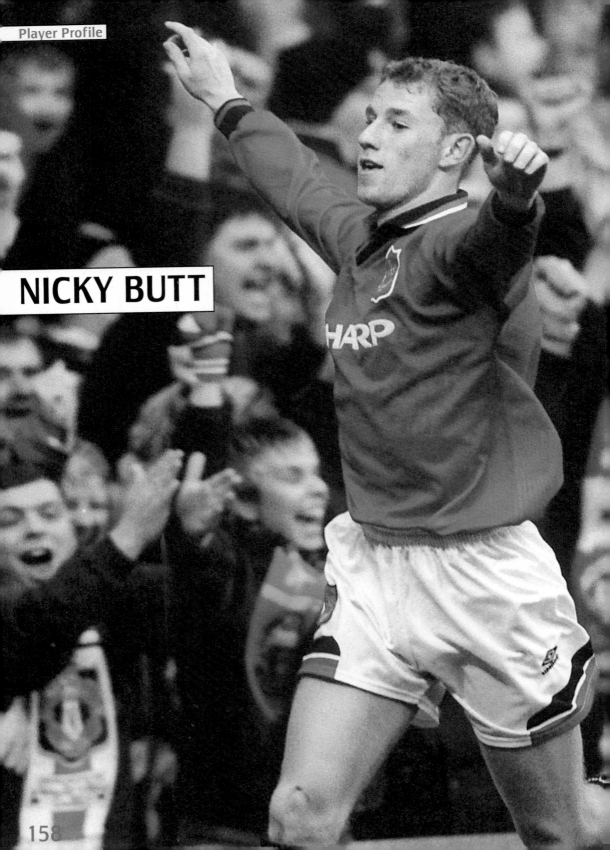

NICKY BUTT

NICKY BUTT

PROFILE

Sturdy midfielder Nicky Butt was one of the first of Fergie's Fledglings to break through the Reserves ranks and make regular appearances for the first team. Second only to Ryan Giggs in the soaraway success stakes, Butt has now firmly established himself in the midfield at United.

> "Nicky's a tough little character. I think he's got a tremendous future at international level."
> KEVIN KEEGAN

As well as Youth and Reserve team victories, Nicky has worn an England shirt at every level up to the Under-21 team, where he was essential to the side that did everything but qualify for the junior version of Euro '96. He was also part of the 1993 Junior World Cup in Australia which came third after a semi-final defeat by Ghana.

At United, Nicky's midfield exploits have been just as rewarding. An outstanding performance in a disappointing FA Cup final against Everton in May 1995 only earned him a loser's medal. He was an immediate selection for Alex Ferguson in the 1995/96 season, cementing a strong partnership with Roy Keane. Ferguson has felt confident enough in the tough-tackling youngster to let Paul Ince's mantle fall on his shoulders and Nicky has so far proved himself worthy. Most notable was his glorious midfield performance with Keane at Old Trafford for the visiting Championship contenders Newcastle on 27 December 1995. Other memorable offerings include a goal from a Cantona cross after one minute against Liverpool on 1 October 1995 and an 11th-hour goal against Bolton Wanderers.

Nicky's exploits have caught everyone's attention. On leaving United to take up the manager's position at Middlesbrough, Bryan Robson singled out one young player he considered destined for future greatness... Nicky Butt, of course.

BEST MOMENT OF 95/96

Scoring in the first minute in Cantona's comeback match v Liverpool, 1 October 1995

I can't believe it's not Butt

FACT FILE

Born:
21 January 1975 | Manchester

Height: **5' 10"**

Weight: **11st 3lb**

Signed for United:
23 January 1993

Signed as trainee:
8 July 1991

United League debut:
21 November 1992 | Oldham Athletic (h)

Previous clubs:
None

1995/96 RECORD

39(1) apps | 3 goals

MANCHESTER UNITED RECORD

61(7) apps | 4 goals

ERIC CANTONA

ERIC CANTONA

PROFILE

When Eric Cantona returned to London SE25 to play Wimbledon 14 months after the infamous Selhurst Park incident of 25 January 1995, it was the final chapter of an incredible year. In 1995, Eric was banished from all competitive football for eight months, lost the captaincy of the French national team and was condemned by pundits as a sinner who should never be forgiven. Eric's comeback match on 1 October against Liverpool saw him set up a goal within a minute and later dance around the goal-pole after converting a penalty equaliser.

No one really doubted that Cantona would regain his influential role in the United side (what percentage of goals scored by United in open play involve a Cantona trick, flick or pass?), but many were surprised by how quickly he caught up with the pace of Premiership football. Even more pleasing was the way Eric managed to tame the fire in his belly despite unprecedented hostility from opposing fans. Obviously taking up Alex Ferguson's wise counsel not to tackle and to concentrate on orchestrating United's attacking manouvres, Eric picked up just one yellow card in his first six months back. He even adopted the role of peacemaker on a number of occasions – most memorably after Nicky Butt's sending off at West Ham, when he stepped in to defuse an explosive situation.

That Eric's return was miraculous was officially confirmed when he was voted Football Writers' Player of the Year. His most testing year yet ended on a high note with United's 4–2 win at Wimbledon. It was a moment to send Red pulses racing: he dived into the crowd, this time to celebrate his second goal, wearing a broad grin and embraced by his disciples. We still believe in you, Eric.

> **"He stands in front of the camera like he is about to take a penalty."**
>
> ETIENNE CHATILLIEZ, THE DIRECTOR OF CANTONA'S FILM DEBUT

BEST MOMENT OF 95/96

The return of the Magnificent Seven, 1 October 1995.

FACT FILE

Born:
24 May 1966 | Marseille

Height: **6' 0"**

Weight: **14st 3lb**

Signed for United:
27 November 1992

Transfer fee:
£1 million

United League debut:
**6 December 1992 |
Manchester City (h)**

Previous clubs:
**Auxerre | Martigues |
Olympique Marseilles |
Bordeaux | Montpellier |
Nîmes | Leeds United**

1995/96 RECORD
29(0) apps | 18 goals

MANCHESTER UNITED RECORD
131(1) apps | 65 goals

INTERNATIONAL RECORD
43 apps | 19 goals
Team: **France**
Debut:
12 August 1987 | W Germany

Classic Cantona: another vital goal tames the Magpies

ANDY COLE

ANDY COLE

PROFILE

It must be some time since a player has been under such prolonged and intense pressure as Andy Cole was subjected to in the 1995/96 season. Ever since his transfer from Newcastle in January 1995 for a record £6 million, the spotlight has never left him.

> **"His positional play is terrific and his movement off the ball is superb."**
> ALEX FERGUSON

Unfortunately for Andy and United, what has left him are the striking exploits that earned him that huge price-tag in the first place. At a high-profile club (and they don't get any higher than Manchester United), in a tense Championship struggle, an out-of-form £6-million striker is a godsend for a sensationalist media who can wallow in his every mistake with the benefit of endless, agonizing, slow-motion replays.

There are those who say that if Paul Scholes had been playing regularly in the first team, the Championship would have come to Old Trafford by January. But those people forget that Andy Cole is more than just a goalscorer. The faith that Fergie has kept in Andy since his arrival in Manchester may not have been rewarded with a flood of goals but rather with a consistently high work-rate, a flurry of vital assists and a steady growth in his overall game. One element of Andy's play that has shown marked improvement is his running off the ball, which caused panic in opposition defences throughout the 1995/96 season and created those spaces that allowed Eric, Giggsy and Keano to have their free runs on goal.

Despite the barrage of criticism directed at Andy for his finishing problems, he never hid from the limelight. When he jumped off the bench to score with his first touch against Middlesbrough in the final League match of 1995/96, he may finally have laid to rest the ghost of Upton Park, May 1995.

Always look on the bright side...

FACT FILE

Born:
15 October 1971
Nottingham

Height: **5' 11"**

Weight: **11st 2lb**

Signed for United:
12 January 1995

Transfer fee:
£6 million

United League debut:
22 January 1995 |
Blackburn Rovers (h)

Previous clubs:
Bristol City |
Newcastle United

1995/96 RECORD

39(2) apps | 13 goals

MANCHESTER UNITED RECORD

56(3) apps | 25 goals

INTERNATIONAL RECORD

1 app | 0 goals

Team: **England**

Debut:
29 March 1994 | Uruguay (h)

BEST MOMENT OF 95/96

Cole's last-minute winner in the FA Cup Third Round replay against Sunderland, 16 January 1996

RYAN GIGGS

RYAN GIGGS

PROFILE

It seems ridiculous now, but there was talk at the end of the 1994/95 season suggesting Ryan Giggs had peaked at the age of 20 and was in the process of losing his prowess. There are a lot of possible reasons for Ryan's undoubted lack of form during the 1994/95 season: injury, the huge public scrutiny, the wear and tear of three full seasons on a player just out of his teens, and the diminishing freedom he could enjoy on the pitch as opposition defences paid him more and more attention.

It took him a couple of years, but by the 1995/96 season Giggsy was back on top of his game. There is no better sight in the British game than United's number 11 flying down the left flank, skipping past defenders and turning defence into attack in a matter of breathtaking moments. And during the 1995/96 season, Old Trafford thrilled to this sight more times than ever as Giggsy's relationship with Eric the Provider blossomed with almost telepathic understanding.

> **"People forget he's years away from his prime, which is frightening for defenders."**
>
> TOMMY DOCHERTY

Ryan's team-play also blossomed. He's now happy to forego the half-chance of a shot in order to pass to a team-mate in a better position. It's a sign of the growing maturity that is evident in other aspects of his game, notably his improved defensive play: the Giggs of today is willing to get back and muck in to ease the strain on United's back four, as he did in the FA Cup semi final against Chelsea in March.

Ryan will always have those dazzling individual tricks to keep Old Trafford happy, but it is the addition of more generous skills to his repertoire that makes a player great, and makes the prospect of the 1996/97 season that much more enticing.

FACT FILE

Born:
29 November 1973 | Cardiff
Height: **5' 11"**
Weight: **10st 7lb**
Signed for United:
29 November 1990
Signed as trainee:
9 July 1990
United League debut:
2 March 1991 | Everton (h)
Previous clubs:
None

1995/96 RECORD
40(3) apps | 12 goals
MANCHESTER UNITED RECORD
214(23) apps | 52 goals
INTERNATIONAL RECORD
15 apps | 3 goals
Team: **Wales**
Debut:
13 March 1993 | Belgium | (h)

Always ready to stretch himself further...

BEST MOMENT OF 95/96

Giggs' goal from a near-impossible angle against Manchester City, 6 April 1996

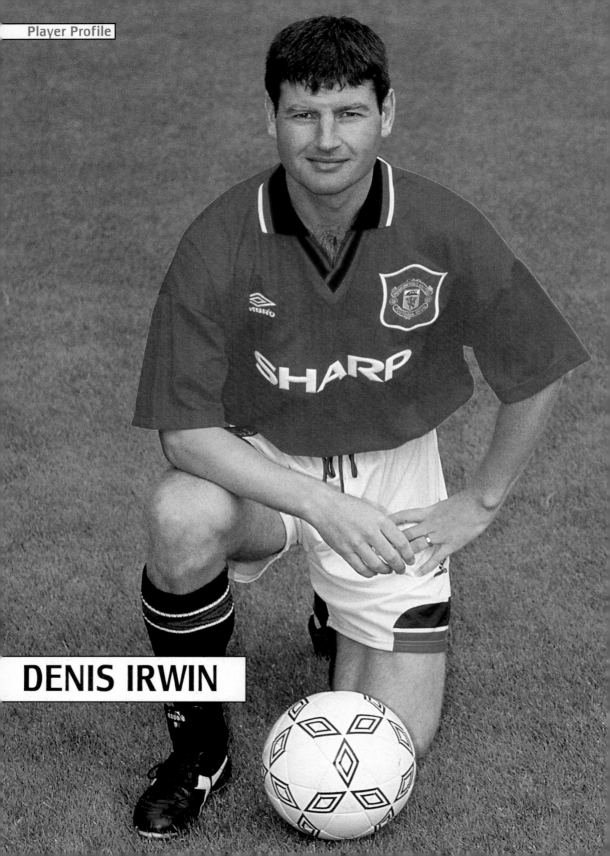

DENIS IRWIN

DENIS IRWIN

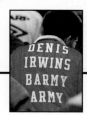

PROFILE

Denis Irwin ranks the birth of his children as his proudest moments. "They exceed anything I've achieved as a footballer," he says. They must be special kids, because few players have achieved as much as the Corker has: World Cup quarter finalist, UEFA Cup winner, twice Premiership medallist and winner of numerous domestic cups. And all this after a disastrous start to his career when he suffered the humiliation of a free transfer from his first club, Leeds. But it was the determination with which he battled to put that humiliation behind him at Oldham Athletic that attracted Ferguson to the Irishman. Denis signed for United in June 1990 for £625,000, and by the time he played his first game for the Red Devils he had already made a mockery of that price-tag with stirring displays for Jack Charlton's side in the Italian World Cup tournament.

> **"For me, the highlight of Christmas TV is watching a documentary about Denis Irwin...** *Mr Bean's Christmas*, **I think it was called."**
>
> CHOCCY McCLAIR'S DIARY

Expectations at Old Trafford were high for the quiet defender and he did not disappoint, showing a handy ability to play on either side of the park along with deceptive pace and a fine understanding of the game. Over the years we have come to see another part of Denis's play: the cracking free-kick drives that endear him to fantasy football managers around the country, eager to have a high-scoring defender on their books.

Denis has withstood pressure from the youngsters, and it's understandable that Fergie should remain faithful to a player who has served him so well. Perhaps the saying should really be: "If they're good enough, they're young enough."

BEST MOMENT OF 95/96

Irwin's 20-yard blast against Coventry, 22 November 1995

FACT FILE

Born:
31 October 1965 | Cork

Height: **5' 8"**

Weight: **10st 8lb**

Signed for United:
8 June 1990

Transfer fee:
£625,000

United League debut:
**25 August 1990 |
Coventry City (h)**

Previous clubs:
Leeds United | Oldham Athletic

1995/96 RECORD

39(1) apps | 1 goal

MANCHESTER UNITED RECORD

299(4) apps | 20 goals

INTERNATIONAL RECORD

40 apps | 1 goal

Team: **Republic of Ireland**

Debut:
12 September 1990 v Morocco

Denis puts the boot in for United

ROY KEANE

ROY KEANE

PROFILE

Boom Boom Keano earns his nickname. In a part of the pitch shared by accredited geniuses Cantona and Giggs, Roy holds his own with his particular brand of muscular midfield play. With Keano's consistently powerful performances throughout the season, the Guvnor's midfield presence was not seriously missed.

Because of Fergie's edict forbidding Eric from doing any troublesome tackling, Roy's ball-winning prowess had to be stretched across the entire width of the pitch. It's a credit to his strength and passion that United enjoyed so much possession during the season.

With the glamour boys doing their dazzling work up front, you could easily miss the antics in the engine room. But Roy is rarely out of the spotlight – and not always because of trouble with referees. His inimitable style of celebrating other players' goals will always attract attention: at times, Giggs, Cole et al have looked positively alarmed as the stocky figure of Keane bears down, grinning fiercely, to hurl them to the ground as a sign of his appreciation. His knack of scoring corkers himself at important moments, like his right-footed winner against Leeds in the third last match of the 1995/96 Premiership, means he will remain a firm favourite with the Old Trafford faithful. The enduring problem for Keano is his ever-increasing collection of bookings. But with the amount of work that he gets through in a game, it is a testament to his timing and fitness that he is not punished more often. The bigger testament to his overall skill and influence is how much he is missed during his absences through suspension.

> **"I love it when the team scores... The lads are always giving me stick, but I'm just so happy I can't help it."**
>
> ROY KEANE

FACT FILE

Born:
10 August 1971 | Cork
Height: **5' 10"**
Weight: **11st 1lb**
Signed for United:
19 July 1993
Transfer fee:
£3.75 million
United League debut:
15 August 1993 |
Norwich City (a)
Previous clubs:
Cobh Ramblers |
Nottingham Forest

1995/96 RECORD

37(1) apps | 6 goals

MANCHESTER UNITED RECORD

120(8) apps | 17 goals

INTERNATIONAL RECORD

25 apps | 1 goal
Team: **Republic of Ireland**
Debut:
22 May 1991 v Chile

BEST MOMENT OF 95/96

Scoring the match-clinching second goal against Newcastle at Old Trafford, 27 December 1995

Keane pulls his weights for the Reds

DAVID MAY

DAVID MAY

PROFILE

When David May was lured away from Blackburn by Manchester United in the summer of 1994, United secured one of Jack Walker's prime assets. David had struck up an awesome central defensive partnership with Colin Hendry during Blackburn's spirited challenge for the 1993/94 Premiership. He could tackle, was dominant in the air and poached his share of goals. At just £1.2 million, it appeared Alex Ferguson had scored again with a shrewd bit of business in the transfer market. Fergie was clearly planning ahead for the day when Captain Courageous Steve Bruce would finally hang up his boots, leaving a gaping hole in United's back ranks.

> "When David first joined, I asked a few Blackburn players what he was like. They all said: 'Crazy... '"
>
> RYAN GIGGS

However a year later, when David's old team-mates, inspired by Dalglish and Shearer, beat United to the Premiership title, a few football observers were looking for a scapegoat and the Rovers old boy fitted the bill. David had filled a number of roles during an unsettled first season for the Reds, but he rarely played in his favoured central defensive position. Understandably, David found it difficult to slot anonymously into a back four that had been dominated for so long by Parker, Irwin, Pallister and Bruce. The media wrote him off as a "Trojan donkey" sent by the millionaires of Blackburn to scupper United's trophy aspirations.

Such ill-informed criticism ignored the fact he had been playing out of position and also his determination to make his move work. In 1995/96, the return of Parker and the emergence of the Neville Brothers has shored up the flanks and given David more opportunity to operate in the centre. Fine performances, such as his assured display in the Cup semi-final thriller against Chelsea, suggest David may be the one to lead the new generation of United stoppers.

Despite his respectable appearance, David has a wacky sense of humour and his presence in the squad can only serve to keep United spirits high.

May the force be with you

FACT FILE

Born:
24 June 1970 | Oldham
Height: **6' 0"**
Weight: **12st 10lb**
Signed for United:
1 July 1994
Transfer fee:
£1.2 million
United League debut:
20 August 1994 | QPR (h)
Previous club:
Blackburn Rovers

1995/96 RECORD

12(5) apps | 1 goal

MANCHESTER UNITED RECORD

34(9) apps | 4 goals

BEST MOMENT OF 95/96

Scoring the vital first goal against Boro in United's final League match

BRIAN McCLAIR

Squad Number: 9 | Forward

BRIAN McCLAIR

PROFILE

It's easy to forget Brian's early top-scoring days at United. Arriving from Celtic for a bargain fee of £850,000 and with a frightening reputation as a striker, Choccy made an immediate impact. Since grabbing the limelight with 24 League goals in his first season for the Reds, Brian has adopted a progressively more withdrawn midfield role. But he still poaches vital goals and boasts an excellent goal ratio of one every three and a bit games. Perhaps his finest moment in United colours came when his goal pipped Nottingham Forest in the 1992 League Cup final.

> "Choccy is such a clever, witty person, with a dry sense of humour and an oddball mentality."
>
> ALEX FERGUSON

Often labelled "Boss's pet" by team-mates in his early days, Brian is a dream to manage. He's played in virtually every position under Fergie – even volunteering to have a go in goal when Schmeichel was injured last season. His football intelligence means he can be trusted to fill a variety of tactical roles; his natural winning instinct makes him a valuable squad member. When he's not turning out for the first team, he plays with equal gusto for the Reserves, helping to bring on the rich vein of young talent at the club. Recognising Brian's guiding influence, the crowd chanted: "Choccy is their leader" as he led a youthful bunch of United pupils to victory against Port Vale in a 1994 Coca-Cola Cup tie.

There'll be no shortage of options when Choccy's playing days come to an end. He's already heavily involved in PFA work, and his caustic, occasionally surreal wit has found a hilarious outlet in the club's official magazine, where his day-to-day diary has made many innocent victims of United staff.

Choccy on the chase

FACT FILE

Born:
8 December 1963 | Airdrie

Height: **5' 10"**

Weight: **12st 12lb**

Signed for United:
1 July 1987

Transfer fee:
£850,000

United League debut:
15 August 1987 | Southampton (a)

Previous clubs:
Motherwell | Celtic

1995/96 RECORD

13(10) apps | 3 goals

MANCHESTER UNITED RECORD

382(39) apps | 126 goals

INTERNATIONAL RECORD

30 apps | 2 goals

Team: **Scotland**

Debut:
2 December 1987 | Luxembourg

BEST MOMENT OF 95/96

Scoring two against Coventry City, 22 November 1995

GARY NEVILLE

GARY NEVILLE

PROFILE

It's unusual to discover two talented footballers in the same family. The Charlton brothers were notable exceptions, as are United's current sibling double-act... the Neville brothers.

The older of the two is Gary Neville who, despite his size, is already a supremely accomplished defender. At the age of 20 he is now a regular selection for Terry Venables' England squad and for Manchester United's first team.

Gary's leadership qualities showed through in the Youth honours he helped bring to Manchester United, which were reflected in his speedy progression to first-team action. His debut (if only for two minutes) came in a 0–0 draw against Moscow Torpedo back in September 1992 when he was just 17. Since then he has proved invaluable as injuries to Parker, Pallister, May and Bruce threatened to shake the normally solid United fortifications.

In the 1995/96 season, Gary's input at the back was critical as United spent several months in second slot behind Premiership leaders Newcastle United. Indeed, throughout the season he fitted neatly into the first-team jigsaw alongside more experienced stars such as Bruce and Parker without any difficulties.

In addition to technical and tactical skill, it's those little extras that make you invaluable. Gary has doubled up his role as defender to do his bit for the United attack force: strong shoulders make him a master of the long throw-in – as seen in the April 1995 FA Cup semi final against Crystal Palace, when a fine example enabled Pallister to head for glory.

> ## "Gary has risen to the challenge of being an international. He looks as if he's always belonged in United's defence."
>
> TERRY VENABLES ON GARY NEVILLE

Gary's contribution to England's Euro '96 campaign has been just as effective. His first England call-up came for a match against Japan in June 1995 and, when the good news arrived, Gary says he couldn't believe it. It's clear El Tel was pleased with the result. Since then he's been a permanent fixture in the England right-back position. The future looks bright for Neville the elder.

The two Garys, Flitcroft and Neville, enjoy an arcade game duel

FACT FILE

Born:
18 February 1975 | Bury
Height: **5' 10"**
Weight: **11st 11lb**
Signed for United:
23 January 1993
Signed as trainee:
8 July 1991
United League debut:
8 May 1994 |
Coventry City (h)
Previous clubs:
None

1995/96 RECORD

36(1) apps | 0 goals

MANCHESTER UNITED RECORD

60(7) apps | 0 goals

INTERNATIONAL RECORD

8 apps | 0 goals
Team: **England**
Debut:
3 June 1995 | Japan (h)

BEST MOMENT OF 95/96

Becoming a regular for his country at the age of 20

PHIL NEVILLE

PHIL NEVILLE

PROFILE

The younger son of Neville Neville, the Commercial Manager at Bury FC, Phil Neville has showed he is capable of achieving the same outstanding results as his brother, fledging England right back Gary Neville.

Phil has successfully stood in both full back positions at United. And despite starting out in the shadow of his brother's formidable success, there is no doubt Phil is also blessed with outstanding sporting abilities. He was not far from choosing a career at the crease, his batting apparently of a high enough standard to enable him to reach full international status. Indeed, sporting ability runs in the family: twin sister Tracy is already an accomplished England netball international.

> "I went on two courses, one for cricket and one for football. I had to chose: as you can see, I chose football."
>
> PHIL NEVILLE

In contrast to a difficult first-team season, the Youth team fared better in 1995. Phil's contribution to United's FA Youth Cup victory that year was considerable – he captained the side to defeat Tottenham Hotspur after a daunting penalty shoot-out. Phil's League debut for United came in the same season against Man City on 11 February 1995. He was pitched into the fray in late January that year against Wrexham in his first FA Cup tie, and his 26th-minute pass helped Giggs to find the net and secure a 5–2 win for the Reds.

Finding his form in the 1995/96 season, Phil has been regularly picked in brother Gary's right-back position. He shows encouraging attacking tendencies and he has laid on a number of goals for United. He memorably set up Cantona's match-clincher against Newcastle at St James' Park, and is never afraid to get to the byline.

Football pundits have tipped the Neville brothers to form a dynamic duo in the England defence. Phil Neville was a regular for the England Youth team and trained with the senior squad, missing active service against Bulgaria only because of a twisted ankle.

Phil keeps tabs on Cottee of the Hammers

FACT FILE

Born:
21 January 1977 | Bury
Height: **5' 10"**
Weight: **11st 10lb**
Signed for United:
1 June 1994
Signed as trainee:
5 July 1993
United League debut:
11 February 1995 |
Man City (a)

1995/96 RECORD

28(5) apps | 0 goals

MANCHESTER UNITED RECORD

30(6) apps | 0 goals

BEST MOMENT OF 95/96

His call-up to the England squad for the Bulgaria game

GARY PALLISTER

GARY PALLISTER

PROFILE

Sometimes you only realise just how good a footballer is when he isn't playing. An unsettled back four was the bane of Alex Ferguson's life last season, and it was no coincidence that Gary Pallister was sidelined by injury when Man United suffered two of their heaviest defeats, at The Dell and White Hart Lane.

> **"There is no better central defender in the country than Gary Pallister. He's been outstanding in the last three seasons. A lot of credit for my large number of clean sheets must go to Gary."**
>
> PETER SCHMEICHEL

Pally is so horizontally laid-back and carries out his defensive duties with such disarming efficiency that it's easy for his consistent performances to pass you by. Always a calming influence at the back, Gary is equally comfortable carrying the ball forward. At corners, he's a constant threat, flicking on from the near post. His height and power make him a natural deterrent against aerial threats from Ferdinand and co; his speed on the ground means precious few attackers beat him for pace; but probably his greatest asset is his tackling ability. An impeccable disciplinary record is as much a testament to split-second timing – which means he takes the ball first and man second – as to his cool temperament.

Gary's come a long way since joining United from Middlesbrough as a scrawny 24 year old in 1990. Now weighing in at close to 15 stone, Gary is said to have curbed his junk-food tendencies and sticks to a diet designed by MUFC nutritionist Trevor Lea. Spinal sciatica disrupted Gary's 1993/94 campaign and he often had to defy pain in pursuit of glory, and he was keen to stay healthy for England's Euro '96 campaign after time out due to injury during 1995/96.

Gary's most embarassing moment occurred on international duty: he stripped off his tracksuit ready to come on as sub against the USA at Wembley, only to find he wasn't wearing his England shirt. It's not often that Pally is left red-faced on a football pitch.

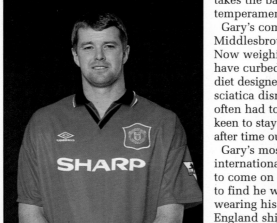

Long tall Pally

FACT FILE

Born:
30 June 1965 | Ramsgate

Height: **6' 4"**

Weight: **14st 13lb**

Signed for United:
28 August 1989

Transfer fee:
£2.3 million

United league debut:
30 August 1989 | Norwich City (h)

Previous clubs:
Darlington (loan) | Middlesbrough

1995/96 RECORD

27(0) apps | 1 goal

MANCHESTER UNITED RECORD

349(4) apps | 12 goals

INTERNATIONAL RECORD

20 apps | 0 goals

Team: **England**

Debut:
30 August 1988 | Hungary

BEST MOMENT OF 95/96

Scoring against his old club Middlesbrough, 28 October 1995

PAUL PARKER

Squad Number: 2 | Defender

PAUL PARKER

PROFILE

Paul's man-marking expertise has always been second to none, but it was that plus his pace and crosses that earned him a place in the England 1990 World Cup team. At a time when attacking backs were as rare as United Championships, Paul stood out as a player who could bring an extra element to the England side. In that semi final against West Germany, it was Paul who, after unluckily deflecting a hopeful shot into England's net, pulled the team round when he delivered the perfect cross to set up Gary Lineker's equaliser.

> "Apart from being the worst-dressed man at the club – you should see his suits! – he's a great player. He's very tough and agressive."
>
> GARY PALLISTER

Within two seasons of coming to Old Trafford from QPR in 1991, Paul had become a fixture at right back in the Championship sides of 1992/93 and 1993/94. The man known as Busby (because he's always on the phone) was in the thick of it, relied upon to break up opposition attacks as well as to create them for United.

For a man with this kind of pedigree, the last two seasons must have been frustrating for Paul. In 1994/95, injuries kept his first-team appearances to a miserly three. The 1995/96 season has hardly been an improvement, but for a different reason. Keeping his admirable faith in the club's youth, Fergie has preferred playing the Neville brothers to Paul, who has spent a lot of the season on the bench. He may well have to get used to that if he wants to stay at United. But even as a substitute, Paul has shown he still has the capacity to influence a game, scoring at Reading in the FA Cup Fourth Round. Busby may be giving way to the babes, but he's still got a lot to offer.

FACT FILE

Born:
4 April 1964 | West Ham
Height: **5' 7"**
Weight: **11st 7lb**
Signed for United:
6 August 1991
Transfer fee:
£2 million
United League debut:
17 August 1991 | Notts County (h)
Previous clubs:
Fulham | QPR

1995/96 RECORD
7(3) apps | 1 goal
MANCHESTER UNITED RECORD
136(9) apps | 2 goals
INTERNATIONAL RECORD
18(1) apps | 0 goals
Team: **England**
Debut:
26 July 1989 | Albania

Going cone-shaped

BEST MOMENT OF 95/96

Scoring against Reading in the Fourth Round of the FA Cup, 27 January 1996

PETER SCHMEICHEL

PETER SCHMEICHEL

PROFILE

Intimidation is an integral part of the game, and football in the Premiership is famed throughout the world for its tough atmosphere. But it sometimes seems that Peter Schmeichel forgets it's the opposition who should be the target of abuse and not his own defenders. For some opposition fans, the red-faced fury with which he publicly attacks his defence is incomprehensible. And yet United can pull out a number of justifications for his behaviour.

> ## "One goal and suddenly he's a superstar!"
> ANDY COLE AFTER SCHMEICHEL'S GOAL

First up, of course, is that this guy is a great keeper, the world's number one. If anyone has earned the right to shout at his team-mates, it's Schmikes.

Maybe if his tactic didn't work, questions would be asked. But the plain fact is that his abrasive method of motivation does the trick: United's defence has consistently matched Arsenal's low goal-concession figures since Peter came to Old Trafford in 1991.

The battleaxe from Gladsaxe

But the main reason for the shouting is something most mere mortals can relate to, and the reason for the Great Dane's popularity at the club. As Gary McAllister said after United's 3–1 defeat at Elland Road: "He was really having a go at his team-mates during the game. That shows how much he cares about winning. He's an emotional guy and he wears his heart on his sleeve."

And the emotions were there for all to see in one of the most memorable moments of last season. 2–1 down with minutes remaining in the second leg of the UEFA Cup tie against Rotor Volgograd, Schmikes soared above everyone to connect with a corner and score a stunning goal. Although the effort was in vain given the final result, the sheer elation on Peter's face was a picture few United fans will forget in a hurry.

FACT FILE

Born:
18 November 1963 | Gladsaxe | Denmark
Height: **6' 4"**
Weight: **15st 13lb**
Signed for United:
6 August 1991
Transfer fee: **£550,000**
United League debut:
17 August 1991 | Notts County (h)
Previous club: **Brondby IF**

1995/96 RECORD

44 apps | 1 goal | 21 clean sheets

MANCHESTER UNITED RECORD

245 apps | 1 goal | 118 clean sheets

INTERNATIONAL RECORD

82 apps | 63 goals conceded
Team: **Denmark**
Debut:
20 May 1987 | Greece

BEST MOMENT OF 95/96

An outstanding display to deny Newcastle at St James' Park, 4 March 1996

PAUL SCHOLES

Squad Number: 24 | Forward

PAUL SCHOLES

PROFILE

Salford born and bred, Paul Scholes is at the vanguard of United's exciting youth division which has now come into its own. At the beginning of the 1995/96 season, in the absence of many of the Reds' confirmed headliners, Paul established himself as a first-teamer by intelligent attacking and building up a goal ratio to rival the very best in the Premiership. Quite simply, Paul Scholes got on a roll.

He signed as a trainee for United in July 1991 and made eight appearances for the Youth A team in the 1991/92 season, scoring five goals. By the following year, "Goalsey Scholesy" was the Youth team's top scorer, knocking in 25 goals in the 25 games and helping the side (which included other Youth prodigies such as David Beckham and Nicky Butt) to claim the Lancashire League Division One Championship.

> **"The lad has the goalscorer's instinct people saw I had, and the maturity to go with it. He's very sharp..."**
>
> DENNIS LAW ON PAUL SCHOLES

Paul's commanding performances for United's Reserves and Youth were smoothly transferred to the Premiership. He came close to making history by securing United's second double in a row when, in his first season in the first team, his timely shots at Upton Park and Wembley were denied at important games against West Ham and Everton.

Despite that disappointing finish, because Eric was away by the start of 1996 Scholesy had become the first team's leading goalscorer, with a total of 10 goals in 16 matches. Superb games against West Ham and in particular Manchester City, where he scored with a fourth-minute header, proved Scholes was a consistent goal machine as well as a useful link player.

Described by the papers as a "carrot-topped terror", Paul is a first-rate home-grown striker who has the skills vital to United's future glory.

FACT FILE

Born:
16 November 1974 | Salford
Height: **5' 7"**
Weight: **11st**
Signed for United:
23 January 1993
Signed as trainee:
8 July 1991
United League debut:
24 September 1994 | Ipswich Town (a)
Previous clubs:
None

1995/96 RECORD
18(12) apps | 14 goals
MANCHESTER UNITED RECORD
28(27) apps | 21 goals

BEST MOMENT OF 95/96

Scoring two goals in the first nine minutes at Stamford Bridge, 21 October 1995

The future is orange

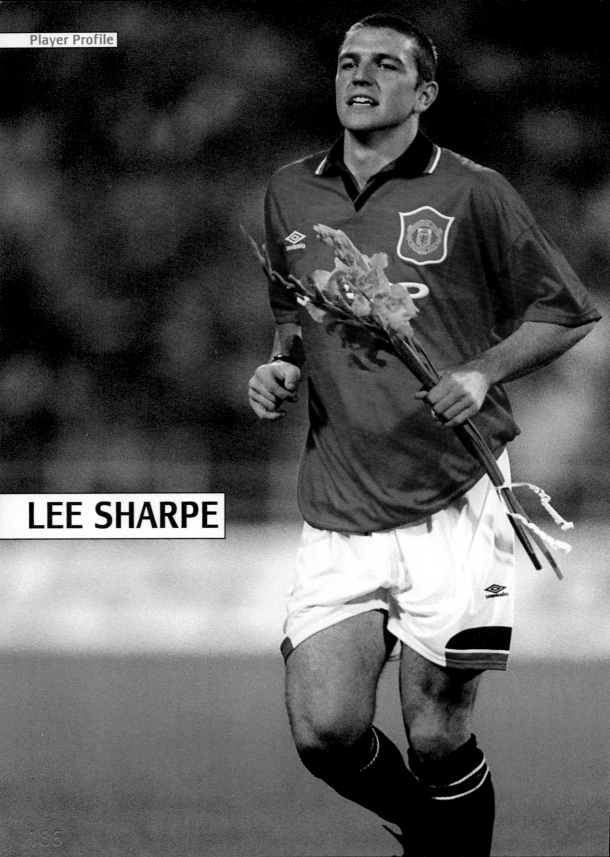

LEE SHARPE

LEE SHARPE

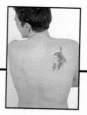

PROFILE

December 1995 probably marked the lowest point of Lee Sharpe's rollercoaster career. In the past he had been sidelined by illness and injury, but never before had he suffered the wrath of the Old Trafford crowd.

Two thumping defeats in a row by Liverpool and Leeds during the vital Christmas period put the skids under United's Premiership title challenge. As Newcastle sped ahead, some United supporters were looking for a scapegoat. Suprisingly, considering his longterm rapport with fans, Lee Sharpe bore the brunt. He was disturbed by the level of abuse he received – "it was hard and it did hurt me," he said. He looked a mere shell of the the confident character who broke into the England team at the age of 19.

> "My settee – it's a big, lolloping, casual sort of a thing... and it's not too fancy. That just about sums me up."
>
> LEE SHARPE

Although Lee admits he was playing badly, he had bravely kept quiet about a nagging back injury which was hampering his mobility. Eventually it took a tip from a friend, local golf pro Mark Russell, to persuade Lee to blank out the taunts of the crowd and regain his true form. As Lee puts it: "Mark helped me kick all the bad stuff out of my head and feed the good vibes back in." Whatever he said, it worked. Who could forget Lee's classy right-foot finish which sunk neighbours City 2–1 in the FA Cup Fifth Round tie in February? And who can forget the diving celebration?

His improvement didn't go unnoticed by Terry Venables: Lee came back into the reckoning for the England squad. Everyone knows about Lee's natural talent and versatility, but he's shown that beneath his happy-go-lucky exterior, there is a committed professional who reacts positively to any setback and who doesn't slap in a transfer request whenever times get tough. Sharpey's here to stay.

FACT FILE

Born:
27 May 1971 | Halesowen

Height: **6' 0"**

Weight: **12st 6lb**

Signed for United:
1 June 1988

Transfer fee:
£185,000

United League debut:
24 September 1988 | West Ham (h)

Previous clubs:
Torquay United

1995/96 RECORD

29(12) apps | 6 goals

MANCHESTER UNITED RECORD

212(50) apps | 36 goals

INTERNATIONAL RECORD

8 apps | 0 goals

Team: **England**

Debut:
27 March 1991 | Republic of Ireland

BEST MOMENT OF 95/96

Scoring the winner against Blackburn on 10 February 1996, which marked his return to form

True-Lee, mad-Lee, deep-Lee

CHRIS CASPER

PROFILE

Chris Casper is still waiting patiently for the real crack at first-team football which Gary Neville, his sidekick and room-mate from the Youth team glory days of 1992, has enjoyed with club and country. While the elder Neville's success has been at right back, Casper, loyal to his centre-back roots, has had his progress checked by the durability of Pallister and Bruce and the signing of David May.

In 1994/95, Chris followed the Coca-Cola Cup road into the limelight as one of the fledglings pitched into battle against Port Vale. In 1995/96, his Reserve-team partner Pat McGibbon pipped him to the dubious pleasure of facing York City in the same competition. A commanding player at the back, Chris has also used his height at the other end of the field to notch up the odd goal from set-pieces. He netted an important one for the Reserves at Everton in January before heading off to the south coast for a spell on loan to Second Division Bournemouth, where he scored on his debut. Youth team coach Eric Harrison credits Chris with being in the "Alan Hansen mould".

FACT FILE

Born:
28th April 1975 | Burnley
Height: **6' 0"**
Weight: **11st 11lb**
Signed as trainee:
8 July 1991
Signed Professional:
23 January 1993
United League debut:
None to date
Previous clubs:
None

1995/96 RECORD

0 apps | 0 goals

MANCHESTER UNITED RECORD

1 app | 0 goals

Squad Number: 27 | Midfielder

TERRY COOKE

PROFILE

Terry Cooke entered the 1995/96 season on the crest of a wave, after playing the starring role in United's only trophy-winning campaign of 1994/95. He made the FA Youth Cup final against Spurs his own by scoring a goal in each of the two legs and the crucial penalty in the Old Trafford shoot-out in front of more than 20,000 fans. During that run, he benefited from switching to a centre forward's role. But now Cookie's back in his usual right-wing position and pushing for a first-team place.

He made his only start for the seniors against Bolton on 16 September 1995, when the Wanderers were found wanting on the backfoot as Terry streaked past them with electrifying pace. A cheeky flick and cross set Giggsy up for a goal and thrust Terry into the *Match of the Day* spotlight, his skills earning praise from Alan Hansen. The former Liverpool captain wasn't the only one who made a mental note for the future. Ex-City manager Peter Reid also declared his admiration, and took the 19-year-old Brummie to Sunderland on loan. Keep your eyes on Terry Cooke.

FACT FILE

Born:
5 August 1976
Height: **5' 7"**
Weight: **9st 9lb**
Signed as trainee:
13 July 1992
Signed Professional:
1 July 1994
United League debut:
16 September 1995 | Bolton Wanderers (h)

1995/96 RECORD

2(5) apps | 1 goal

MANCHESTER UNITED RECORD

2(5) apps | 1 goal

Squad Number: 18 | Midfielder

SIMON DAVIES

PROFILE

    1995/96 was a frustrating campaign for the Cheshire-born midfielder Simon Davies, who spent most of the time kicking his heels in the Reserves. He did come up for some first-team air as a sub on several occasions, but he only made two starts: in the goalless draw with Sheffield Wednesday at Hillsborough, and in the match the fans preferred to forget: 0–3 at home to York City.

    Simon's talents are a long way from being forgotten or overlooked, but it's difficult to bed down in a house crammed full of midfield talent. Few pros would relish the challenge of having to outbid Ryan Giggs, Lee Sharpe, David Beckham and Ben Thornley for a spot in the first team, and that's the size of Simon's task if he decides to persevere at the club he's been with for the last six years. Perhaps his route to fame and fortune will require a detour via the international scene; he increased his chances of being capped by declaring himself to be Welsh, making himself available for Bobby Gould's brave new regime.

FACT FILE

Born: **23 April 1974 | Middlewich**

Height: **6' 0"**

Weight: **11st 8lb**

Signed as trainee: **9 July 1990**

Signed Professional: **1 July 1992**

United League debut: **19 November 1994 | Crystal Palace (h)**

1995/96 RECORD

0(2) apps | 0 goals

MANCHESTER UNITED RECORD

10(8) apps | 1 goal

INTERNATIONAL RECORD

1 app | 0 goals | Wales
Debut:
24 April 1996 | Switzerland

Squad Number: 13 | Goalkeeper

TONY COTON

PROFILE

    The £500,000 signing of Tony Coton in January 1996 came out of the blue... literally. The keeper's cross-town switch from City to United raised more than a few eyebrows, particularly in the Blue half of the City. Many questioned the wisdom of Tony's decision to swap the shadow of one international goalkeeper – Germany's Eike Immel – for the shadow of another. But Tony merely shrugged and said: "You don't turn Manchester United down."

    The call for Coton, a veteran of nearly 500 League appearances for Birmingham, Watford and City, came when Alex Ferguson weighed up the fitness of Peter Schmeichel and decided he needed experienced cover for his number one. Gary Walsh had moved to Boro and Kevin Pilkington was the oldest of the club's five other keepers, at the tender age of 21. Fergie looked across the city to Moss Side to see that TC, fully recovered from a career-threatening injury, was twiddling his thumbs. The name of Les Sealey rang a few bells for both parties. As Tony said himself, he didn't need to be asked twice.

FACT FILE

Born:
19 May 1961 | Tamworth

Height: **6' 2"**

Weight: **13st 7lb**

Joined United: **18 January 1996 from Manchester City**

Transfer fee: **£500,000**

United League debut: **None to date**

Previous clubs: **Birmingham City | Watford Manchester City**

1995/96 RECORD

0 apps | 0 clean sheets

PAT McGIBBON

PROFILE

The Red hearts of the home support bled for Pat McGibbon when his debut against York City ended in disaster after 48 minutes. The young Northern Ireland international tripped the lively Paul Barnes and turned to see referee Jim Rushton's red card ushering him away. It was a cruel twist, but in keeping with the spirit of a night where nothing seemed to go right for Manchester United.

Signed from Portadown in August 1992, Pat was close to a recall at Christmas when United prepared to face Newcastle without Bruce and Pallister. "Pat is big and quick and certainly wouldn't be overawed by the importance of the occasion," said Fergie. On the night, however, a new pairing of David May and Gary Neville kept Kevin Keegan's men at bay. The subsequent return to fitness of Bruce and Pallister reduced Pat's chances of making amends in the first team, although his fine performances for the Reserves kept him in the frame. He made a solid partnership with Colin Murdock in the centre of defence as Jim Ryan's team homed in on the Pontin's League title.

FACT FILE

Born:
6 September 1973 | Lurgan
Height: **6' 1"**
Weight: **13st 2lb**
Joined United:
1 August 1992 from Portadown, N Ireland
Transfer fee:
£500,000
United League debut:
None to date
1 app | 0 goals

1 app | 0 goals
INTERNATIONAL RECORD

4 apps | 0 goals
Team: Northern Ireland
Debut: **22 May 1995 |**
Canada

Squad Number: 30 | Defender

JOHN O'KANE

PROFILE

John was among the first 13 United players to wear the grey change strip in the heat of a League battle, coming on as sub in the first match of the season at Aston Villa. The 3–1 defeat was no reflection on John's defensive abilities – they were already three goals down when he joined the fray.

John reappeared at right back against Rotor on another day of disappointment as the Reds tumbled out of the UEFA Cup. The defence was stripped of three international full backs – Paul Parker, Gary Neville and Denis Irwin were all out injured. so John stepped up to fill the gap. Conceding two goals in the first half gave United a mountain to climb and the manager had to gamble by throwing in some extra forwards. O'Kane and Beckham were replaced by Scholes and Cooke; the tactic nearly worked as United drew level, only to bow out on the away-goals rule.

John didn't feature in the first team again in 1995/96; instead he returned to the Reserves to aid their successful League campaign.

FACT FILE

Born:
15 November 1974 | Nottingham
Height: **5'10"**
Weight: **12st 2lb**
Signed as trainee:
8 July 1991
Signed Professional:
23 January 1993
United League debut:
19 August 1995 v Villa (a)
Previous clubs:
None
1995/96 RECORD

1(1) apps | 0 goals
MANCHESTER UNITED RECORD

3(2) apps | 0 goals

Squad Number: 25 | Goalkeeper

KEVIN PILKINGTON

PROFILE

Kevin is another young player who could be forgiven for feeling a bit bemused by the club's use of its spending power. The signing of Tony Coton pushed Kevin down the goalkeeping ladder – where he had been tucked just behind Peter Schmeichel – but not before he had taken over when the Great Dane made a false start against Tottenham Hotspur on New Year's Day 1996. He also played in home draws against Chelsea, Sheffield Wednesday and Sunderland, and in the ill-fated Coca-Cola Cup match against York City.

Kevin was sent out to face some more Endsleigh strikers when he was loaned to Third Division Rochdale in February, on the condition that he would be used by 'Dale in first-team matches. Alex Ferguson had already witnessed the positive effect of the "Endsleigh experience" when David Beckham and Ben Thornley came back from loan toughened up by life in the lower divisions. It's hoped that Kevin's stint at Spotland will stand him in similarly good stead whenever he's next called up to protect the United goal.

FACT FILE

Born:
8 March 1974 | Hitchin
Height: **6' 2"**
Weight: **13st 0lbs**
Signed Professional:
1 July 1992
United League debut:
**19 November 1994 v
Crystal Palace (h)**

1995/96 RECORD

4(1) apps | 0 clean sheets

MANCHESTER UNITED RECORD

4(2) apps | 1 clean sheet

Squad Number: 29 | Midfielder

BEN THORNLEY

PROFILE

Football has been rather cruel to Ben Thornley since his debut for Manchester United in the club's illustrious double-winning season. The talented winger has had to grit his teeth on the long, hard route back from injury, but the damage to cruciate ligaments in his knee was initially so grave that it's no surprise to see him take each game as it comes with a big, beaming, cheery grin.

Ben has slid down a few snakes in the last couple of years, but he's now game to climb a few more ladders and put some pressure on his old mate from Salford Schoolboys, Ryan Giggs. He used loan spells with Stockport County and Huddersfield Town in 1995/96 to remind us of his potential, crossing the ball well with both feet and showing an electric turn of pace. Whether he can make it all the way back into the United first team remains to be seen, but there are plenty of other clubs who would jump at the chance to have Ben running down their left wing. Stockport manager Dave Jones says: "If Alex Ferguson ever decided to sell him, we'd be first in the queue."

FACT FILE

Born:
21 April 1975 | Bury
Height: **5' 9"**
Weight: **11st 12lb**
Signed as trainee:
8 July 1991
Signed Professional:
23 January 1993
United League debut:
**26 February 1994 |
West Ham Utd (a)**

1995/96 RECORD

0(1) apps | 0 goals

MANCHESTER UNITED RECORD

0(2) apps | 0 goals

PHILIP MULRYNE

PROFILE

Manchester United's tradition of breeding fine wingers shows no sign of ending if lads like Phil Mulryne are still coming through. A regular in the A team's number 11 shirt and Belfast-born, Phil may yet have to endure comparisons with the finest winger of them all, George Best.

For now, Eric Harrison is likening him to a more recent model in the form of Ben Thornley. Like Ben, Phil is a right-footer plying his trade on the left wing. Eric says: "He's very talented, he can dribble and cross with either foot. He's a good prospect."

As early as his first year with United, Phil's prospects looked good. He broke into the FA Youth Cup team and scored twice *en route* to the 1995 FA Youth Cup. In the Lancashire League, he netted five in 11 appearances for Pop Robson's B team.

In 1995/96 he stepped up to the Reserves, playing his first full match in the Pontin's League during March. Later that month, he joined Reserve team defenders Pat McGibbon and Colin Murdock in the Northern Ireland B squad for a game against Norway.

Following in Keith Gillespie's footsteps would be a good plan. A Youth Cup winner with the Reds in 1992, Keith is now one of Northern Ireland's most exciting players. United fans bemoaned Keith's loss to Newcastle; it would be a shame if Phil also has to move on to find first-team football.

FACT FILE

Born: **1 January 1978 | Belfast**

Height: **5' 9"**

Weight: **10st 0lb**

Signed as trainee: **11 July 1994**

Signed Professional: **17 March 1995**

1995/96 RECORD

RESERVES
3(1) apps | 0 goals

A TEAM
25 apps | 9 goals

B TEAM

Northern Ireland B
INTERNATIONAL TEAM

MICHAEL CLEGG

PROFILE

Still in his teens, Michael Clegg has already earned the highest of accolades at Old Trafford: he has been mentioned in Brian McClair's diary for the club magazine ("Cleggy takes another victim: Jason Wilcox leaves the field after he treads on his toe!").

Michael knows that the bigger they are, the harder they fall: he made a habit of humbling experienced wingers in the 1995/96 Pontins' League campaign. A regular at right back in the Reserves, his best position is arguably in the centre of defence. But, like Gary Neville, modest Michael's not blessed with the tallest of frames, and he may have to settle for a place on either flank. It didn't do Gary any harm – just ask Terry Venables!

In the FA Youth Cup triumph of 1995, Michael was a quietly confident key member of the cup-winning team, and helped tame Tottenham's lively young forwards in the second leg of the final at Old Trafford. Eric Harrison calls Clegg's contribution during that Cup run "outstanding" and sees him as "a determined character and a solid defender."

To crown his 1995/96 season, Michael dented the scoresheet in a match for the A team. Eric Harrison laughed: "Michael's only played two games for us this season, so one in two isn't bad for a full back!"

FACT FILE

Born: **3 July 1977 | Tameside**

Height: **5' 8"**

Weight: **10st 12lb**

Signed as trainee: **5 July 1993**

Signed Professional: **1 July 1995**

1995/96 RECORD

RESERVES
22(4) apps | 0 goals

A TEAM
2 apps | 1 goal

B TEAM

RONNIE WALLWORK

PROFILE

Local lad Ronnie Wallwork joined Manchester United after leaving school in the summer of 1994. By the summer of 1995, the stocky defender had picked up his first winners' medal after forcing his way into the FA Youth Cup side. Predominantly a B team League player in his first season, Ronnie caught the eye in the Cup. In the fifth round, he scored against Villa in a youth game described by Eric Harrison as "the best that I've seen for a couple of years".

In 1992, United's Youth Cup-winning team contained no less than nine players who went on to play for the first team, including Ryan Giggs and Gary Neville. The class of '95 has so far yielded Terry Cooke and Phil Neville, and Ronnie Wallwork is one player who should follow them into the senior ranks.

Ronnie has already played for England many times. As a schoolboy he was a key member of the Under-16 team, and since then he's been capped at Under-18 level.

"I don't see many better players at that age than Ronnie," says Eric Harrison. "He's the sort of modern centre half you need."

In the 1995/96 season Ronnie was a mainstay of the A team defence, but he also made a handful of appearances for the Reserves. In April he collected United's Young Player of the Year award. Promotion for Ronnie could be just around the corner.

FACT FILE

Born: **10 September 1977 | Manchester**

Height: **5" 11"**

Weight: **12st 0lb**

Signed as trainee:
11 July 1994

Signed Professional:
17 March 1995

1995/96 RECORD

RESERVES
4(2) apps | 1 goal

A TEAM
24 apps | 5 goals

England Under-18s
INTERNATIONAL TEAM

DES BAKER

PROFILE

With two players in the first team, two in the Reserves and two at Youth level, the Irish are still well represented at Manchester United, a club worshipped like no other in the Emerald Isle.

One up-and-coming Irish Youth star is centre foward Des Baker. He is rapidly developing the same goalscoring knack as Paul Scholes, arguably the best goalpoacher to emerge from the youth academy in recent years. In his first year as a trainee, Baker scored 18 goals in 21 appearances for the B team. He was also a regular in the 1995 FA Youth Cup-winning team.

Des played a handful of games for the Reserves in 1995/96 but he was chiefly employed as a frontline leader by the A team and Youth team. Even though he was only 18 himself, Des had the look of a mature and experienced player, especially when he made a brief return to the B team to score four goals in a 5–1 win over Burnley in September.

"Quite simply, he puts the ball in the net. That's what he's best at," says Youth team coach Eric Harrison. "He's always been a consistent goalscorer, right the way through school, junior football in Ireland and now over here. You always need someone like Des in your team."

The day when the first team needs someone like Des Baker may not be far away.

FACT FILE

Born: **25 August 1977 | Dublin**

Height: **5' 7"**

Weight: **11st 0lb**

Signed as trainee:
5 July 1993

Signed Professional:
25 August 1994

1995/96 RECORD

RESERVES
8(5) apps | 2 goals

A TEAM
14(6) apps | 8 goals

B TEAM
1 app | 4 goals

INTERNATIONAL TEAM

Eire Under-18s

ALEX FERGUSON

PROFILE

When the 1995/96 season began without a cent being spent to replace Sparky, Incey and Kan-kan, we were left in a state of anxious concern. Of course, we should have realised that the manager had a plan as bold and brilliant as the football his teams play. We should have had faith. After all, faith is Fergie's greatest management tool. He proved in 1995/96 that, with the right players, faith will be rewarded – and just look at the proof.

He believed he could rebuild the team with a group of youngsters and lay foundations for the future. Sure enough, Butt, Beckham and the brothers Neville rewarded his trust, taking to the first team like ducks to water and then some. He entrusted to Keane and Butt the ball-winning role vacated by Incey and was repaid by their dominance of midfield battles throughout the season. He gave Giggsy the freedom of the pitch and watched as the Welsh wizard refound his sparkling form. He stuck with Andy Cole through thick and thin and reaped the dividends as the once out-and-out striker developed his all-round game until it was unrecognisable from the season before.

And then of course there was Eric. If anyone needed careful handling Eric was the one. Overseeing his comeback required the manager's paternal guidance, a lot of patience and, above all, faith. Once again the gamble paid off with huge dividends, and surely Eric's Player of the Year award was due to Fergie's genius as well as his own.

FACT FILE

Born:
31 December 1941 | Govan

Previous clubs as player:
Dunfermline Athletic
Glasgow Rangers | Falkirk
Ayr United

Previous clubs as manager:
East Stirling | St Mirren
Aberdeen | Scotland

HONOURS WITH MANCHESTER UNITED

FA Cup 1990 | FA Cup 1994
European Cup Winners'
Cup 1991
European Super Cup 1991
Football League Cup 1992
FA Premier League 1993
FA Premier League 1994
FA Charity Shield 1993
FA Charity Shield 1994

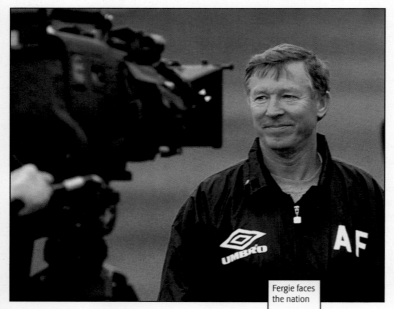

Fergie faces the nation

Taking Sir Matt's philosophy into the Nineties, Fergie regularly fielded sides with an average age in the low 20s, so this team could stay together for years. If you consider the results of the 1995/96 season came during a transitional period, who would bet against Fergie's Fledglings achieving as much success as the Busby Babes? To have your team mentioned in the same sentence as the Babes is achievement enough, but with Fergie's vision and such young talent at his command, such success should soon become a reality.

BRIAN KIDD

PROFILE

Nominated by Alex Ferguson as his likely successor to the Old Trafford hot seat, Brian Kidd has been an important cog in the United winning machine of the Nineties. Kiddo experienced the finest moment of his playing career on his 19th birthday, when he scored the clincher in United's historic 1968 European Cup triumph over Benfica. Perhaps he never realised his early potential as a player, but his fascination with the techniques of the game unlocked a rewarding new career at the end of his playing days.

One of Alex Ferguson's biggest tasks when he took on the United manager's job was to instil a stronger work ethic in the players, and Kiddo was the man to assist him. Brian's time at Old Trafford began as a PFA-sponsored talent-spotter. His restless enthusiasm for developing gifted young players and his imaginative training methods impressed Fergie enough to appoint him as his assistant in 1991. Brian has become the Boss's trusted confidant, often leading scouting missions and travelling abroad with Ferguson to seek out alternative training routines.

United's think-tank

Modest and shy of the media limelight, Brian feels most at home at the Cliff, United's training ground. A confirmed fitness freak, Kiddo regularly goes on individual five-mile runs after training, and bran flakes and baked beans are his favoured snacks.

His expertise at disguising long runs as something more exciting has fooled many United players into improving their fitness. Not Brian McClair, however, who regularly launches bitter tirades against him within the pages of the club's official magazine. After being described by Choccy as Sergeant Kiddo and pictured as a martinet, Kiddo gets his own back at the Cliff.

Seriously though, Brian commands the respect of all the players and deserves a lot of credit for ending the flabby, complacent attitudes of United squads in the late Seventies and early Eighties.

FACT FILE

Born:
29 April 1949 | Manchester

Signed for United as player:
June 1996

Other clubs as player:
Arsenal | Manchester City
Everton | Bolton Wanderers
Atlanta Chiefs, USA
Fort Lauderdale Strikers, USA
Minnesota Kicks, USA

Managerial/coaching career:
Preston North End |
Manchester United B team,
1989 | Manchester United
Youth Development, 1990 |
Manchester United assistant
manager, 1991

MANCHESTER UNITED RECORD
255 apps | 70 goals

INTERNATIONAL RECORD

2 apps
Team: **England**

MANCHESTER UNITED
RESERVES

TEAM REPORT

United's strength in depth was there for all to see as the Reserves clinched their second Pontin's League title in three years. The team sheet for the decisive 2–0 win over Newcastle United was a typical mix of fresh and familiar names. "We've had the full spectrum of players from the club playing for the Reserves this season," reports coach Jim Ryan. "It's really a credit to all of them, in particular the senior professionals like Paul Parker and Brian McClair. The way they have played and behaved in the Reserve team has been terrific."

The Reds made certain of their prize at Gigg Lane, their home venue for much of the season. Once again, United were grateful to Bury Football Club for their hospitality, even if the pitch didn't always suit their passing style. The coach admits the team generally played better football away from home. "When we've played away on nice pitches, we've controlled the game with our passing," says Jim. "But even on the bad pitches we've adjusted our play to be effective. The team's performances have been good all season."

Jim picks out the away match at Leeds, played on The Shay ground at Halifax, as a key highlight. "It was an absolutely smashing game played at a fantastic pace," he enthuses. "We imposed our style on the game against a fairly experienced team, and although we had a few narrow escapes around the goalmouth, we won it in the end because we kept playing football."

At one stage, United's brand of attacking play brought them seven successive wins. This glorious run started in early January and ended in March with a disappointing 2–1 defeat at Derby. "I felt we had played well enough to certainly get a draw out of the game," says Jim. "But those things will always happen during a season and maybe it's good for the young players, because part of their

SCORERS

Jovan Kirovski	16
Terry Cooke	10
Graeme Tomlinson	8
Michael Appleton	3
Paul Scholes	3
Ryan Giggs	2
Pat McGibbon	2
Chris Casper	2
Lee Sharpe	2
Des Baker	2
John O'Kane	2
Ben Thornley	2
Simon Davies	2
Own goals	2
Ronnie Wallwork	1
Brian McClair	1
Jamie Wood	1
David Beckham	1
Neil Mustoe	1
Gary Neville	1

PONTIN'S LEAGUE 1995/96   RESULTS

Date	Opponent	Venue	Score	Date	Opponent	Venue	Score
16 Aug	Bolton Wanderers Res	Home	3-0	9 Jan	Everton Res	Away	1-0
30 Aug	Nottingham County Res	Home	2-2	17 Jan	Liverpool Res	Home	2-1
2 Sep	Liverpool Res	Away	2-3	24 Jan	Bolton Wanderers Res	Away	2-0
6 Sep	Blackburn Rovers Res	Away	1-1	31 Jan	Blackburn Rovers Res	Home	2-1
27 Sep	Oldham Athletic Res	Away	2-0	15 Feb	Everton Res	Home	2-0
7 Oct	Leeds United Res	Home	2-0	26 Feb	Sheffield United Res	Away	3-0
11 Oct	West Brom Albion Res	Away	4-2	7 Mar	Sheffield Wednesday Res	Home	2-1
18 Oct	Birmingham City Res	Home	3-0	19 Mar	Derby County Res	Away	1-2
25 Oct	Nottingham Forest Res	Away	1-1	28 Mar	Stoke City Res	Away	1-1
1 Nov	Shefield Wednesday Res	Away	3-5	4 Apr	Notts County Res	Away	1-0
15 Nov	Sheffield United Res	Home	6-0	10 Apr	West Brom Albion Res	Home	4-1
20 Nov	Wolves Wanderers Res	Home	2-0	20 Apr	Nottingham Forest Res	Home	4-0
29 Nov	Tranmere Rovers Res	Away	3-1	22 Apr	Birmingham City Res	Away	0-1
6 Dec	Leeds United Res	Away	2-1	24 Apr	Newcastle United Res	Home	2-0
11 Dec	Oldham Athletic Res	Home	2-2	29 Apr	Stoke City Res	Home	1-0
20 Dec	Derby County Res	Home	3-1	1 May	Tranmere Rovers Res	Home	9-9
3 Jan	Newcastle United Res	Away	0-2	6 May	Wolves Wanderers Res	Away	8-7

football education is learning how to handle defeat."

The Reserves handled the defeat well enough to pick up 10 points from the next 12 on offer. A 1–1 draw at Stoke City followed by wins over Notts County, West Brom and Nottingham Forest moved them ever closer, and a 4–0 drubbing of Forest at Old Trafford summed up the difference between winning and losing titles. "This season we've had goals from a lot of different people, whereas last year we weren't getting them," says Jim.

Among those who chipped in a few goals was this year's Reserve team Player of the Year, Michael Appleton. "Michael's had a good season; he also picked up an A team winner's medal," says Jim. "He's been quite versatile for me, and wherever he's played he's had a real go at it."

The near future could well see some young Reserve players like Michael having a go with the big boys in the Premiership. The team's displays in the Pontin's League suggest they're up to the task.

PONTINS LEAGUE DIVISION ONE
as at 7 May 1996

	P	W	D	L	F	A	Pts
Manchester United	34	22	5	7	71	35	71
Derby County	33	17	9	7	58	42	60
Stoke City	34	17	8	9	57	42	59
Leeds United	32	16	8	8	39	29	56
Tranmere Rovers	33	17	4	12	70	60	55
Liverpool	33	15	8	10	55	42	53
Everton	33	14	9	10	49	40	51
Bolton	34	12	9	13	51	52	45
Newcastle United	34	13	6	15	55	59	45
Oldham Athletic	33	11	10	11	50	52	44
Birmingham City	34	13	5	16	57	64	44
Sheffield Wednesday	33	11	8	14	66	62	41
Nottingham Forest	33	11	8	14	43	55	41
Blackburn Rovers	33	9	12	12	48	44	39
Sheffield United	34	8	13	13	40	61	37
Wolves Wanderers	34	10	5	19	42	48	35
Notts County	33	9	7	17	46	59	34
West Bromwich Albion	33	5	5	23	33	84	20

At the time of going to print, some teams had not completed their fixtures, but United's position in the League was guaranteed.

The Reserves celebrate League victory

MANCHESTER UNITED
YOUTH TEAMS

TEAM REPORTS

A TEAM: The A team extended Eric Harrison's haul of honours by retaining the Lancashire League Championship. The team's record under Eric's guiding hand – nine titles and four runner-up spots – is truly phenomenal. But the coach's obvious delight is still tempered with caution.

"Once you think you've cracked it," he says sagely, "You're on a slippery slope. We're all sensible enough to realise that we've got to keep digging in all the time."

This year the A team had to dig that little bit deeper, with eight more games to play than last season. They were pushed all the way to the summit by Crewe Alexandra and Stoke City Reserves, who both took maximum points from United. "They're both strong, very formidable sides so we've certainly done well to win it this year," chirps Eric.

Crewe, Stoke, Burnley and Everton all took their turn at the top until United's young lads gained control in the home straight. The Reds clinched it with a clinical performance at Bury A, which was typical of the whole campaign in that goals were shared out.

"All the time I've been here, the goals have been spread out," says Eric. "It's a good thing in many ways, but it's still a mystery to me why nobody scores more than 30 for us in a season!"

COMBINED YOUTH TEAM: Players from the A and B teams joined forces to bring home the Lancashire Youth Cup for the third time in four years, despite being "outplayed" by Blackburn Rovers in the final at Ewood Park. From 2–0 down, the Reds roared back with goals from Ryan Ford, Jonathan Macken and Grant Brebner.

The triumph went some way to making up for the massive disappointment of losing to Liverpool – the eventual winners – in the FA Youth Cup quarter final at Anfield.

A TEAM SCORERS

Michael Twiss	9
Philip Mulryne	9
Des Baker	8
Tommy Smith	6
Ronnie Wallwork	5
Jonathon Macken	5
David Brown	4
Ben Thornley	3
John O'Kane	2
Neil Mustoe	2
Terry Cooke	2
Grant Brebner	2
Mark Wilson	2
Alex Notman	2
Jovan Kirovski	2
Jamie Wood	2
Danny Hall	1
Michael Appleton	1
Graeme Tomlinson	1
Michael Clegg	1
Own goal	1

B TEAM SCORERS

Alex Notman	21
David Brown	19
Jamie Wood	13
Mark Wilson	7
Jonathon Macken	6
Gary Bickerton	5
Des Baker	4
David Healey	3
Jonathon Phillips	3
Gavin Naylor	3
Ross Millard	2
Jamie Byers	2
Tommy Smith	2
Ryan Ford	2
Alan Griffin	2
Grant Brebner	2
Stuart Brightwell	1
Richard Wellens	1
Danny Higginbotham	1
Michael Twiss	1
Robert Trees	1
Own goal	1

LANCS DIVISION ONE
as at 7 May 1996

	P	W	D	L	F	A	Pts
Manchester United A	30	21	3	6	70	22	66
Stoke City A	30	19	6	5	66	27	63
Crewe Alexandra Res.	29	19	3	7	70	41	60
Everton A	30	16	6	8	70	51	54
Tranmere Rovers A	27	16	1	10	52	40	49
Burnley A	30	14	6	10	48	38	48
Blackburn Rovers A	29	13	7	9	54	39	46
Blackpool A	30	13	6	11	44	49	45
Preston North End A	30	11	8	11	45	48	41
Bury A	30	11	7	12	42	53	40
Wrexham A	30	11	6	13	68	60	39
Liverpool A	29	9	8	12	52	51	35
Oldham Athletic A	29	6	6	17	34	63	24
Manchester City A	30	5	6	19	30	58	21
Morecambe Reserves	30	5	5	20	39	82	20
Marine Reserves	29	4	2	23	20	82	14

LANCS DIVISION TWO
as at 7 May 1996

	P	W	D	L	F	A	Pts
Blackburn Rovers B	36	28	4	4	90	27	88
Manchester United B	36	25	6	5	104	39	81
Manchester City B	36	24	8	4	74	26	80
Liverpool B	35	22	2	11	90	43	68
Bolton Wanderers A	35	20	8	7	72	46	68
Crewe Alexandra A	35	20	4	11	82	53	64
Carlisle United A	36	18	9	9	74	46	63
Burnley B	36	15	5	16	61	66	50
Everton B	36	13	9	14	79	62	48
Tranmere Rovers B	35	14	5	16	47	57	47
Preston North End B	36	12	8	16	58	78	44
Chester City A	36	11	10	15	57	63	43
Blackpool B	36	11	8	17	48	72	41
Oldham Athletic B	36	9	11	16	44	62	38
Wigan Athletic A	36	9	9	18	56	71	36
Stockport Town A	36	10	5	21	39	76	35
Marine Youth	36	5	6	25	23	102	21
Rochdale A	36	5	5	26	41	93	20
Bury B	34	3	8	23	30	84	17

At the time of going to print, some teams had not completed their fixtures, but United's position in each League was guaranteed.

A TEAM RESULTS
LANCASHIRE LEAGUE DIVISION ONE

Date	Opponent	H/A	Score		Date	Opponent	H/A	Score
19 Aug	Morecambe Reserves	Home	8-0		13 Jan	Crewe Alexandra Reserves	Away	0-2
26 Aug	Tranmere Rovers A	Home	0-0		20 Jan	Blackburn Rovers A	Away	5-0
2 Sep	Blackburn Rovers A	Home	1-1		3 Feb	Manchester City A	Away	1-0
9 Sep	Blackpool A	Away	2-1		17 Feb	Oldham Athletic A	Home	3-0
16 Sep	Wrexham A	Home	3-2		24 Feb	Marine Reserves	Home	3-1
7 Oct	Crewe Alexandra Reserves	Home	0-1		2 Mar	Bury A	Home	2-0
14 Oct	Tranmere Rovers A	Away	2-0		9 Mar	Burnley A	Away	0-1
21 Oct	Everton A	Home	5-1		16 Mar	Preston North End A	Away	2-1
28 Oct	Stoke City A	Away	0-2		23 Mar	Everton A	Away	2-0
11 Nov	Marine Reserves	Away	6-1		30 Mar	Burnley A	Home	2-1
18 Nov	Manchester City A	Home	0-0		6 Apr	Stoke City A	Home	1-3
24 Nov	Morecambe Reserves	Away	2-0		17 Apr	Liverpool A	Away	2-0
2 Dec	Wrexham A	Away	2-0		20 Apr	Oldham Athletic A	Away	2-1
16 Dec	Liverpool A	Home	3-1		24 Apr	Bury A	Away	6-1
6 Jan	Preston North End A	Home	5-0		27 Apr	Blackpool A	Home	0-1

B TEAM RESULTS
LANCASHIRE LEAGUE DIVISION TWO

Date	Opponent	H/A	Score		Date	Opponent	H/A	Score
19 Aug	Preston North End B	Home	2-2		6 Jan	Marine Youth	Away	4-0
21 Aug	Bolton Wanderers A	Away	5-2		13 Jan	Rochdale A	Away	1-1
26 Aug	Rochdale A	Home	6-1		20 Jan	Wigan A	Home	3-2
30 Aug	Blackburn Rovers B	Home	1-1		10 Feb	Manchester City B	Home	0-1
2 Sep	Stockport A	Away	1-1		17 Feb	Everton B	Home	0-3
16 Sep	Oldham Athletic B	Home	2-0		24 Feb	Liverpool B	Away	1-3
23 Sep	Burnley B	Home	5-1		2 Mar	Bury B	Away	3-1
7 Oct	Liverpool B	Home	4-2		9 Mar	Carlisle A	Home	2-1
14 Oct	Blackburn Rovers B	Away	1-3		16 Mar	Tranmere Rovers B	Away	1-0
21 Oct	Blackpool B	Home	6-0		23 Mar	Carlisle A	Away	4-1
28 Oct	Wigan A	Away	3-2		30 Mar	Burnley B	Away	4-1
4 Nov	Bury B	Home	5-0		4 Apr	Everton B	Away	3-1
11 Nov	Manchester City B	Away	2-0		6 Apr	Chester City A	Home	2-1
18 Nov	Crewe Alexandra A	Home	2-2		13 Apr	Preston North End B	Away	3-0
25 Nov	Oldham Athletic B	Away	2-0		16 Apr	Stockport County A	Home	2-0
2 Dec	Carlisle A	Home	0-0		20 Apr	Bolton Wanderers A	Home	6-1
9 Dec	Chester City A	Away	0-2		27 Apr	Marine Youth	Home	7-0
16 Dec	Tranmere Rovers B	Home	5-1		4 May	Blackpool B	Away	6-1

B TEAM: If Neil Bailey's first season in charge didn't end with a title, it certainly ended in style. The B team won all of their last 12 matches, including eight aways, and recorded a over century of goals for the season. But they were still beaten to the Division Two title by a clear points margin. "It just illustrates the standards you've got to keep up at this place," says Neil. "They're disappointed when you finish second!" A barren spell of three defeats in February effectively ended their hopes of winning the League for the first time since 1989, even though they were unstoppable in March, April and May, playing some fine football. "To beat Bolton 6–1 in April was a good performance," praises Neil. "Right from the first minute they were ready to prove a point."

Earlier in the season, there were times when the defenders had to shine just as brightly as the goalscorers.

"One example was the Manchester City game away where we won 2–0. The lads in defence really earned their corn that day."

The first years have still got plenty of corn to earn, but nobody can deny they've made a very promising start to their United careers.

Start as you mean to go on: the triumphant A team Champs

THE OPPOSITION

NEWCASTLE UTD

Magpies | Founded 1881

FACT FILE

Stadium: **St James' Park** | **Newcastle-upon-Tyne** | **NE14ST**

Capacity: **36,649**

Record attendance: **3 September 1930** | **68,386 v Chelsea** | **Division 1**

Club number: **0191 262 8361**

Tickets: **0191 261 1571**

Ticket prices: **Adult: £12–£20 Child/Senior citizen: £11.50–£20**

Nearest BR station: **Newcastle Central**

TEAM LINE-UP

Shaka Hislop | Pavel Srnicek | Darren Peacock | Philippe Albert | John Beresford | Steve Howey | Warren Barton Robert Lee | David Batty Keith Gillespie | David Ginola Les Ferdinand | Peter Beardsley | Paul Kitson Steve Watson | Faustino Asprilla | Lee Clark | Robbie Elliott | Darren Huckerby

TEAM REPORT

With Chairman Hall's flexible friend on his side, how could Kevin Keegan fail? Over the past two seasons, manager Keegan has been able to transform his team through a process of ruthless replacement (Ferdinand for Cole, Ginola for Fox, Albert for Venison) and inspired acquisitions (Barton, Gillespie, Hislop, Asprilla). The squad in the 1994/95 season had flair and started exceptionally. But come the inevitable mid-season injuries and front-running inexperience, the team floundered, and in May missed out on a place in Europe.

1995/96 saw a new depth to the squad. While they kept their attacking flair, there was an added steeliness that had been sorely missed before. With Albert marshalling one of the most economic defences in the League and the arrival of Blackburn ball-winner David Batty to add realism to their fantasy football, Newcastle started saving those games in which they played poorly. All channels – Beresford and Ginola down the left, Barton and Gillespie down the right, Beardsley, Lee and, eventually, Asprilla down the middle – led to one man. Les Ferdinand, PFA Player of the Year, got the season he deserved, finally rewarded with service equal to his striking talent after all those loyal but lonely years with the Superhoops.

The team faltered towards the end of the season and lost to a passionate Manchester United both home and away. With a team-sheet that would not look out of place in Milan, the Magpies have every right to look forward to next season in Europe with high expectations.

STAR PLAYER

FAUSTINO ASPRILLA

1995/96 RECORD

HOME TEAM SCORE SHOWN FIRST

Final League position: **2nd**

Cup results:
**R3 | Chelsea (h) | 1–1
R3R | Chelsea (a) | 2–2
(Chelsea won 4–2 pens)**

Top Scorer:
Les Ferdinand | 25

RESULTS v MANCHESTER UNITED

Old Trafford:
26 December 1995 | 2–0

St James' Park:
4 March 1996 | 0–1

Black and white and red all over

LIVERPOOL

Reds or Pool | Founded 1892

FACT FILE

Stadium:
Anfield | Anfield Road | Liverpool | L4 0TH

Capacity: **41,000**

Record attendance:
2 February 1952 | 61,905 v Wolves | FA Cup

Club number: **0151 263 2361**

Tickets: **0151 260 8680**

Ticket prices: **Adult: £15**
Family (adult + child): £22.50

Nearest BR station:
Kirkdale

TEAM LINE-UP

David James | Rob Jones | Jason McAteer | Mark Wright Phil Babb | Stan Collymore | John Barnes | John Scales | Jamie Redknapp | Michael Stensgaard | Michael Thomas Steve McManaman | Phil Charnock | Mark Kennedy Stig Inge Bjornebye | Steve Harkness | Dominic Matteo Robbie Fowler | Lee Jones | Neil Ruddock | Tony Warner

TEAM REPORT

The sad death of Bob Paisley this year brought back memories of an era in which Liverpool were, quite simply, the best football team in the world. It's fitting that one of the boot-room boys of that era has been responsible for the renaissance of the Liverpool team from the stale, smug mediocrity of the Sounness regime to the sparkling enthusiasm of the 1995/96 side. In two seasons he has rebuilt virtually the entire squad, not only with bright young talent but, more importantly, with players who are proud to pull on the red shirt. Even Stan Collymore (at the time of his transfer, at £8.5 million the most expensive player in British history) came through a phase of sulking to show a genuine desire to play for this team. His relationship with the ebullient Fowler (at the cost of legendary Ian Rush) has blossomed to the point that both are just as happy to assist as to strike.

The midfield is a rich mixture of old and new, in which Barnes, McManaman, Thomas and Redknapp combine with growing confidence. There are moments when the team forgets that a single pass can be more dangerous than 20 and their intricate triangular passing becomes ineffective. But on their day, they are irrepressible – as United discovered to their cost when they were beaten 2–0 at Anfield in December. Fowler was the outstanding talent, bubbling with lethal confidence, and such confidence is justifiable when behind him stands the defensive foundation of Babb, Ruddock, Jones, Scales and Wright (who had the comeback of the year).

1995/96 was the final installment of Liverpool's transformation. If Roy Evans can keep the team together and retain its spirit, he'll take them towards the kind of success his old mentor would recognise.

1995/96 RECORD

HOME TEAM SCORES SHOWN FIRST

Final League position: **3rd**

Cup results:
R3 | Rochdale (h) | 7-0
R4 | Shrewsbury (a) | 0-4
R5| Charlton Ath (h) | 2-1
R6 | Leeds United (a) | 0-0
R6R| Leeds United (h) | 3-0
Semi | Aston Villa (OT) | 3-0

Top Scorer:
Robbie Fowler | 28

RESULTS v MANCHESTER UNITED

Old Trafford:
1 October 1995 | 2-2
Anfield: **17 Dec 1995 | 2-0**

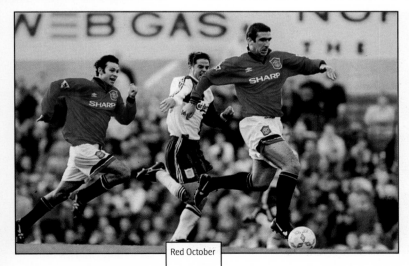

Red October

ASTON VILLA

The Villans | Founded 1874

STAR PLAYER
DWIGHT YORKE

FACT FILE

Stadium:
Villa Park | Trinity Road | Birmingham | B6 6HE

Capacity: **40,310**

Record attendance:
2 March 1946 | 76,588 v Derby County | FA Cup

Club number: **0121 327 2299**

Tickets: **0121 327 5353**

Ticket prices: **Adult: £13–£15 Child/Senior citizen: £6.50–£8**

Nearest BR station:
Witton or Aston

TEAM LINE-UP

Mark Bosnich | Ugo Ehiogu | Paul McGrath | Gareth Southgate | Gary Charles | Ian Taylor | Mark Draper | Andy Townsend | Alan Wright | Savo Milosevic | Tommy Johnson | Franz Carr | Riccardo Scimeca | Nigel Spink | Garry Parker | Julian Joachim | Bryan Small | Steve Staunton

TEAM REPORT

Since Brian Little controversially left Leicester to return to his spiritual football home, Villa have developed from relegation material into fringe Championship contenders and Coca-Cola Cup victors.

United fans will remember how the Villans denied the treble dream in 1994, when Ron Atkinson's side out-manouvred the Reds at Wembley to win 3–1 in the Coca-Cola Cup final. Inevitably, chairman "Deadly" Doug Ellis struck again in the following season to arrest Villa's slide towards the relegation zone. Big Ron was given the chop and Little's services were ruthlessly acquired.

After narrowly avoiding the drop, Villa made rapid strides last season. Little's masterstroke was to promote the effervescent Dwight Yorke to the position of out-and-out striker, a move which reaped a positive glut of goals. With players like Tommy Johnson, Mark Draper and Andy Townsend all adept at shooting from distance, opposition goalkeepers are usually kept busy. The exception came at Old Trafford in January when Villa's turgid, defensive strategy suggested their ambition was just to pinch a point. Although the goalless draw failed to inspire, it emphasised the solidity of Villa's back four, arguably the stingiest in the Premiership last season.

For Brian Little, a passionate Villa man, this job represents the pinnacle of his career and no more walk-outs are forecast. If Yorke's form holds, Serb striker Savo Milosevic finds a finishing touch to match his approach work and the defence continues to stand firm, Villa will be a match for anyone.

1995/96 RECORD

HOME TEAM SCORES SHOWN FIRST

Final League position: **4th**

Cup results:
R3 | **Gravesend (a)** | 0–3
R4 | **Sheffield Utd (a)** | 0–1
R5 | **Ipswich Town (a)** | 1–3
R6 | **Notts Forest (a)** | 0–1
Semi | **Liverpool (OT)** | 0–3

Top Scorer:
Dwight Yorke | 17

RESULTS v MANCHESTER UNITED

Villa Park:
19 August 1995 | 3–1

Old Trafford: **13 Jan 1996 | 0–0**

Give the boy a big hand

ARSENAL

Gunners | Founded 1886

FACT FILE

Stadium:
**Arsenal | Highbury |
London | N5 1BU**

Capacity: **38,500**

Record attendance:
**9 March 1935 | 73,285 v
Sunderland | Div 1**

Club number: **0171 226 0304**

Tickets: **0171 354 5404**

Ticket prices: **Visitors: £11 – £25
Child/Senior citizen: £5 – £5.50**

Underground: **Arsenal or
Highbury & Islington**

TEAM LINE-UP

David Seaman | Lee Dixon |
Nigel Winterburn | Steve Bould |
Tony Adams | David Platt | Ian
Wright | Paul Merson | Dennis
Bergkamp | Glenn Helder |
Andy Linighan | Ray Parlour |
Martin Keown | John Hartson |
David Hillier | Chris Kiwomya |
Ian Selley | Paul Dickov | Scott
Marshall | Lee Harper | Paul
Shaw | Stephen Hughes | Adrian
Clarke | Gavin McGowan

TEAM REPORT

When the Arsenal board of directors interpreted the "unsolicited Christmas gifts" George Graham received in brown paper bags from Rune Hauge as nothing less than sleazy bungs, it left a massive gap to be filled at Highbury. Whatever anyone said about Arsenal's uninspiring style of play, it was undeniable that Graham's tactics paid dividends in the form of seasonal silverware.

The man charged with saving a potentially disastrous situation was Bruce Rioch, who had masterminded Bolton Wanderers' promotion to the Premiership. He immediately made his high intentions plain with the mega-bucks purchases of Dennis Bergkamp and David Platt. Although Brucey had survived on a shoestring at Bolton, he knew he'd have to spend on quality to continue the success that Gunners fans had come to expect.

Some people may condemn Rioch's first season in charge as a failure, but that view ignores his introduction of a more watchable, attacking style. He was the first to admit that some members of the 1995/96 squad were not good enough to play the fluid pass-and-move game that he sees as the future for Arsenal, and he's not afraid to spend big money if the right player becomes available.

Two things Rioch doesn't want to lose are Arsenal's defence – which still lives up to its Scrooge-like reputation – and the potent Bergkamp/Wright partnership (which depends on Rioch and Wright resolving their differences over the summer). Lack of creativity in midfield is the major problem he inherited, and he'll hope to add craft to graft in that area this season.

STAR PLAYER

DENNIS BERGKAMP

1995/96 RECORD

HOME TEAM SCORES SHOWN FIRST

Final League position: **5th**

Cup results:
**R3 | Sheffield Utd (h) | 1 – 1
R3R | Sheffield Utd (a) | 1 – 0**

Top Scorer:
Ian Wright | 15

RESULTS v MANCHESTER UNITED

Highbury:
4 November 1995 | 1 – 0

Old Trafford:
20 March 1996 | 1 – 0

Gunner believe it

TOTTENHAM

Spurs | Founded 1882

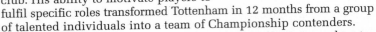

FACT FILE

Stadium:
White Hart Lane | 748 High Road | London | N17 0AP

Capacity: **35,000**

Record attendance:
5 March 1938 | 73,038 v Sunderland | FA Cup

Club number: **0181 365 5000**

Tickets: **0181 365 5050**

Ticket prices: **Adult: £15–£27**

Nearest station:
White Hart Lane or Northumberland Park

TEAM LINE-UP

Ian Walker | Dean Austin | Justin Edinburgh | David Howells | Colin Calderwood | Gary Mabbutt | Ruel Fox | Darren Anderton | Teddy Sheringham | Chris Armstrong | Jason Dozzell | Erik Thorstvedt | Sol Campbell | Stuart Nethercott | Clive Wilson | Ronny Rosenthal | Gerry McMahon | David Kerslake | Andy Sinton

TEAM REPORT

After the brief fantasy football reign of Osvaldo Ardiles when Spurs fans got "tennis spectator's neck", from their heads jerking to one side then the other as goals flew in at both ends, Gerry Francis brought much needed stability to the club. His ability to motivate players to fulfil specific roles transformed Tottenham in 12 months from a group of talented individuals into a team of Championship contenders.

As well as tightening their defensive line, Francis can now boast one of the most potent striking partnerships in the Premiership. Following Klinsmann's controversial departure a year into his two-year contract, many people thought Spurs would lack firepower. In fact, Chris Armstrong and Teddy Sheringham have, if anything, struck up an even more telepathic understanding up front.

Manchester United were given a nasty shock on New Year's Day 1996 at White Hart Lane, when an understrength Spurs blasted our boys to a shocking 4–1 defeat. Both Sheringham and Armstrong were on target in the match that convinced Alex Ferguson that William "Plum Tree" Prunier wasn't the ideal long-term replacement for Steve Bruce in central defence.

Under the more pragmatic Francis regime, Spurs have added steel to their legendary flair. It has often been said in the past that the Spurs board of directors were keener on buying crowd-pleasers than creating a winning team. The arrival of Alan Sugar has changed all that, and his ambition is shared by former England captain Francis, who craves Premiership success for his club.

STAR PLAYER

TEDDY SHERINGHAM

1995/96 RECORD

HOME TEAM SCORES SHOWN FIRST

Final League position: **8th**

Cup results:
R4 | Wolves (h) | 1–1
R4R | Wolves (a) | 0–2
R5 | Notts Forest (a) | 2–2
R5R | Notts Forest (h) | 1–1
(Notts Forest won 3–1 pens)

Top Scorer:
Teddy Sheringham | 16

RESULTS v MANCHESTER UNITED

White Hart Lane:
1 January 1996 | 4–1

Old Trafford:
24 March 1996 | 1–0

Butt and Walker in aerial combat

EVERTON

Toffees | Founded 1878

FACT FILE

Stadium: **Goodison Park |
Liverpool | L4 4EL**

Capacity: **40,180**

Record attendance:
**18 September 1948 | 78,299 v
Liverpool | FA Cup**

Club number: **0151 330 2200**

Tickets: **0151 330 2300**

Ticket prices: **Adult: £14–£17
Child/Senior citizen: £6**

Nearest BR station:
**Kirkdale or Liverpool
Lime Street**

TEAM LINE-UP

Neville Southall | Gary Ablett |
Andy Hinchcliffe | Dave Watson
David Unsworth | Graham Stuart
Paul Rideout | Duncan Ferguson
Barry Horne | Anders Limpar |
Danniel Amokachi | John Ebbrell
Mathew Jackson | Vinny
Samways | Andrei Kanchelskis |
Joe Parkinson | Mark Hottiger |
Craig Short | Graham Allan |
Mark Grugel | Christopher Price |
Andy Weathers | Mathew Woods

TEAM REPORT

Joe Royle hopes for a season with honours this time. His team failed to capitalise on Joe's first triumphant year, when the Toffees lifted the 1995 FA Cup.

The fruits of that success weren't harvested. Everton joined the rest of the British teams who failed in European club cup competitions when they lost on aggregate to the Dutch masters of Feyenoord. However, their most embarrassing result of 1995/96 must be the humiliating defeat by Port Vale in the FA Cup replay.

The big talking point at Goodison last season was the prison sentence given to Everton's £4-million signing Duncan Ferguson. The big Scottish forward put his nightmare experience behind him with some excellent performances, which helped Everton secure a solid position in the Premiership. And the recognition helped him get into the Scottish squad for the European Championship, only to be ruled out by injury.

United fans will remember Everton best for last season's acrimonious signing of ex-United favourite Andrei Kanchelskis. The unhappiness with the way he left the club was made clear at Old Trafford, when the United faithful booed the Russian constantly throughout Everton's February visit to the Theatre of Dreams. The hostile atmosphere seemed to shake the visitors and United went on to win the game. It was an unhappy reunion for Andrei with his old club, and all of us remember his horrifying early departure at Goodison Park with a bad injury the September before.

Everton have some very good players and, with a probable cash injection in the summer for new blood, Joe Royle's men are a hot prospect to win something in 1996/97.

STAR PLAYER

DUNCAN FERGUSON

Stuart and Keane gurning for glory

1995/96 RECORD

HOME TEAM SCORES SHOWN FIRST

Final League position: **6th**

Cup results:
**R3 | Stockport (h) | 2–2
R3R | Stockport (a) | 2–3
R4 | Port Vale (h) | 2–2
R4R | Port Vale (a) | 2–1**

Top Scorer:
Andrei Kanchelskis | 17

RESULTS v MANCHESTER UNITED

Goodison Park:
9 September 1995 | 2–3

Old Trafford:
21 February 1996 | 2–0

BLACKBURN ROVERS

Rovers | Founded 1875

STAR PLAYER

ALAN SHEARER

FACT FILE

Stadium:
Ewood Park | Blackburn | BB2 4JF

Capacity: **31,089**

Record attendance:
2 March 1929 | 61,783 v Bolton | FA Cup

Club number: **01254 698888**

Tickets: **01254 671666**

Ticket prices: **Adult: £14–£17**

Child/Senior Citizen: £7–£8

Nearest BR station:
Blackburn

TEAM LINE-UP

Tim Flowers | Chris Coleman | Jeff Kenna | Colin Hendry | Tim Sherwood | Graeme Le Saux | Stuart Ripley | Kevin Gallacher | Alan Shearer | Mike Newell | Jason Wilcox | Nicky Marker | Bobby Mimms | Graham Fenton | Matty Holmes | Chris Sutton | Billy McKinlay | Adam Reed | Niklas Gudmundsson | Henning Berg | Paul Harford | Ian Pearce | Lars Bohinen | Paul Warhurst

TEAM REPORT

Over the first 26 matches of the 1995/96 season, Rovers won just one match away from home. Something funny happened at Ewood Park after Dalglish moved upstairs. A gleeful United fan would call it Leeds Syndrome: a team falling to bits after a freakish League win. They've been voted the third-least popular visitors at Old Trafford, and the harsh verdict is that they give fairweather football to fairweather fans.

Rovers' 1994/95 triumph looks even more threadbare 12 months on. By the end of that season, while United were loping up the League, Blackburn's game had been sussed by the rest of the Premiership and they were beginning to fray. Over 1995/96 things just fell apart. Europe was humiliating and brief. The only Rovers who kept their grip were Alan Shearer and heroic, feel-no-pain centre back Colin Hendry. Sherwood lost his edge; Chris Sutton, the £5-million hope to partner Shearer, didn't often get on the field; winger Ripley was injured; and fighting broke out between Le Saux and Batty, before Batty left for Tyneside.

At the moment, they are grim to watch. They dish up a long-ball game over the heads of an inept midfield, and if you took Shearer away they'd be nowhere. He gets half the goals and no help from his team-mates. All good Reds believe Billy Moneybags turned down United because the Blackburn money was better (why else would you do it?), and you have to wonder whether even Jack Walker's wallet is deep enough to keep his goal prodigy from walking.

Here's some advice, then: get rid of your manager, sell Colin Hendry while he's still worth something, and hope that the rumours about your youth policy bearing fruit are true.

1995/96 RECORD

HOME TEAM SCORES SHOWN FIRST

Final League position: **7th**

Cup results:
R3 | Ipswich Town (a) | 0–0
R3R | Ipswich Town (h) | 0–1

Top Scorer:
Alan Shearer | 31

RESULTS v MANCHESTER UNITED

Ewood Park:
28 August 1995 | 1–2

Old Trafford:
10 February 1996 | 1–0

Coleman's ball

NOTTINGHAM FOREST

Reds | Founded 1865

FACT FILE

Stadium:
City Ground | Nottingham | NG2 5FJ

Capacity: **30,539**

Record attendance:
2 March 1946 | 76,588 v Derby County | FA Cup

Club number: **0115 952 6000**

Tickets: **0115 952 6002**

Ticket prices: **Adult: £16–£18**

Child/Senior Citizen: £8–£10

Nearest BR station:
Nottingham Midland

TEAM LINE-UP

Mark Crossley | Des Lyttle | Stuart Pearce | Colin Cooper | Steve Chettle | Scott Gemmill | Steve Stone | Ian Woan | Stephen Howe | Paul McGregor | Bryan Roy | Chris Bart-Williams | Kevin Campbell | David Phillips | Alf Inge Haaland | Richard Irving Andrea Silenzi | Jason Lee | Vance Warner

TEAM REPORT

Many people thought Forest would struggle following the departure of Stan the Man to Liverpool for a British record transfer fee of £8.5 million. In fact, shrewd manager Frank Clark has coolly re-modelled his troops into an impressive unit, aided by the welcome emergence of several talented young players to add to the platform of scary Stuart "Psycho" Pearce and the mercurial Bryan Roy.

It was no coincidence that Steve Stone and Colin Cooper got their first taste of international football in 1995, the same year that Pearce regained his England place. It reflected not only the outstanding form of those individuals, but also the success of the whole team. Youngsters like Jason Lee (despite being mercilessly ridiculed by Messrs Skinner, Baddiel, Astle and Statto on BBC2's *Fantasy Football League*) and Paul McGregor all performed creditably in demanding League and European matches. In addition, Kevin Campbell has paid back Frank Clark for rescuing him from Arsenal obscurity by adding extra power in the last third of the pitch.

The Colly-free Forest team ended the season satisfied with a respectable League position, and extended runs in the UEFA and FA Cups (to their credit, they were the last English side left in Europe). In addition, the Midland Reds have built up a fearsome home record at the City Ground. Manchester United discovered this to their cost last November when only a late Eric Cantona penalty, his 50th goal for United, salvaged a 1–1 draw.

Chris Bart-Williams tracks Cantona

1995/96 RECORD

HOME TEAM SCORES SHOWN FIRST

Final League position: **9th**

Cup results:
R3 | Stoke City (a) | 1–1
R3R | Stoke City (h) | 2–0
R4 | Oxford Utd (h) | 1–1
R4R | Oxford Utd (a) | 0–3
R5 | Spurs (h) | 2–2
R5R | Spurs (a) | 1–3 (pens)
R6 | Aston Villa (h) 0–1

Top Scorer:
Ian Woan | 9

RESULTS v MANCHESTER UNITED

City Ground: **27 Nov 95 | 1–1**

Old Trafford: **28 Apr 96 | 5–0**

WEST HAM UNITED

Hammers | Founded 1895

STAR PLAYER
JULIAN DICKS

FACT FILE

Stadium:
**Upton Park | Boleyn Ground |
London | E 13 9AZ**

Capacity: **25,634**

Record attendance:
**17 October 1970 | 42,322 v
Tottenham (h)**

Club number: **0181 548 2748**

Tickets: **0181 548 2700**

Ticket prices: **£14–£25**

Child/Senior Citizen:

Nearest Underground:
Upton Park

TEAM LINE-UP

Ludek Miklosko | Tim Breacker |
Julian Dicks | Steve Potts |
Alvin Martin | Ian Bishop |
Marc Rieper Tony Cottee |
John Moncur | Keith Rowland |
Iain Dowie | Kenny Brown |
Dani | Neil Finn | Ilie
Dumitrescu Robbie Slater |
Danny Williamson | Dale
Gordon | Michael Hughes |
Frank Lampard | Slaven Bilic |
Les Sealey

TEAM REPORT

Accompanied by the good looks and unrivalled skills of Portuguese international Dani, the Hammers celebrated a shock defeat of London rivals Tottenham Hotspur on 12 February 1996. Just days later, the same team were nursing a 3–0 FA Cup defeat by lowly First Division Grimsby.

This erratic form was typical of West Ham's season. In August 1995, the bookies had them odds-on for relegation at the season's close, and this was duly confirmed by a defeat by Manchester United on 23 August when the Reds celebrated their first League success of the season with a 2–1 win. Paul Scholes showed his formidable attacking abilities by scoring in the 50th minute, and Keane's decider came in the 68th. United's repeat performance on 22 January was another strongly fought victory for the Reds. Eric Cantona's masterful play, including an eighth-minute goal, ensured a win, although the Irons struck back with gutsy determination. West Ham have been difficult opponents for United in recent years, having denied them the Championship back in May 1995; United were happy to get two League victories in 1995/96.

The presence of Dani and Romanian international Ilie Dumitrescu lifted the Hammers' form. The side went on to win five games on the trot in the following months, including a 2–0 defeat of Newcastle on 21 February, which closed the gap between United and the League leaders. Harry Redknapp is now confident of future success, having strengthened his squad with class players including Croatian central defender Slaven Bilic.

1995/96 RECORD

HOME TEAM SCORES SHOWN FIRST

Final League position: **10th**

Cup results:
**R3 | Southend Utd (h) | 2–0
R4 | Grimsby Town (h) | 1–1
R4R | Grimsby Town (a) | 0–3**

Top Scorer:
Tony Cottee & Julian Dicks | 10

RESULTS v MANCHESTER UNITED

Old Trafford:
23 August 1995 | 2–1

Upton Park:
22 January 1996 | 0–1

Cottee edges it
away from Butt

CHELSEA

The Blues | Founded: 1905

STAR PLAYER

RUUD GULLIT

FACT FILE

Stadium:
Stamford Bridge | London | SW6 1HS

Capacity: **31,791**

Record attendance:
12 October 1935 | 82,905 v Arsenal | Division One

Club number: **0171 385 5545**

Tickets: **0891 121011**

Ticket prices: **Visitor: £14–£35; Child/Senior Citizen: £6.50–£8**

Nearest Underground:
Fulham Broadway

TEAM LINE-UP

Craig Burley | Steve Clarke | Paul Furlong | Michael Duberry | Ruud Gullit | Kevin Hitchcock | Mark Hughes | Mustafa Izzet | Erland Johnsen | Dmitri Kharine | David Lee | Christian McCann | Scott Minto | Jody Morris | Andy Myers | Eddie Newton | Mark Nicholls | Gavin Peacock | Dan Petrescu | Terry Phelan | Frank Sinclair | Terry Skiverton | John Spencer | Dennis Wise | Russell Kelly

TEAM REPORT

Like Jürgen Klinsmann before him, dreadlocked Dutchman Ruud Gullit has proved to be the catalyst for some exciting football down south. Gullit may not be the long-term answer to Chelsea's prayers, but he stands as the ultimate example of what ex-manager Glenn Hoddle wanted to achieve.

Gullit has often commented on the pleasure he has taken from seeing the rest of the Blues' boys learning new skills, enjoying their football more and getting better results. It remains to be seen whether Chelsea can continue to develop their new-found continental style now that Hoddle has strapped on his flak jacket and gone to manage England.

Almost as fun as watching the new Chelsea play is to witness the Ken Bates/Matthew Harding soap opera. One day they are kissing each other in front of 30,000 people at Stamford Bridge; the next, one is fighting the other in the pages of the tabloid press.

Chelsea have often invited ridicule for fielding so many vertically-challenged players (Wise, Peacock, Spencer etc), but it suits their ball-to-feet pattern. If needs must, the dynamic Bates-Harding duo surely won't hesitate to spend big money on big players to bolster their dwarfish squad. But the find of last season was home-grown Mike Duberry, an unusually composed 20-year-old defender who deputised so impressively when Gullit was injured that he became a permanent fixture in the first team.

Chelsea were the only team to defeat United home and away during the 1993/94 double season. Whoever follows Hoddle will aim to keep the flair but add steel, for more Premiership consistency.

Faster than a speeding Gullit?

1995/96 RECORD

HOME TEAM SCORES SHOWN FIRST

Final League position: **11th**

Cup results: **R3 | Newcastle (h) | 1–0**
R3R | Newcastle (a) | 2–4
R4 | QPR (a) | 1–2
R5 | Grimsby Town (a) | 0–0
R5R | Grimsby Town (h) | 4–1
R6 | Wimbledon (h) | 2–2
R6R | Wimbledon (a) | 1–3
Semi | Manchester Utd (Villa Park) | 2–1

Top Scorer:
John Spencer | 13

RESULTS v MANCHESTER UNITED

Stamford Bridge: **21 October 1995 | 1–4**

Old Trafford: **2 December 1995 | 1–1**

MIDDLESBROUGH

Boro | Founded 1876

STAR PLAYER
NICK BARMBY

FACT FILE

Stadium: **Cellnet Riverside Stadium | Middlesbrough | Cleveland | TS3 6RS**

Capacity: **30,000**

Record attendance:
27 December 1949 | 53,596 v Newcastle Utd | Division 1

Club number: **01642 227227**

Tickets: **01642 207014**

Ticket prices: **Adult: £12.50–£19**

Child/Senior citizen: £7.50–£12.50

Nearest station: **Middlesbrough**

TEAM LINE-UP

Alan Miller | Neil Cox | Chris Morris | Steve Vickers | Nigel Pearson | Derek Whyte | Nick Barmby | Jamie Pollock | Jan Aage Fjørtoft | John Hendrie | Robbie Mustoe | Alan Moore | Gary Walsh | Curtis Fleming | Phil Whelan | Graham Kavanagh | Jaime Moreno | Philip Stamp | Craig Hignett | Craig Liddle | Ben Roberts | Chris Freeston | Branco | Michael Barron | Juninho

TEAM REPORT

It would come as quite a shock if we discovered that Bryan Robson's school reports concluded with the customary "could do better". And yet the feeling inspired by his Middlesbrough side at the end of the 1995/96 season is that it should have done better than the lower mid-table place it reached, especially when you consider the extraordinary heights achieved during the first few months in the Premiership after graduation from the First Division. Then, Boro burst to the head of the class, boasting the spanking new Riverside stadium and thrilling the fans with attractive, attacking football. In Barmby and Fjørtoft, Middlesbrough had a strike-force that epitomized a growing phenomenon in the Premier League – experienced youth – and showed immediate signs of understanding each other's play. The excitement multiplied when Robson pulled off the most audacious transfer coups in recent years and brought Juninho and Branco, the brilliant Brazilians, from the sunny shores of South America to the not-so-sunny banks of the Tees.

And yet, as Spurs had discovered in 1994/95, matches are played in both halves of the field. The early season's flame was extinguished by a worrying leak in defence. There were mid-term injuries to Fjørtoft and Barmby, while Robson seemed distracted by rumours linking him to the England job. Middlesbrough's flight in the top half of the Premiership was virtually grounded in a dismal drop down the table. However, with sensible spending to strengthen defence, Middlesbrough could well sustain their flight in the forthcoming season. And at Old Trafford we learned that if Bryan Robson is involved, you don't bet against success.

1995/96 RECORD

HOME TEAM SCORES SHOWN FIRST

Final League position: **12th**

Cup results:
R3 | Notts County (a) | 1–2
R4 | Wimbledon (h) | 0–0
R4R | Wimbledon (a) | 1–0

Top Scorer:
Nick Barmby | 7

RESULTS v MANCHESTER UNITED

Old Trafford:
28 October 1995 | 2–0

Riverside Stadium:
5 May 1996 | 0–3

Whelan slides in on Scholes

LEEDS UNITED

United | Founded 1919

FACT FILE

Stadium: **Elland Road** | **Leeds LS 11 OES**

Capacity: **40,000**

Record attendance: **15 March 1967** | **57,892 v Sunderland** | **FA Cup**

Club number: **0113 271 6037**

Tickets: **0113 271 0710**

Ticket prices: **Adult: £14–£25**

Child/Senior citizen: £7–£13

Nearest BR station: **Leeds City**

TEAM LINE-UP

Gary Kelly | Tony Dorigo | David Wetherall | John Pemberton | Carlton Palmer | Gary McAllister | Gary Speed | Tony Yeboah | Brian Deane | Rod Wallace | Tomas Brolin | Philomen Masinga | Lucas Radebe | Paul Beesley | Nigel Worthington | Mark Ford | Andy Gray | Mark Beeney | Mark Tinkler

TEAM REPORT

Probably the only thing United fans have ever thanked Leeds for is Eric Cantona. Since his departure, consistency has been elusive. True to form, the Leeds team of 1995/96 succumbed to defensive frailty and, although their season was saved in fine Cup runs, in the League they finished in mid-table obscurity.

And yet it had started so well. In the first quarter of the season, the safest bet in the world was that Tony Yeboah would score the Goal of the Month. With his pace, his balance and his explosive power, the Ghanaian produced some footballing fireworks, spectacular enough to draw attention away from the glamour signings of Collymore, Ferdinand and Bergkamp.

The Leeds attack was, as always, marshalled by Gary McAllister. The Scottish midfielder has consistently been the best player for Leeds since King Eric crossed the Pennines to Manchester. His thinking is quicker than just about any other player's in Britain, and his experience will be vital as youthful talents like Andy Gray are introduced int the team. Unless major signings are made in the summer, Leeds fans dream of a team playing a fast, passing game with a cutting edge will remain just fantasy.

In 1995/96, on days when the Leeds attack was on song, the team was effective. Manchester United found that out the painful way when they lost 3–1 at Elland Road on Christmas Eve 1995. But too often last season the final ball was wasted. With a shaky defence letting in goals too easily and a poor away record, the Leeds fans will be looking back to the 1991/92 season for some time to come.

Deane and Keane struggle for supremacy

1995/96 RECORD

HOME TEAM SCORES SHOWN FIRST

Final League position: **13th**

Cup results:
R3 | Derby County (a) | 2–4
R4 | Bolton (a) | 0–1
R5 | Port Vale (h) | 0–0
R5R | Port Vale (a) | 1–2
R6 | Liverpool (h) | 0–0
R6R | Liverpool (a) | 3–0

Top Scorer:
Tony Yeboah | **12**

RESULTS v MANCHESTER UNITED

Elland Road: **24 Dec 95** | **3–1**
Old Trafford: **17 April 96** | **1–0**

WIMBLEDON

The Dons | Founded 1889

FACT FILE

Stadium:
Selhurst Park | South Norwood | London | SE25

Capacity: **26,000**

Record attendance:
3 February 1996 | 32,852 v Man Utd | Premier League

Club number: **0181 771 2233**

Tickets: **0181 771 8841**

Ticket prices: **Adult: £20–£40**

Child/Senior citizen: £10

Nearest BR station:
Selhurst or Thornton Heath

TEAM LINE-UP

Neil Sullivan | Chris Perry | Kenny Cunningham | Alan Kimble | Oyvind Leonhardsen | Dean Holdsworth | Marcus Gayle | Alan Reeves | Neil Ardley | Andy Clark | Steve Talboys | Jon Goodman | Jason Euell | Andy Pearce | Paul Heald | Alan Kimble | Vinny Jones | Robbie Earle | Efan Ekoku | Gary Elkins | Andy Thorn | Chris Perry | Hans Segers

TEAM REPORT

Wimbledon, every big club's bogey team, struggled last season amid rumours about a proposed move away from the capital. The Dons' temporary home at Selhurst Park has led to a lack of support from their fans, who are unwilling to travel to a distant foreign ground outside their own London borough. Sam Hamman, the colourful Wimbledon chairman, has blamed this situation for the club's financial decline, which in turn has affected the team's progress on the field. Sam has declared that a new city with new support would help the club in its fight for survival in the top flight.

Wimbledon's difficult 1995/96 campaign was highlighted at Old Trafford when United beat the Crazy Gang 3–1. The performance was noted for Roy Keane's outstanding game in midfield; he scored two goals and secured the Reds a victory.

The Dons' future in this division seems brighter after Joe Kinnear turned down his self-confessed managerial dream offer to become the manager of his beloved Ireland. And although the last recognised member of the Crazy Gang, Vinny Jones, is likely to leave, Wimbledon have still got some skilful players in their squad to overcome the loss of his renowned spirit. They include the England goalscorer Dean Holdsworth, the Norwegian international Oyvind Leonhardsen and the strong midfield dynamo Robbie Earle.

Wimbledon appeared to be sliding towards Division One last season, but their famous Crazy Gang spirit re-surfaced and they hauled themselves out of the relegation zone. It is time this shoestring club received the credit it deserves for taking on the financial muscle of the big clubs and stubbornly refusing to buckle.

STAR PLAYER

DEAN HOLDSWORTH

1995/96 RECORD

HOME TEAM SCORES SHOWN FIRST

Final League position: **14th**

Cup results:
R4 | Middlesbrough (a) | 0–0
R4R | Middlesbrough (h) | 1–0
R5 | Huddersfield (a) | 2–2
R5R | Huddersfield (h) | 3–1
R6 | Chelsea (a) | 2–2
R6R | Chelsea (h) | 1–3

Top Scorer:
Robbie Earle | 11

RESULTS v MANCHESTER UNITED

Old Trafford: **26 Aug 95 | 3–1**
Selhurst Park: **3 Feb 96 | 2–4**

Not so crazy after all

SHEFFIELD WED

The Owls | Founded 1867

FACT FILE

Stadium:
Hillsborough | Sheffield | S6 1SW

Capacity: **36,020**

Record attendance:
17 February 1934 | 72,841 v Manchester City | FA Cup

Club number: **0114 234 3122**

Tickets: **0114 233 7233**

Ticket prices: **Adult: £8.50–£17**

Child/Senior citizen: £5–£11.50

Nearest BR station:
Sheffield Midland

TEAM LINE-UP

Kevin Pressman | Peter Atherton | Ian Nolan | Steve Nicol | Chris Waddle | David Hirst | Mark Bright | Marc Degryse | Des Walker | Guy Whittingham | Lee Briscoe | John Sheridan | Graham Hyde | Mark Pembridge | Dan Petrescu | Andy Pearce | Regi Blinker | Chris Woods | Dejan Stefanovic | Darko Kovacevic | O'Neill Donaldson | Grant Watts

TEAM REPORT

Wednesday were caught at the wrong end of the table last season, as David Pleat took over as manager from ex-England forward Trevor Francis. The team needed rebuilding as Pleat tried to come to terms with the squad's deficiencies.

David Pleat is a respected manager in the game, who found success at Luton Town with few resources and did well at Tottenham in the short period he was there. Although the Owls had a poor season, his credentials suggest it will not be long before he turns Wednesday's fortunes around.

Wednesday have many star performers. If David Hirst can stay clear of injury, he could rediscover the form that once made him a target for Fergie. Although this has still to be found, Wednesday's fans will be encouraged by Hirst's longest season in the first team for a number of years. Regi Blinker, a late arrival in the 1995/96 season from Feyenoord, was an instant hit. Fans quickly bought up local supplies of dreadlock wigs to emulate their favourite new winger. Marc Degryse still seems the pick of the foreign contingent: the Belgian international looked a really classy player as he helped the Owls to survive the relegation battle. Steve Nicol was brought in mid-season to strengthen the team's defence. This experienced footballer has shown he can still perform at the highest level, even though some thought he was finished a year or two ago.

Despite Wednesday's poor form, they did well against United in the 1995/96, gaining two draws. And although some of Wednesday fans are baying for David Pleat's blood, the Owls' board have stood firm behind their man in the hope that Sheffield will do better this time around.

1995/96 RECORD

HOME TEAM SCORES SHOWN FIRST

Final League position: **15th**

Cup results:
R3 | Charlton Ath (a) | 2–0

Top Scorer:
David Hirst | 13

RESULTS v MANCHESTER UNITED

Hillsborough:
23 September 1995 | 0–0

Old Trafford:
9 December 1995 | 2–2

Owls well that ends well

COVENTRY CITY

Sky Blues | Founded 1883

STAR PLAYER
DION DUBLIN

FACT FILE

Stadium:
Highfield Road | Richard Street | Coventry | CV2 4FW

Capacity: **22,600**

Record attendance:
29 April 1967 | 51,455 v Wolves | Division Two

Club number: **0203 223535**

Tickets: **0203 225545**

Ticket prices: **Adult: £12–£20 Child/Senior citizen: £6–£10**

Nearest BR station:
Coventry

TEAM LINE-UP

Steve Ogrizovic | David Burrows David Rennie | Kevin Richardson | Paul Telfer | Marques Isaias | Peter Ndlovu | Dion Dublin | John Salako | Noel Whelan | Ally Pickering | Steve Morgan | Willie Boland | David Busst Jonathan Gould | Gordon Strachan | Paul Williams John Filan | Marcus Hall | Iyseden Christie | Nii Lamptey

TEAM REPORT

The stalwart of Highfield Road over the last few seasons has been ex-Manchester United forward Dion Dublin. Coventry's current star striker, who was also a top 10 goalscorer in all football competitions for the 1995/96 season, has been the trusty captain of the Sky Blues for almost two seasons. But apart from charming the Coventry faithful, Dion struggled to keep his team above the dreaded relegation zone in 1996.

When Man United visit Highfield Road the occasion is always treated with a sense of awe. The Reds duly complied with tradition in November 1995, treating the Sky Blues to a 4–0 pasting made up of a brace of goals from Brian McClair plus one each from Beckham and Irwin.

As the Reds went to within three points of Newcastle, Big Ron's team was dumped at the bottom of the Premiership table. And there they remained, losing and drawing the following three games.

But the tide turned in their favour on 9 December with five goals from Busst, Dublin, Rennie, Ndlovu and Salako seeing off the 1995 Championship winners Blackburn. The wind was in Coventry's sails as they cruised up to 17th place, but they were still fighting for their place in the Premiership.

Big Ron's team just survived on the edge. With class players like Dion Dublin, Peter Ndlovu and John Salako on their books, Coventry should be safe in their billet at the lower end of the Premiership table.

1995/96 RECORD

HOME TEAM SCORES SHOWN FIRST

Final League position: **16th**

Cup results:
R3 | Plymouth (a) | 1–3
R4 | Man City (h) | 2–2
R4R | Man City (a) | 2–1

Top Scorer:
Dion Dublin | 14

RESULTS v MANCHESTER UNITED

Highfield Road:
22 November 1995 | 0–4

Old Trafford:
8 April 1996 | 1–0

Cantona reaps doom on Coventry

SOUTHAMPTON

Saints | **Founded 1885**

STAR PLAYER
MATT LE TISSIER

FACT FILE

Stadium:
The Dell | Milton Road | Southampton | SO15 2XH

Capacity: **15,000**

Record attendance:
8 October 1969 | 31,044 v Man Utd | Division One

Club number: **01703 220505**

Tickets: **01703 220505**

Ticket prices: **Adult: £11–£18**
Child/Senior citizen: £5–£6

Nearest BR station:
Southampton Central

TEAM LINE-UP

Dave Beasant | Jason Dodd | Francis Benali | Jim Magilton | Barry Venison | Richard Hall | Ken Monkou | Gordon Watson | Neil Shipperley Neil Heaney | Tommy Widdrington | Matt Le Tissier | David Hughes | Bruce Grobbelaar | Neil Maddison | Frankie Bennett | Matthew Oakley | Simon Charlton

TEAM REPORT

Southampton's 1995/96 season was an unusual one. Despite their annual dogfight against the drop, the Saints' star striker Matt Le Tissier had a quiet season: he only managed an average of one goal every four games for the club. Perhaps the gifted one should have considered moving to United when the offer was still open.

But when the Saints came marching in to Old Trafford in November 1995, the end result was convincing enough without another new signing. Strangely, the 13th Premiership game for the Reds proved unlucky for the men in red and white. Within 10 minutes, United had the game all wrapped up with two from Giggs in the first and the fourth, plus a third from Scholes in the eighth. Cole's goal in the 69th minute meant a more-than-convincing 4–1 victory for the Reds. As Dave Merrington said: "We could have done without the first 15 minutes."

1995/96 was yet another season of battling to stay above water in the League. Having started in 12th place, the Saints dropped briefly to bottom in late August. Barry Venison's team dwindled in the relegation zone, seemingly unable to lift themselves from the ground floor of the table. But they re-discovered their form and managed to move themselves up to 14th place, where they fiercely defended their lower mid-table position. Indeed, they nearly de-railed United's Championship plans by destroying the invisible greys in a shocking 3–1 result, a win that probably saved them from the drop.

The Saints seem condemned to remain in the lower mid-table blues for the forthcoming season, unless Le Tiss can find his old goal-scoring form.

1995/96 RECORD

HOME TEAM SCORES SHOWN FIRST

Final League position: **17th**

Cup results:
R3 | Portsmouth (h) | 3–0
R4 | Crewe Alex (h) | 1–1
R4R | Crewe Alex (a) | 2–3
R5 | Swindon (a) | 1–1
R5R | Swindon (h) | 2–0
R6 | Man United (a) | 2–0

Top Scorer:
Matthew Le Tissier | 7

RESULTS v MANCHESTER UNITED

Old Trafford:
18 November 1995 | 4–1
The Dell: **13 April 1996 | 3–1**

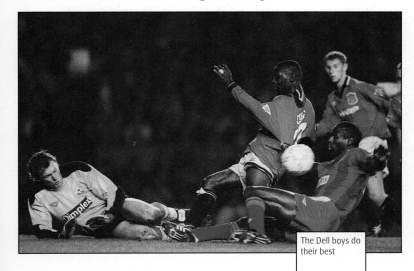

The Dell boys do their best

SUNDERLAND

Rokermen | Founded 1879

STAR PLAYER

MICHAEL GRAY

FACT FILE

Stadium:
**Roker Park Ground |
Sunderland | SR6 9SW**

Capacity: **22,657**

Record attendance:
**8 March 1933 | 75,118 v Derby
County | FA Cup**

Club number: **0191 514 0332**

Tickets: **0191 514 0332**

Ticket prices: **Adult: £15 – £13**

Child/Senior citizen: £9

Nearest BR station: **Seaburn**

TEAM LINE-UP

Alec Chamberlain | David Preece
John Kay | Dariusz Kubicki |
Martin Scott | Richard Ord |
Andy Melville | Michael Gray |
Steve Agnew | Gordon
Armstrong | Brian Atkinson |
Martin Smith | Martin Gray | Paul
Bracewell | Terry Cooke | Gareth
Hall | Lee Howey | Phil Gray |
David Kelly | Stephen Brodie |
Craig Russell

TEAM REPORT

When Sunderland's North Eastern rivals Newcastle and Middlesbrough both returned to the Premiership, the Wearsiders must have thought they had missed the boat to the big time.

The Rokermen's last jaunt in the top flight was the 1990/91 season, when they went up by default after unlucky Swindon Town were found guilty of financial irregularities and stripped of their promotion by the FA. But Sunderland relinquished their chance to settle when they were relegated in the next season, just before the Premiership was formed.

Peter Reid was appointed manager at Roker Park in 1995. The ex-Manchester City boss and Everton player turned the now ambitious club's fortunes around. He successfully guided the team away from relegation and made the Rokermen into First Division Championship contenders just one season later.

United fans already know a lot about Sunderland, after it took the Red Devils two torrid games to beat the tough Wearsiders in last season's FA Cup. In the first match at Old Trafford, United were just 10 minutes from going out, but a Cantona goal saved the day for the Reds though plucky Sunderland probably deserved the win. In the replay at Roker Park, the famous Roker roar failed to subdue United. Paul Scholes, an inspired substitution by Alex Ferguson, levelled the match, and the barrage of abuse directed at Andy Cole by the Sunderland fans stopped after he scored the last -minute winner.

The Wearsiders are used to near-misses in the FA Cup: it was only in 1992 that caretaker manager Malcom Crosby took them all the way to the final, only to be beaten 2–0 by Liverpool. This sleeping giant is ready to roar once again.

1995/96 RECORD

HOME TEAM SCORES SHOWN FIRST

Final Endsleigh League
Division One position: **1**

Cup results:
R3 | Man United (h) | 2–2
R3R | Man United (a) | 1–2

Top Scorer:
Craig Russell | 13

Roker and roll

DERBY COUNTY

The Rams | Founded 1884

FACT FILE

Stadium:
**Baseball Ground |
Shaftesbury Crescent | Derby
DE3 8NB**

Capacity: **19,500**

Record attendance:
**20 September 1969 | 41,826
v Tottenham | Division One**

Club number: **01332 340505**

Tickets: **01332 340505**

Ticket prices: **Adult: £7–£12**

Child/Senior Citizen: £4–£6

Nearest BR station: Derby

TEAM LINE-UP

Russell Hoult | Darren Wassall |
Chris Powell | Dean Yates | Igor
Stimac | Sean Flynn | Ashley
Ward | Ron Willems Marco
Gabbiadini | Lee Carsley |
Jason Kavanagh | Gary Rowett |
Darryl Powell | Andrew Tretton |
Paul Trollope | Martin Taylor |
Wayne Sutton | Dean Sturridge |
Paul Simpson | Robin van der
Laan | Chris Boden | Will Davies
Matt Carbon

TEAM REPORT

County guaranteed automatic promotion to the top flight by beating fellow contenders Crystal Palace in their penultimate game, thereby avoiding the nerve-jangling lottery of the play-offs. Jim Smith's sigh of relief on that day was audible throughout the country. He, more than any other manager, knows the despair of football's cruellest pantomime, having been the loser in play-off tournaments when managing Newcastle and Portsmouth.

The elation may be brief however as the struggle to maintain a position in the Premiership will be as tough as any play-off. Derby was, by Endsleigh League standards, a wealthy club, capable of capturing players for hundreds of thousands of pounds. but to ensure Premiership success these days clubs must pay for the multi-million pound player. After the £20-million overhaul of the Baseball Ground to boost its 19,500 capacity, Jim Smith will have to sell many players to buy only a few new ones.

One player the manager will be keen to keep is skipper Van der Laan. The Dutchman was the Rams' inspiration last season, dominating midfield battles with his ball-winning prowess. And Smith is unlikely to let go of his forward trio of Simpson, Sturridge and the experienced Gabbiadini, who may cause a few problems for their Premiership opposition. But Derby's defence will give Smith himself the jitters unless he can generate some much-needed stability.

It doesn't look promising for Derby. They read more like Bolton than Boro. But Jim Smith has finally earned the right to pit his wits against the best in the country, and no one would begrudge him the opportunity.

STAR PLAYER

**ROBIN
VAN DER LAAN**

Wham, bam, thank you Rams

1995/96 RECORD

HOME TEAM SCORES SHOWN FIRST

Final Endsleigh League
Division One position: **2**

Cup results:
R3 | Leeds United (h) | 2–4

Top Scorer:
Dean Sturridge | 20

CRYSTAL PALACE

TEAM PROFILE

After the disappointment of the 1994/95 season, Ron Noades acted swiftly to bring back Steve Coppell. His much-trumpeted arrival was largely symbolic, with coach Ray Lewington in charge of team affairs. Despite a number of impressive performances, results were not secured in Palace's favour. Hence the arrival of football's very own Mr Motivator, Dave "Harry" Bassett. After his appointment, and with Lewington still on the staff, Palace rose from the pits of the division to clinch a play-off place.

Fans hardly anticipated such success after off-loading several stars at the start of the season, Armstrong and Shaw among them. But the Eagles bought well, including the midfielder-cum-attacker Dougie Freeman, a snip at £800,000 from Barnet, whose form prompted the sale of target-man Gareth Taylor to Sheffield United. Slightly more expensive was the promising England Under-21 player Andy "Fat Boy" Roberts from Millwall who has linked well with experienced skipper Ray Houghton in midfield. Indeed, relegation to the Endsleigh had a silver lining, as it allowed the development of up-and-coming youngsters, such as the exciting Bruce Dwyer, away from the glare of the Premiership. Other youngsters have been successfully blooded during this campaign – Leon McKenzie, son of boxer Duke, a case in point.

STAR PLAYER
DOUGIE FREEDMAN

FACT FILE

Nickname: **Eagles**

Stadium:
Selhurst Park
London | SE25 6PU

Capacity: **26,400**

Club number: **0181 653 1000**

Tickets: **0181 771 8841**

Manager:
Dave Bassett

STOKE CITY

TEAM PROFILE

Lou Macari's return, after a largely unhappy spell with Celtic, has reversed Stoke's fortunes. Starved of funds for new players, the present line-up is a healthy blend of seasoned pros (like defensive stalwarts Vince Overson and Ian Cranson) and young starlets (including forward pairing Martin Carruthers and Simon Sturridge).

Rather surprisingly, deadline day witnessed the off-loading of fans' favourite Paul Peschisolido back to Birmingham City, another example of Barry Fry's peculiar transfer policy. However, Mike Sheron, a signing from Norwich City, formed a more than capable deputy for the departed Canadian. Indeed, Sheron appears to be rediscovering the form which brought him recognition in the top flight with Manchester City. His understanding with the prolific Sturridge guaranteed Stoke's place in the play-offs. Another reborn star is Ray Wallace, one of the family triumvirate whose career was going nowhere at Leeds United with brother Rodney. Macari has switched Ray to midfield from his customary right-back spot, which has resulted in a better-balanced team. But pundits are sceptical of Stoke City's Premiership chances. Their small squad could not sustain the challenge, and the lack of funds to buy players is an obvious handicap. Macari has already complained about the damage suspension has wreaked on their promotion chances.

STAR PLAYER
SIMON STURRIDGE

FACT FILE

Nickname: **Potters**

Stadium:
Victoria Ground | Stoke-on-Trent | STG 4EG

Capacity: **24,071**

Club number: **01782 4135211**

Tickets: **01782 4135211**

Manager:
Lou Macari

LEICESTER CITY

TEAM PROFILE

A season in which the Foxes were widely tipped to bounce straight back to the Premiership looked once again as if it would be wrecked by managerial desertion, when Mark McGhee walked out on the club to take over at Wolves. Chairman Martin George could be forgiven for a heady sense of *déjà vu*, what with Aston Villa prising away Brian Little the previous season.

George's astute choice as replacement was Norwich City's Martin O'Neill. After a none too steady start, the Irishman seems to have won the fans over with his stylish one-touch passing game, first initiated while he was Wycombe manager. The backbone of the side has remained the same since his appointment.

There is the know-how of players like Garry Parker, who has "seen it all, done it all" at two of the country's top clubs, Forest and Villa. Up front, the aggression of Welsh international Iwan Roberts perfectly complements the more delicate approach of former Red Mark Robins.

The fans experienced further heartbreak with the sale of Leicester's favourite son, Julian Joachim, to Aston Villa. A shrewd deadline-day loan signing of Mustafa Izzet from Chelsea propelled the side to the top rankings of the First Division. The young Turk's incisive wing play laid chance on chance for the forward players. Promotion to the Premiership would be celebrated with much passion by Leicester's sizeable support.

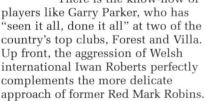

STAR PLAYER
STEVE CLARIDGE

FACT FILE

Nickname: **Filberts or Foxes**

Stadium:
City Stadium | Filbert Street | Leicester | LE2 7FL

Capacity: **22,517**

Club number: **0116 2555000**

Tickets: **0116 2915232**

Manager:
Martin O'Neill

CHARLTON ATHLETIC

TEAM PROFILE

Charlton Athletic's most memorable moment of the 1995/96 season came on 28 February 1996,when they met giants Liverpool in the Fifth Round of the FA Cup. But instead of leaping towards Wembley, the Addicks conceded defeat. The year before, Man United dismissed Charlton 3–0 in the Sixth Round of the FA Cup with goals from Mark Hughes and Andrei Kanchelskis.

Finishing in sixth place, Division One Charlton didn't always look like Premiership pretenders. A surge of nine matches without defeat in December and January equalled an all-time club record of seven away wins, and included a defeat of London rivals Milwall – the turning point in their League form.

A 2–1 thrashing by Liverpool, who played carelessly and missed some easy chances, seemed to underline the vast differences between the First Division and the Premiership. But Charlton have had experience of top League football: Eighties manager Lennie "Houdini" Lawrence regularly steered the team clear of relegation in the old Division One.

Current manager and ex-Charlton player Alan Curbishley hasn't bought any new players for some time. But an outstanding youth policy produces outstanding home-grown talent, such as Lee Bowyer and Richard Rufus. Youth player Kevin Nicholls is another player to watch in the future.

STAR PLAYER
LEE BOWYER

FACT FILE

Nickname: **Addicks**

Stadium:
The Valley | Floyd Road | Charlton | London | SE7 8BL

Capacity: **15,000**

Club number: **0181 293 4567**

Tickets: **0181 858 5888**

Manager:
Alan Curbishley

MANCHESTER UNITED

Manchester United Football Club plc
Old Trafford | Manchester | M16 ORA

Chairman & Chief Executive
C M Edwards

Directors
C M Edwards
J M Edelson
Sir Bobby Charlton CBE
E M Watkins LLM
R L Olive
R P Launders

Manager
Alex Ferguson

Secretary
Kenneth Merrett

USEFUL TELEPHONE NUMBERS

General enquiries	**0161 872 1661**
Ticket information	**0161 872 0199**
Development Association	**0161 872 4676**
	0161 873 8378
	0161 873 8379
Commercial Department	**0161 872 3488**
Membership Office	**0161 872 5208**
Executive Suite	**0161 872 3331**
United Megastore	**0161 848 8181**
United Superstore	**0161 872 3398**
Mail Order Hotline	**0161 877 4002**
Club Call	**0891 121 161**
Subscriptions to official magazines **ManchesterUNITED** and **Glory Glory Man United**	**0990 442 442**